,75

D0338339

THE LOGICAL DESIGN
OF OPERATING SYSTEMS

Prentice-Hall
Series in Automatic Computation

George Forsythe, editor

AHO, editor, *Currents in the Theory of Computing*
AHO AND ULLMAN,   *The Theory of Parsing, Translation, and Compiling*,
   Volume I: *Parsing;* Volume II: *Compiling*
ANDREE,   *Computer Programming: Techniques, Analysis, and Mathematics*
   and Applications to Integral Equations
ARBIB,   *Theories of Abstract Automata*
BATES AND DOUGLAS,   *Programming Language/One*, 2nd ed.
BLUMENTHAL,   *Management Information Systems*
BRENT,   *Algorithms for Minimization without Derivatives*
BRINCH HANSEN,   *Operating System Principles*
COFFMAN AND DENNING,   *Operating Systems Theory*
CRESS, et al.,   *FORTRAN IV with WATFOR and WATFIV*
DAHLQUIST, BJÖRCK, AND ANDERSON,   *Numerical Methods*
DANIEL,   *The Approximate Minimization of Functionals*
DEO,   *Graph Theory with Applications to Engineering and Computer Science*
DESMONDE,   *Computers and Their Uses*, 2nd ed.
DESMONDE,   *Real-Time Data Processing Systems*
DRUMMOND,   *Evaluation and Measurement Techniques for Digital Computer Systems*
EVANS, et al.,   *Simulation Using Digital Computers*
FIKE,   *Computer Evaluation of Mathematical Functions*
FIKE,   *PL/1 for Scientific Programers*
FORSYTHE AND MOLER,   *Computer Solution of Linear Algebraic Systems*
GAUTHIER AND PONTO,   *Designing Systems Programs*
GEAR,   *Numerical Initial Value Problems in Ordinary Differential Equations*
GOLDEN,   *FORTRAN IV Programming and Computing*
GOLDEN AND LEICHUS,   *IBM/360 Programming and Computing*
GORDON,   *System Simulation*
HANSEN,   *A Table of Series and Products*
HARTMANIS AND STEARNS,   *Algebraic Structure Theory of Sequential Machines*
HULL,   *Introduction to Computing*
JACOBY, et al.,   *Iterative Methods for Nonlinear Optimization Problems*
JOHNSON,   *System Structure in Data, Programs, and Computers*
KANTER,   *The Computer and the Executive*
KIVIAT, et al.,   *The SIMSCRIPT II Programming Language*
LAWSON AND HANSON,   *Solving Least Squares Problems*
LORIN,   *Parallelism in Hardware and Software: Real and Apparent Concurrency*
LOUDEN AND LEDIN,   *Programming the IBM 1130*, 2nd ed.
MARTIN,   *Design of Man-Computer Dialogues*
MARTIN,   *Design of Real-Time Computer Systems*
MARTIN,   *Future Developments in Telecommunications*
MARTIN,   *Programming Real-Time Computing Systems*
MARTIN,   *Security, Accuracy, and Privacy in Computer Systems*
MARTIN,   *Systems Analysis for Data Transmission*

MARTIN, *Telecommunications and the Computer*

MARTIN, *Teleprocessing Network Organization*

MARTIN AND NORMAN, *The Computerized Society*

MATHISON AND WALKER, *Computers and Telecommunications: Issues in Public Policy*

MCKEEMAN, et al., *A Compiler Generator*

MEYERS, *Time-Sharing Computation in the Social Sciences*

MINSKY, *Computation: Finite and Infinite Machines*

NIEVERGELT et al., *Computer Approaches to Mathematical Problems*

PLANE AND MCMILLAN, *Discrete Optimization: Integer Programming and Network Analysis for Management Decisions*

PRITSKER AND KIVIAT, *Simulation with GASP II: a FORTRAN-Based Simulation Language*

PYLYSHYN, editor, *Perspectives on the Computer Revolution*

RICH, *Internal Sorting Methods: Illustrated with PL/1 Program*

RUSTIN, editor, *Algorithm Specification*

RUSTIN, editor, *Computer Networks*

RUSTIN, editor, *Data Base Systems*

RUSTIN, editor, *Debugging Techniques in Large Systems*

RUSTIN, editor, *Design and Optimization of Compilers*

RUSTIN, editor, *Formal Semantics of Programming Languages*

SACKMAN AND CITRENBAUM, editors, *On-line Planning: Towards Creative Problem-Solving*

SALTON, editor, *The SMART Retrieval System: Experiments in Automatic Document Processing*

SAMMET, *Programming Languages: History and Fundamentals*

SCHAEFER, *A Mathematical Theory of Global Program Optimization*

SCHULTZ, *Spline Analysis*

SCHWARZ, et al., *Numerical Analysis of Symmetric Matrices*

SHAW, *The Logical Design of Operating Systems*

SHERMAN, *Techniques in Computer Programming*

SIMON AND SIKLOSSY, *Representation and Meaning: Experiments with Information Processing Systems*

STERBENZ, *Floating-Point Computation*

STERLING AND POLLACK, *Introduction to Statistical Data Processing*

STOUTEMYER, *PL/1 Programming for Engineering and Science*

STRANG AND FIX, *An Analysis of the Finite Element Method*

STROUD, *Approximate Calculation of Multiple Integrals*

TAVISS, editor, *The Computer Impact*

TRAUB, *Iterative Methods for the Solution of Polynomial Equations*

UHR, *Pattern Recognition, Learing, and Thought*

VAN TASSEL, *Computer Security Management*

VARGA, *Matrix Iterative Analysis*

WAITE, *Implementing Software for Non-Numeric Application*

WILKINSON, *Rounding Errors in Algebraic Processes*

WIRTH, *Systematic Programming: An Introduction*

To Heather, David, and Elizabeth

THE LOGICAL DESIGN

OF OPERATING SYSTEMS

ALAN C. SHAW

Computer Science Group
University of Washington

PRENTICE-HALL, INC.

ENGLEWOOD CLIFFS, N. J.

Library of Congress Cataloging in Publication Data
SHAW, ALAN C

   The logical design of operating systems.

   (Prentice-Hall series in automatic computation)
   Bibliography: p.
   1. Electronic digital computers—Programming.
2. Multiprogramming (Electronic computers)   I. Title.
QA76.6.S52   001.6'42   74–537
ISBN 0–13–540112–7

© 1974 by Prentice-Hall, Inc., Englewood Cliffs, N.J.

Current printing (last digit):

19 18 17 16 15 14 13 12 11

Printed in the United States of America

PRENTICE-HALL INTERNATIONAL, INC., *London*
PRENTICE-HALL OF AUSTRALIA PTY. LTD., *Sydney*
PRENTICE-HALL OF CANADA, LTD., *Toronto*
PRENTICE-HALL OF INDIA PRIVATE LIMITED, *New Delhi*
PRENTICE-HALL OF JAPAN, INC., *Tokyo*

CONTENTS

6   PROCEDURE AND DATA SHARING IN MAIN STORAGE   152

7   PROCESS AND RESOURCE CONTROL   166

8   THE DEADLOCK PROBLEM   203

9 FILE SYSTEMS   244

Appendix: A MULTIPROGRAMMING PROJECT   277

REFERENCES   287

INDEX   293

PREFACE

Computer operating systems are among the most complex "systems" devised by humans, and it is only recently that we have been able to understand and coherently organize this complexity. This book is a text on the *principles* of operating systems, with particular emphasis on multiprogramming. I have tried to present the concepts and techniques required for engineering and understanding these systems rather than discuss in detail how operating system x is implemented on machine y; however, many examples from real systems are given to illustrate the application of particular principles. The title "logical design" was selected to stress my concern with the logical organization and interactions of the elements of operating systems and with methods of "reasoning" about them.

The book is intended for computer science students and professionals with a basic knowledge of machine organization, assembly language, programming languages, and data structures. The prerequisite background can be obtained in an introductory one-term course in each of the above subjects, approximately equivalent to courses B2, I1, I2, and I3 of the curriculum proposed in *Curriculum 68* by the Association for Computing Machinery[1]. While the book was being written, I used it as the primary text for a one-term graduate course at Cornell University and at the University of Washington. The book is suitable for a one- or two-term course at either the graduate or advanced undergraduate level, and contains almost all the topics suggested in course I4 of *Curriculum 68*[1] and in the more recent COSINE report[2].

[1]ACM Curriculum Committee on Computer Science. *Curriculum 68*, recommendations for academic programs in computer science. *Comm. ACM*, **11**, 3 (March 1968), 151–197.

[2]COSINE Committee of the Commission on Education. An undergraduate course on operating systems principles (Denning, P. J., chairman). Commission on Education, National Academy of Engineering, Washington, D.C., 1971.

My global view is that the subject of operating systems is most conveniently divided into three related areas: process management, resource management, and file systems. Each of the nine chapters of the book is concerned with some aspects of one or more of these areas. Chapter 1 provides an overview of the organization of systems hardware and software, including a historical perspective and rationale. In Chapter 2, I use the simple setting of a job-at-a-time batch system to present some basic ideas on linking loaders and input-output methods. The model of interacting processes as a means for describing systems and as a framework for solving problems of process communication and synchronization (including some problems introduced in Chapter 2) is developed in Chapter 3. Chapter 4 is an introduction to multiprogramming systems; building upon the material developed in the preceding chapters, it discusses hardware and software requirements for multiprogramming, the "virtual" machines viewed by users and by systems programmers, and design methodologies. Techniques for the management of real and virtual memories are investigated in Chapter 5; the following chapter (Chapter 6) continues the study of the main memory resource, looking at the problems of single-copy sharing of information in real and virtual memory systems. Process and resource management ideas are consolidated in Chapter 7, where a comprehensive nucleus is described and used as a model for examining systems data structures, input-output processes, interrupt handling, and scheduling methods. Chapter 8 gives a detailed treatment of systems deadlock; methods for deadlock detection, recovery, and prevention are described for both serially-reusable (conventional) and consumable (message-like) resources. The last chapter (Chapter 9) discusses the basic elements of file systems, including a section on recovery from failure.

The book contains many exercises which the reader is strongly encouraged to do. In learning new ideas on computer systems, it is particularly important that students be given the opportunity to apply these ideas through programming projects. Nontrivial but tractable projects are not easy to design; for this reason, I have included an appendix containing a detailed specification of a large but manageable multiprogramming project which I have used successfully several times.

I have tried to reference all the material carefully so that the reader can pursue some area in further depth or obtain another point of view, and so that proper credit is given to the source of each technique or idea. I sincerely regret any errors or omissions in the latter. All references are collected at the end of the book and are cited in the text by the last name of the author followed by a date, e.g., Dijkstra, 1965b.

ACKNOWLEDGEMENTS

I am very grateful to a number of people for their help, encouragement, and intellectual influence during the preparation of this manuscript. W. F. Miller first introduced me to the pleasures and satisfaction of research and scholarship, and provided early support of my book writing in operating systems. I had the privilege of assisting N. Wirth in a systems programming class at Stanford University in 1965–66 and produced a set of notes based on his lectures;† these notes contained some of the principal ideas underlying the design and construction of operating systems and compilers. I am also indebted to Wirth for showing me that systems design and programming can be a scientific activity.

J. George and J. Horning read the manuscript and offered many constructive suggestions. The book developed from the "laboratories" of my operating systems classes at Cornell University and the University of Washington; I thank the students in these classes for their stimulation, energy, curiosity, good humor, and willingness to help define and organize a new field. G. Andrews, R. Holt, N. Weiderman, and T. Wilcox were especially helpful, not only in the above capacity but also as active research colleagues. In particular, parts of Chapter 7 use the results of the Ph.D. work of Weiderman and Chapter 8 is based on Holt's Ph.D. research.

My final acknowledgements go to the many researchers and practitioners who have contributed to the development of the field of operating systems. I have been most influenced by the published works of E. W. Dijkstra, and discuss his contributions throughout the book.

ALAN C. SHAW
Seattle, Wash.

†Shaw, A. C., *Lecture Notes on a Course in Systems Programming*. Tech. Report No. 52, Computer Science Dept., Stanford University, Stanford, Calif. Dec. 1966. (Available from the Clearinghouse for Federal, Scientific, and Technical Information, U.S. Dept. of Commerce, National Bureau of Standards, Springfield, Virginia 22151 (Accession No. PB176762)).

1 THE ORGANIZATION OF COMPUTING SYSTEMS

The term *logical design* is used by computer designers to describe a systematic methodology, based on Boolean algebra, for designing switching networks. This book uses the term in a broader sense to denote a general method of *reasoning* about operating systems which allows their systematic design, and the study of their organization and behavior. Our emphasis is on general principles as opposed to *ad hoc* "tricks;" thus, coding techniques are not discussed in great detail, nor do we present a case study of a particular commercial system, even though many examples from the latter are given to illustrate particular points.

This chapter introduces the subject by examining the historical development of hardware and software components, by briefly outlining the organization and functions of computing systems, and by discussing systems programs from several different points of view. First, some basic terminology is defined.

1.1. SOME DEFINITIONS

Words such as "operating system," "time-sharing,"or "multiprogramming" do not have widely accepted precise definitions, except perhaps within the context of a theoretical study restricted to some small aspect of systems. Instead, these terms denote certain types of organization, functions, behavior, and/or methods of operation. With this in mind, we informally define several important terms commonly used to describe systems.

An *operating* (supervisory, monitor, executive) *system* (OS) is an *organized* collection of (systems) programs that acts as an interface between machine hardware and users, providing users with a set of facilities to simplify the design, coding, debugging, and maintenance of programs; and, at the same time, controlling the allocation of resources to assure efficient operation.

There are three categories of "pure" OS's, each of which may be characterized by the type of interaction permissible between a user and his job, and by the tolerances on system response time:

1. A *batch processing* OS is one in which user jobs are submitted in sequential batches on input devices and there is no interaction between a user and his job during processing. The user is completely isolated from his job and, as a result, equates system response with job turnaround time. The latter is generally satisfactory if it can be measured in small numbers of minutes or hours. Consequently, the OS can follow a relatively flexible scheduling policy.

2. A *time-sharing* OS is a system that provides computational services to many on-line users concurrently, allowing each user to interact with his computations. The effect of simultaneous access is achieved by sharing processor time and other resources among several users in a manner that guarantees some response to each user command within a few seconds. The computer is allocated to each user process for a small "time-slice," normally in the millisecond range; if the process is not completed at the end of its slice, it is interrupted and placed on a waiting queue, permitting another process its turn at the machine.

3. A *real-time* OS is one that services on-line external processes having *strict* timing constraints on response. Interrupt signals from external processes command the attention of the system; if they are not handled promptly (in microseconds, milliseconds, or seconds, depending on the process), the external process is seriously degraded or misrepresented. These systems are often designed for a particular application, for example, process control.

A particular OS might provide for any or all of batch processing, time-sharing or real-time jobs. For example, both real-time and time-sharing systems usually process batch jobs in the "background" when there is no on-line or external activity.

The most common method for implementing OS's is through multiprogramming. A *multiprogrammed* (multiprogramming) *OS* (MS) is one that maintains more than one user program in main storage simultaneously, sharing processor time, storage space, and other resources among the active user jobs. This resource sharing extends into the operating system; the programs comprising the OS are themselves multiprogrammed in most large systems.

Another way for an OS to process several jobs at once is by swapping. A *swapping OS* maintains several jobs on secondary storage and only one job in main storage at any time; the system switches to another job by moving the current job out of main store and loading a selected job from auxiliary storage. If the previous job is not completed, it will be swapped back in at a later time. This technique has been used mainly in small time-sharing systems.

Our last definition, multiprocessing, describes the hardware configuration of a system and is sometimes confused with multiprogramming. A *multiprocessing computer system* is a computer hardware complex with more than one independent processing unit. This includes central processors (CPU's), input-output (IO) processors, data channels, and special purpose processors, such as arithmetic units. Most often, the term refers to multiple central processing units.

This book is concerned primarily with multiprogrammed operating systems—the advantages and disadvantages of this organization as compared to others, and the techniques and requirements for time, space, and other resource sharing.

1.2. NOTATION FOR ALGORITHMS

The programming language Algol 60 (Naur, 1963), and recognizable variations thereof, will be our primary means for specifying algorithms. Algol, rather than English, flow charts, assembly language, or some other higher level language, was selected for the following reasons:

1. The syntax and semantics of Algol are clearly defined, with little ambiguity, in the public literature.

2. It has been used successfully for many years as an international publication language for algorithms.

3. Algol-like descriptions can be sufficiently "high-level" to eliminate many housekeeping details, if that is desired. Conversely, it can be used in a "low-level" manner that maps into machine language in a straightforward way.†

4. The author and many of his students and colleagues have found this to be a powerful notation for deriving, organizing, and analyzing algorithms. [For an introduction to Algol 60 and a copy of the original report, see Rosen (1967, pp. 48–117).]

---

†While we ascribe to the general philosophy of structured programming (see, for example, Dijkstra, 1969 and SIGPLAN, 1972), the reader will still find **go to** statements in some of our programs. **go to**'s have not been totally eliminated in favor of some other constructs because they are useful for describing machine level activities in a clear way and for explicitly exhibiting flow of control, yet they can also be used in a *disciplined* manner to yield well-structured programs.

Example of an Algol procedure

Tree-like data structures are often used in operating systems, for example, to represent process hierarchies (Chapter 7) or file directories (Chapter 9).

A *binary tree* consists of a finite set of nodes that is either empty or can be divided into a root node and two disjoint binary trees, the left and right subtrees (Knuth, 1968). Let each node n in a binary tree be represented by the triple ($Data[n]$, $Left[n]$, $Right[n]$), where $Data[n]$ is a positive integer, $Left[n]$ is a nonnegative pointer to the root of the left subtree, and $Right[n]$ is a nonnegative pointer to the right subtree. Reserve the node pointer $n = 0$ for the empty tree. Assume that for each node n:

(1)
$$Data[n] < Data[x] \quad \text{for all } x \in Leftsubtree(n) \quad \text{and}$$
$$Data[n] > Data[x] \quad \text{for all } x \in Rightsubtree(n).$$

Figure 1-1 contains an example of such a tree. [Symbol tables are some-

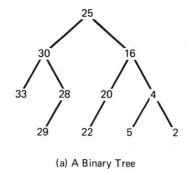

(a) A Binary Tree

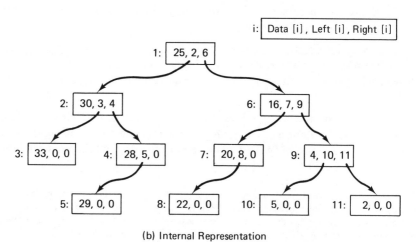

(b) Internal Representation

Fig. 1-1 Binary tree organized for fast sorting, searching, and inserting.

times organized in this manner so they may be expanded and searched easily (Gries, 1971)]. Below is an Algol procedure *Treesearch(root, arg, m)* which will search the tree with root *root* for a node *n* such that $Data[n] = arg$; it will return **true** and set *m* to the matching node if successful, and **false** otherwise. The algorithm uses the recursive definition of a binary tree directly.

Boolean procedure *Treesearch(root, arg, m)* ;
value *root, arg* ; **integer** *root, arg, m* ;
comment *Data* [ ], *Left* [ ], *Right* [ ] are assumed global to this procedure.
Search the tree with root *root* for the node *n* such that $Data[n] = arg$;
if *root* = 0 **then** *Treesearch* := **false else**
begin
   integer *d* ;
   d := *Data*[*root*] ;
   if *arg* = *d* **then begin** *m* := *root* ; *Treesearch* := **true end**
   else
   if *arg* > *d* **then** *Treesearch* := *Treesearch(Left[root], arg, m)*
   else *Treesearch* := *Treesearch(Right[root], arg, m)*
end

EXERCISE

Write an Algol procedure *Addtotree(root, n)* which takes the binary tree with root *root* and node ordering defined by (1), and adds the isolated node *n* to it retaining the ordering of (1). Write another procedure which prints the data of the tree in ascending sequence; use any convenient primitive, such as *Write(x)*, as an output call to print the variable *x*.

1.3 HISTORICAL PERSPECTIVE

This section briefly describes the historical evolution of computer hardware and software systems. A more detailed discussion and bibliography can be found in S. Rosen (1969) and R. Rosin (1969).

1.3.1 Early Systems

From about 1949, when the first stored program digital computer actually started executing instructions, until 1956, the basic organization and mode of operation of computers remained relatively constant (with some farsighted but mostly unsuccessful exceptions). Their classical von Neumann architecture was predicated on strictly sequential instruction execution including input-output operations. When loading and running programs, users would work at the console directly on-line to the machine, setting registers, stepping through instructions, examining storage locations, and generally interacting with their computation at the lowest machine level. (Time-sharing systems were a recognition of the advantages of operating in this fashion but at a higher level than the "raw" hardware). Programs were written in absolute machine language (decimal or octal notation) and were preceded by an absolute loader.

It is instructive to review the procedures for absolute loading since, even now, they represent the starting point for any software system on a raw machine. Any computer has the equivalent of a Load button; when pressed by an operator, it will cause the computer to read an input data record into some fixed set of contiguous main storage locations and then transfer control, i.e., set the instruction counter of the machine, to a fixed address in that set, usually the first.

Example

Let main storage of a primitive computer be designated $M[0]$, $M[1]$, $M[2]$, . . . , where each location $M[i]$ may contain one byte (8 bits) of information. Suppose that pressing the Load button will cause one 80-column card with 80 bytes of information to be read into $M[0], \ldots, M[79]$, followed by the setting of the instruction counter to zero; i.e.,

$$PressLoad: \quad Read(\textbf{for } i := 0 \textbf{ step } 1 \textbf{ until } 79 \textbf{ do } M[i]) \ ;$$
$$Transferto(M[0]) \ ;$$

In order to read an absolute program, the first card, the one read by *Press-Load*, must contain machine instructions for reading succeeding cards (or at least the next card). Let each address, instruction, and datum in our primitive machine occupy 1 byte. Assume that the absolute program is punched on cards with the following format:

Card columns	Contents
1	loading address LA for 1st byte of program/data part of card.
2	the number of bytes, n, to be loaded; $n \le 78$.
3 to $(n + 2)$	program/data part; the absolute code.

The last card contains $n = 0$, and the "loading address" is interpreted as the first instruction, the entry point, of the program; Fig. 1-2 shows the required cards in order. Finally, let storage locations $M[r], \ldots, M[r + 79]$ be a reserved read-in area where r is arbitrarily assigned as the starting location of the read-in area. Then a one-card absolute loader, appearing on the first card, performs the following actions:

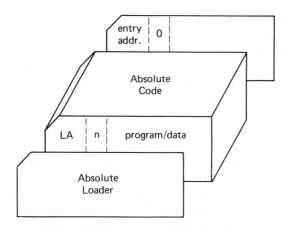

Fig. 1-2 Absolute loader and code cards.

Load: *Read*(**for** $i := 0$ **step** 1 **until** 79 **do** $M[r + i]$) ;
          $LA := M[r]$; $n := M[r + 1]$;
          if $n = 0$ **then** *Transferto*(LA) ;
          for $i := 0$ **step** 1 **until** $n - 1$ **do**
              $M[LA + i] := M[r + 2 + i]$;
          go to *Load* ;

The loading process is a vivid example of bootstrapping—"pulling oneself up by one's own bootstraps."

In these early years, programming aids were either nonexistent or minimal —simple assemblers and interpreters at the most sophisticated installations, with little use of library routines. As the importance of symbolic programming was recognized and assembly systems came into more widespread use, a standard operating procedure evolved: A loader reads in an assembler; the assembler assembles into absolute code symbolic decks of user source programs and library routines; the assembled code is written on tape or cards, and a loader is again used to read these into main storage; the absolute program is then executed. Each step required manual assistance from an operator and consumed a great deal of time, especially in comparison with the computer time to process the cards at that step.

The "first generation" of operating systems was motivated by the above inefficiencies as well as by other considerations. These additional factors included the expense of on-line operation; the availability of other languages (the FORTRAN system being most prominent); the development of library programs and services especially related to input-output operations; and the awkwardness of translating into absolute code, which required that *all* program sections and subroutines needed for a given run be translated together initially and every time a change was made in any program. The first batch systems automated the standard load/translate/load/execute sequence with a central control program to retrieve and load required system programs—an assembler, compiler, loader, or library subroutine—and to handle job-to-job transitions. Language translators were rewritten to produce relocatable rather than absolute code. Linking loaders were developed to allow source and relocatable object language decks to be mixed together; library programs could then also be stored in relocatable object form. Services from a human operator were required for administrating the physical batch input and output equipment, for setup of nonstandard jobs, and for taking corrective action on system failure. The originator of a job was banished, at least in principle, from the machine and gradually was convinced that the "best" way of treating a computer complex was as a large input-output box. In these OS's, protection was a most difficult and frustrating problem; it was relatively easy for the system to be destroyed by itself or by a user, or for one user to read past his job into the next job. Resource allocation, for main storage and IO devices primarily, was the task of language processors and user programs rather than the OS.

1.3.2 Second Generation Hardware and Software

The generations of computer hardware have been defined in terms of their component technology—vacuum tubes in the first generation, transistors in the second, and integrated circuits in the third. From the perspective of operating systems, these distinctions are less important than those that can be made in hardware and software architecture; the time periods are roughly the same.

From about 1959 to 1963, several significant hardware developments came into widespread use and stimulated advances in OS's. Perhaps the most important hardware innovation was the *data channel*—a primitive computer, with its own instruction set, registers, and control, that controls the communication and data transmission between the main computer and IO devices. On receiving an IO request from a CPU, the channel executes and controls the operation, asynchronously and in parallel with continued CPU execution; overlapping of IO and CPU operations is then possible. Main storage is shared by the CPU and channel, containing programs and data for both. Initially, the CPU could interrogate the status of the channel, but it soon became clear that one could operate more efficiently if the channel could also *interrupt* CPU processing to deliver a message, most frequently the completion of an IO operation.

Complicated input-output programming systems were written to take advantage of the potential efficiencies of this new architecture. These included software buffering facilities to permit automatic reading ahead of programs and queuing output for delayed writing of output, and interrupt-handling routines to respond to IO interrupts and return control to interrupted programs.

Interrupts were expanded to signal exceptional internal conditions such as an arithmetic overflow, and instructions were added for the selective *enabling* (turning on), *disabling* (turning off), and *inhibiting* (delaying the action of) the interrupt mechanisms. Internal clocks that could be programmed to interrupt the CPU after a specified time interval became available; these allowed a supervisory routine to control the amount of CPU time allocated for each user, permitting the automatic detection of some erroneous or excessively long programs.

It was natural for users, on the one hand, to delegate interrupt-handling and IO services to a central system, and for installation managers, on the other hand, to begin to insist that users employ these services. A sophisticated programmer would still often write his own packages. System protection remained a serious and unsolved problem; systems crashes were caused by both experienced and beginning programmers, in an almost too easy fashion.

During this period, libraries were expanded considerably to include utility routines, such as sorts or card-to-tape converters, and more language processors; direct access files (usually disks) began to replace magnetic tape for storing the system and libraries. With the added and more complex tasks of the OS—the "machine" viewed by a typical user becoming further removed from the actual hardware—it was necessary to specify in a more systematic way the characteristics and requirements of a job; job control languages were added for this purpose.

We can summarize this generation as a settling-in period for sequential batch processing, with many exploratory efforts to use data channels, interrupts, and auxiliary storage efficiently. However, one-job-at-a-time processing still resulted in low channel activity for heavy compute jobs and low CPU activity for heavy IO jobs, even if maximum overlap of CPU and channel operations was obtained.

1.3.3 Systems of the Third Generation and Beyond

From about 1962 to 1969, a new method of running jobs, *multiprogramming*, came into almost universal use in large OS's; a new way to do computing, *time-sharing*, was also developed as an alternative to batch processing. Large fast-access disk units provided on-line storage for systems and user library programs, as well as for user jobs waiting to be processed. Hardware for storage and instruction protection was incorporated on many computers; main memory systems with relocation hardware that permitted the implementation of large "virtual" memories appeared on some large machines; and multiprocessor configurations became more common. The problems of resource allocation and protection became more critical and difficult in a multiprogramming environment, where many processes were simultaneously requesting both shared and exclusive use of resources of the system, often had to transmit signals to one another, and were potentially malicious or erratic. It was during this period that the subject of operating systems emerged as a central part of software engineering and computer science.

Many hardware and software innovations have appeared since the first machines of the mid-nineteen-forties, and the pace has not slackened in recent years. Advances in large-scale integrated circuit technology and in mass production of standard computer components have made it possible to build inexpensive yet powerful computers; the number and variety of these will proliferate in the near future, requiring economical software to match the hardware. At the same time, large computer networks connected via communication lines are beginning to offer utility-like services; these place even heavier burdens on systems software. Other hardware changes, such as writeable control storage for microprogramming, hierarchies of main storage units with automatic information transfers among levels, increased and programmable parallelism in processing units, and economical associative memories, will lead to new software requirements and force a deeper understanding of OS's. Current software developments include higher-level languages for systems programming; the derivation of adequate OS primitives for process and resource scheduling, which may be implemented by hardware, microprograms, or standard software; human-oriented job-control languages; languages and systems to deal with parallelism; subsystems for measuring OS performance; and more general protection schemes.

For the first time, systematic techniques for designing, analyzing, and simulating OS's are available to a limited extent and are under widespread investigation. We are purposely brief here, since later chapters discuss operating systems at the levels of the late third generation and beyond.

1.4 SOME VIEWS OF OPERATING SYSTEMS

Some of the earliest types of systems programs were language processors —assemblers, macro-assemblers, interpreters, and compilers. These are no longer considered components of an OS but are treated as applications programs; they use services provided by an OS and run under its control. (An important application of language processors is the translation of OS's and subsystems written in assembly and higher level languages, including the case of an OS operating under the control of another OS.)

The major systems modules comprising an OS can be divided into two overlapping classes. First are those which may be called, directly or indirectly, during user program execution. Input-output routines and other file systems services are the most obvious examples. The second class consists of those programs that are invoked, either explicitly through directives or implicitly through declarations, through *control language* statements issued by users or a machine operator. These two classes represent the bulk of an OS† and include:

1. Schedulers to allocate central processing unit(s) to jobs, parts of jobs, and systems processes.

2. Memory management routines that decide and administrate the allocation of main storage.

3. Input-output controllers that service input-output requests for all occupants of the system.

4. Linking and loading procedures to relocate, load, and link together a set of programs.

5. File systems programs for controlling the access, storage, and movement of files of data among the computer storage media.

6. Interrupt handlers for servicing external and internal interrupts.

These programs call each other and interact in complex and, often, subtle ways.

1.4.1 Virtual Machines, Translation, and Resource Allocation

It is useful to distinguish between the actual computer hardware and its principles of operations on the one hand, and the "machines" viewed by different classes of users on the other hand. We shall call the latter *virtual machines*, since they rarely are the real computer but are most often the result of layers of software superimposed upon it.

Examples

1. Consider a higher-level language compile, load, and go subsystem, for example, implementing the Algol language. The Algol programmer equates the computer with this subsystem—a machine that directly executes Algol. Consequently, the user of this virtual machine is not concerned with problems of register and storage allocation, channel programs, interrupts, array mapping functions, and other tasks that appear at "lower" levels.

2. The implementers of the subsystem described in 1 above might have used a macro-assembly system that included a number of "system" macros, for example, for input-output. The macro-assembly language programmers may not have to worry about details of storage allocation for their programs if their virtual machine automatically provides this service; however, it is

---

†We have ignored those modules responsible for systems generation and maintenance.

necessary to design storage administration routines for the Algol machine, e.g., for run-time stack housekeeping.

3. A systems programmer working on a basic module such as an input-output buffering system would typically employ a virtual machine consisting partly of the real machine but augmented by some operating systems "nucleus" primitives, for example, macros for transmitting messages among processes and for queue manipulation.

4. The job control language through which a user expresses his job and resource requirements represents a virtual operating systems machine at the job and job step levels.

5. A user may be given the illusion of working with a very large central memory; the system in turn implements this virtual memory on a much smaller and/or differently organized real main storage.

A user thus has available a number of machines from which he can create more abstract machines. At the lowest level, there is the real computer. A systems programmer using machines at level i and below writes software to implement a new virtual machine at level $i + 1$. Weiderman (1971) has graphically depicted this hierarchy of virtual machines as in the example of Fig. 1-3; M_i designates a machine and S_i designates software at level i. In the figure, software module S_0 implemented in the language of the real computer M_0 realizes a new virtual machine M_1. Similarly, software S_2 written for virtual machine M_2 produces a new virtual machine M_3, whereas S'_2 written for the same machine as S_2 produces a different virtual machine M'_3.

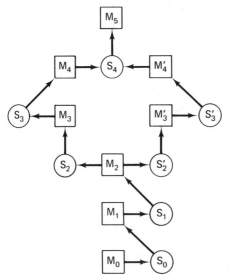

Fig. 1-3 Hierarchies of virtual machines (Weiderman, 1971).

Since operating systems and language processors implement virtual machine interfaces for computer users, their basic function can be defined as one of translation; they successively translate machines at higher levels to lower-level equivalents until eventually the real computer is reached. Consider a possible translation sequence starting with a higher-level language machine. Let M_1, M_2, and M_3 be machines produced by a software loader S_0, an assembler S_1, and a compiler S_2, respectively; this hierarchy is illustrated in Fig. 1-4(a). A higher-level language program x_4 is translated successively into assembly language x_3, relocatable machine code x_2, and an absolute machine language program x_1. The latter is then translated (executed, interpreted) to yield an output string x_0 [Fig. 1-4(b)].

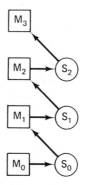

(a) Virtual Machines Leading to a Higher Level Language Processor

$$x_0 = M_0(M_1(M_2(M_3(x_4))))$$

Fig. 1-4   Systems as translators.   (b) Translation From x_4 to x_0

Language processors are essentially translators, but this is a simplistic and peripheral interpretation of the task of an OS (except perhaps from the point of view of a user). Their more fundamental activity is the allocation and administration of resources; we attach a general meaning to "resources" to include not only the hardware resources of the computer but also software resources, such as shared programs and data, and messages transmitted among processes. When the resource is an *active* unit such as a central processor or data channel, the allocator is usually called a scheduler.

At this point, it is worth emphasizing that the most important task of any system is to assist computer *users* in solving their problems—by giving them language facilities that allow algorithms to be expressed efficiently, by performing resource allocation and housekeeping functions centrally so that their problems may be solved economically, and by scheduling their processes to provide rapid response.

1.4.2 Four Key Issues

There are four related problems that are inherent in multiprogramming OS's (Miller, 1968). Two of these, *virtual machine mappings* and *resource allocation*, have been briefly mentioned. The virtual machine translation problem appears in both a *static* form, as in the example of the last section (Fig. 1-4), and a *dynamic* form, such as the execution-time relocation of instruction and data addresses. This translation can be viewed as a name/resource mapping. For example, suppose that peripheral units are identified symbolically and that storage addresses are relocatable at some level above the real machine; these must then be mapped into absolute device and storage addresses, respectively. Resource allocation and scheduling become a problem of matching the efficient use of hardware with user response constraints.

The third issue is that of *protection*. We must ensure the integrity of the OS and user programs from accidental or malicious damage or snooping by users and the system itself. This is not only a question of preventing the destruction of information but must also be concerned with problems of privacy and ownership. Private user files or parts of the OS may require guarantees against unauthorized reading or execution. In addition, an owner of a file—data or program—should be able to permit any of reading, writing, or execution to specified classes of users.

The fourth problem that is characteristic of these systems results from the need to *synchronize* and *communicate* among resident systems processes and, sometimes, user processes. Physically, as well as abstractly, many processes are simultaneously executing. A given independent program, e.g., user job, must always produce the same answer regardless of other programs that may be running at the same time. When programs require synchronization—for example, when an input program provides buffered data for a main program—one must be careful to prevent the situations in which no program runs because each is waiting for a signal from another or in which a program misses a signal.

Throughout the book, the four issues will constantly appear, and a variety of techniques to handle them will be discussed.

1.5   SYSTEMS ORGANIZATION

There are an overwhelming number of possible hardware organizations; fortunately, most of these are extensions and variations of a standard configuration. Figure 1-5 contains a block diagram of perhaps the simplest ar-

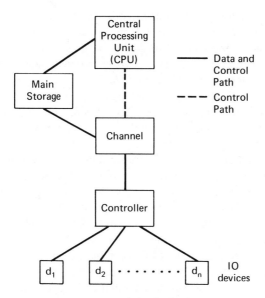

Fig. 1-5 A minimal machine.

rangement of this by now classical machine. Unless we state otherwise, it will be assumed that our OS software is designed *minimally* for such a computer.

The CPU has the normal complement of internal and program-addressable registers, arithmetic unit(s), and the system control. The latter controls instruction sequencing and execution, directly and indirectly activating the rest of the computer hardware. Below is the basic algorithm executed by the CPU control; the algorithm can be implemented by a microprogram or by logic circuitry:

> *loop:*   *Fetch next instruction* ;
> *Increment instruction counter* ;
> *Execute the instruction* ;
> **go to** *loop* ;

Enabled interrupts from IO devices, the controller, channel, and/or the execution cycle itself are serviced at the end of an instruction cycle after the third step. If several interrupts occur simultaneously during a single cycle, a hardware priority mechanism may ignore all but one for at least one more cycle. The CPU is assumed to have an internal timer that may be set by program to cause an interrupt signal after a specified time interval.

Main storage is considered a contiguously addressed set of storage bins, each with capacity of 1 unit (bit, byte, word, digit, character, . . .) of information. The data channel (Section 1.3.2) can transmit data or control information from main storage (and sometimes CPU registers) to the IO controller, and send data or status information from the latter back to main storage or the CPU; this is generally accomplished in parallel with CPU operation. The controller is a device-dependent processor that will select and control the operation of specific devices. The IO devices may include batch peripherals, such as card readers, punches, paper tape equipment, and line printers; and interactive terminals, such as typewriter consoles and graphics devices; it will certainly include some large auxiliary storage units, for example, drum or disk, and perhaps even magnetic tape.

Some of these hardware features are amplified in succeeding chapters when their details and variations significantly affect software design.

There does not exist a standard widely accepted organization for an OS. However, we can make some general comments about their composition at this point. Informally define the *state of an OS* as the collection of states of all processes and resources in the system. The state of a process includes whether it is ready to run, is executing on a processor, or is logically blocked waiting for the allocation of a resource it requested; the state of a class of resources includes the current allocation and a list of processes waiting for their resource requests to be granted. Most changes of state of an OS occur as a result of interrupts that invoke OS processes. In this sense, interrupt handling routines represent the driving force underlying all systems, and we say that OS's are *interrupt-driven*.†

Changes of state are effected by *process and resource management* components of the OS. The third major part is a *file system*, since normally all information transmission through the storage media and IO peripherals is centrally administrated. Other important OS software can be described in terms of the process, resource, and file systems components; one outstanding example is the "job management" portion of a system, which supervises the initiation, execution, termination, and accounting for jobs. Some necessary software, such as dump routines or peripheral utilities, can often be considered as applications programs, even when the OS itself requests them.

---

†There are systems that are not interrupt-driven but instead rely on separate hardware processors to poll a central processor for state change requests; the prime example is the CDC 6400/6500/6600 computer series (CDC, 1969). Although we shall assume an interrupt-driven operation, most of the techniques considered are independent of this choice, and also apply to the polling situation and to systems where a simple call to a systems routine can also change the process and resource states.

2 BATCH PROCESSING SYSTEMS

2.1 INTRODUCTION

The name "batch processing" is derived from the manner in which jobs are collected and run. In the early systems of this type, submitted jobs are collected into batches or sets, and processed sequentially, one job at a time, through the computer. The primary tasks performed by the operating system are

1. *Job control.* This most basic and highest level function provides for the initiation and termination of both jobs and steps within jobs. The primary action here is the interpretation of job control cards to (a) establish and terminate accounting procedures for a job, (b) associate actual input-output device addresses with the symbolic ones employed in the job, and (c) invoke the appropriate systems program to perform the task requested by a job step.

2. *Program loading and linking.* Programs are allocated storage, relocated to reflect this allocation, and loaded into storage. At the same time, linkage among independently translated programs that are used together is established. These programs could be user object programs, operating system modules, or elements of a general user library.

3. *Input-output control.* Except under unusual circumstances, the system is responsible for all input-output. Input-output requests are sent to systems programs that schedule, initiate, and monitor the operations. This task often includes device and auxiliary storage allocation, and software buffering. The intent of this centralization is to improve both the efficiency and protection of the system, as well as to relieve the user from the rather messy details of input-output programming.

17

This chapter is concerned with the fundamental ideas underlying linking loaders and input-output programming within the framework of batch processing systems. This is not meant to be an exhaustive treatment of classical batch systems. Our purpose is to introduce some important ideas and techniques that are useful in their own right and will be applied in later chapters on multiprogrammed systems.

2.2 LINKING AND LOADING

The static structure of a program can be represented by a tree as illustrated in Fig. 2-1, where each node P_i designates either a procedure or a program segment, P_0 is the main program, and the successor nodes of any P_i

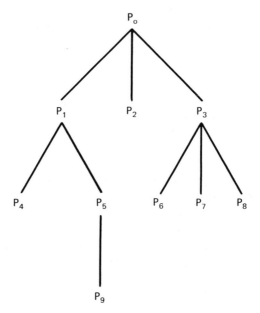

Fig. 2-1   Static tree structure of a program.

contain the procedures called by P_i and program segments transferred to by P_i. For example, P_1 is called by P_0 and, in turn, calls P_4 and P_5 in the figure. Multiple uses of the same procedure, including recursion, are indicated when two or more nodes have the same name. The procedures may be library routines or user programs. Execution of a program requires that there be provision for loading any procedure in the static tree into storage and for linking together calling and called procedures.

The earliest language processors produced object programs in the form of *absolute* machine code; the storage locations where programs and data reside at run time were determined by the language processors. This meant that *all* of the procedures that appeared in the static program structure had to be translated together to ensure that no conflicts in storage allocation arose. Independently translated programs could not be merged, in general, since it was possible for them to have overlapping storage assignments. Thus, a user was compelled to include source language programs for all the library and applications routines referenced by his program, however indirectly.

These difficulties were resolved by changing the output of language processors to relocatable object programs containing symbolic linkage information. Each procedure or program segment is independently translated. Programs are allocated storage, relocated according to this allocation, loaded, and linked together just *prior* to execution. The set of systems programs that performs the relocation, linking, and loading is called a *linking loader*; the process is termed *static* relocation, linking, and loading since these tasks are completely done before program execution. (These tasks may also be accomplished *dynamically* during execution; this case will be treated in Chapters 5 and 6.) The entire process is portrayed in Fig. 2-2.

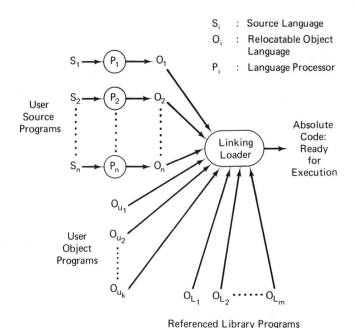

Fig. 2-2 Linking loaders.

2.2.1 Static Relocation

Since storage is not allocated until load time, language processors will translate source programs into a sequence of instruction and data records relative to some arbitrary base location, usually 0. These records are then relocated when storage is assigned.

A translated instruction record generally consists of some variation of the form:

$$Loc \; oc \; a_1 a_2. \ldots a_n$$

where Loc is the relative address of the instruction, oc is the operation code, and the a_i are the instruction operand fields. Loc can be eliminated except when the $(i + 1)$st sequential record does not have a relative address immediately succeeding the ith. If the object program is to be loaded into contiguous storage starting at location α and the program has been translated relative to β, then the instruction part of the above record will be stored in $Loc + k$, where the *relocation constant* $k = \alpha - \beta$. Now consider the address fields. Each a_i can be a register name, an immediate operand, the storage address of an operand, or the storage address of an instruction (we are simplifying the situation somewhat, since other information, such as indirect addressing flags, may be present). In the latter two cases, relocation may be necessary, depending on the structure of the machine and the original source program. Address fields may always be relative, for example, if effective address calculation uses base registers; no relocation is required here. However, when address fields are treated as absolute by the machine, an address a_i must be changed to $a_i + k$ by the loader. The instruction records can be augmented by indicators specifying which a_i are to be relocated, or a global relocation dictionary associated with the program may be used to point to these operands.

Data records are treated in a similar manner. They have the general form

$$Loc \; d_1 d_2. \ldots d_m$$

where Loc is the relative address of the data and the d_i are data items. As before, the data items will be loaded starting at storage location $Loc + k$. A field d_i can also contain a relative address; d_i must then also be relocated by k.

2.2.2 The Linking Process

A program or data segment may both (a) define symbols for possible reference by other programs and (b) reference symbolic information defined by other modules. Examples of (a) are the name of a routine, the entry points to a routine, and the names of data areas; references to external symbols [(b)]

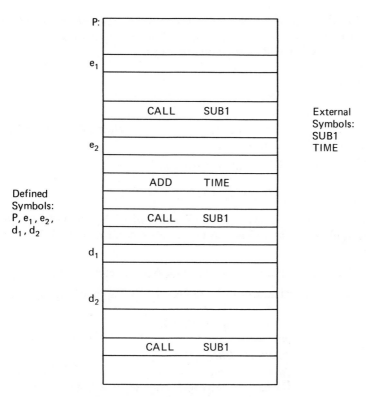

Fig. 2-3 Defined and external symbols in a program or data segment.

occur naturally in calls to procedures and use of global data (Fig. 2-3). Both the internally defined symbols and the external symbols used must explicitly appear in relocatable object modules for use by the linking routine.

Associated with *each* relocatable object segment will be a symbol *definition* table and a symbol *use* table (Fig. 2-4). The definition table lists every symbol of class (a) above. Each entry is a pair (*Dname[i]*, *Dval[i]*), where *Dname* contains the symbols and *Dval* contains their corresponding values; a symbol value is usually a relocatable data or instruction address within the segment. When a segment is relocated by the linking loader, the *Dval* entries are similarly relocated to the absolute storage address defined by the symbol. This table then becomes part of a global *symbol table* that is used to retrieve addresses for externally defined symbols.

The use table consists minimally of a list of all external symbols referenced in the segment. There are two common methods for handling external references when one is creating relocatable segments. The first is to use the locations where the references occur as links in a chain headed by the use table entry [Fig. 2-5 (a)]. When the symbol is defined, the absolute addresses can be easily inserted in the correct locations by tracing through this chain; the last element in the chain will have a null link, say 0.

Example

Let

(a) P be a program segment that has been relocated by the relocation constant k and loaded into storage M,

(b) the use table of P contain n entries:

$$(Uname[i], \ Uval[i]), \ i = 1, \ldots, n,$$

(c) $Uval[i]$ point to the last use of $Uname[i]$ in P (assume that $Uval[i]$ is a relocatable address) and be the header element of a chain of uses of that symbol, and

(d) $Uname[i]$ contain, not the symbol, but its defined value.

Then the external references in P are inserted by the following algorithm:

```
for i := 1 step 1 until n do
begin
    Fixup := Uname[i] ;
    Next := Uval[i] ;
    for adr := Next + k while Next ≠ 0 do
    begin
        Next := M[adr] ;
        M[adr] := Fixup
    end
end ;
```

The second method avoids the above fixup procedure by using indirect addressing for all external symbols [Figure 2-5(b)]. When the symbol is defined, its value is inserted in the indirect address location; the latter is sometimes called a *transfer vector*. Linking is faster and simpler, but at execution time, two memory cycles instead of one are required to reference a symbol.

Linking and loading can be done by either a one-pass or two-pass technique. The two-pass method has the following steps:

A. Pass 1:

1. Get next relocatable object segment P.

2. Relocate and load P.

3. Update global symbol table with defined symbols of P.

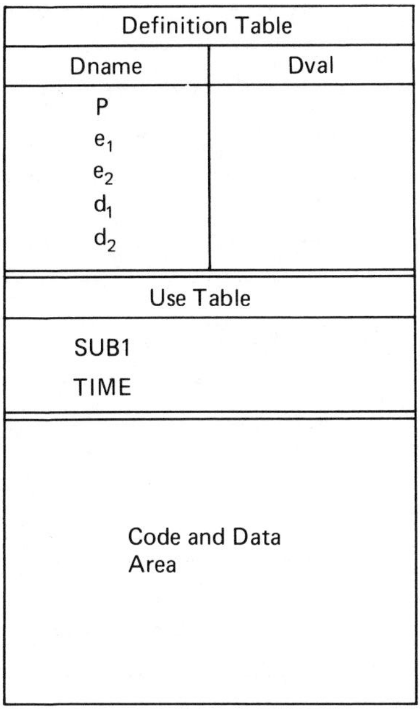

Definition Table	
Dname	Dval
P e_1 e_2 d_1 d_2	
Use Table	
SUB1 TIME	
Code and Data Area	

Fig. 2-4 Form of a relocatable segment.

4. Repeat Steps 1–3 for each segment P.

B. Pass 2:

1. Get use table for next segment P.

2. Fixup external references in P by retrieving definition of each use table entry from the global symbol table.

3. Repeat Steps 1–2 for each loaded segment P.

The symbol processing is similar to that employed in a standard two-pass assembler. The assembler analogy also applies to the one-pass techniques; the principal part of the processing is involved with handling the complexities resulting from symbol forward references (see the exercise below). It should be clear that the linking methods are, to a large extent, concerned with the creation, searching, and manipulation of symbol tables.

The linking and loading operations are often separated into two distinct parts. The first part produces a "load module" consisting of all object segments linked and relocated together relative to a standard base address; the load module is usually placed in auxiliary memory. The final part, the load operation, loads the module into main storage, relocating addresses to reflect memory allocation.

The main components of a linking loader have been described in isolation without mentioning their interaction with other parts of an operating system.

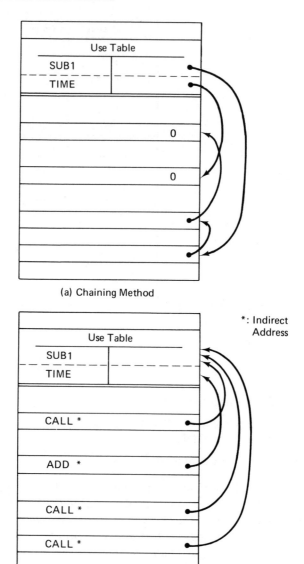

(a) Chaining Method

(b) Indirect Addressing

Fig. 2-5   Treatment of external symbol references.

In particular, much use of the input-output and file systems must be made in order to locate and retrieve the required set of relocatable object modules; we have also ignored main storage allocation, which clearly must be performed before loading.

Many operating systems employ the static relocation and linking techniques outlined in these sections. The more elaborate and dynamic methods described in Chapters 5 and 6 require similar relocation information, and symbol definition and use tables in object programs.

EXERCISE

Write an Algol procedure for a one-pass linking loader. The procedure will successively read the relocatable object programs comprising a job and perform the required relocation linking and loading. Each object segment O_i will be of the form

$$(d, \textit{Dname}[1], \textit{Dval}[1], \textit{Dname}[2], \textit{Dval}[2], \ldots, \textit{Dname}[d], \textit{Dval}[d],$$
$$u, \textit{Uname}[1], \textit{Uval}[1], \textit{Uname}[2], \textit{Uval}[2], \ldots, \textit{Uname}[u], \textit{Uval}[u],$$
$$t, \textit{Text}[1], \textit{Text}[2], \ldots, \textit{Text}[t]),$$

where $d \geq 0$, $u \geq 0$, and $t \geq 1$.

Each definition table value *Dval* points to a relative location (relative to 0) of the assembled code in O_i. Each use table value *Uval* points to the last element in a chain of uses of the corresponding undefined symbol. The array *Text* contains the assembled instructions and relocation information. You are given a routine *Relocate*(t, *Text*) that relocates and loads the code of *Text* into storage M and updates a location counter LC; at any time, LC contains the address of the next word to be inserted in storage; i.e., the next word will be inserted in $M[LC]$. Assume that the global symbol table consists of three arrays, *Name*, *Adr*, and *Flag*, with the following interpretation:

1. If *Flag*[i] = **false**, the symbol given in *Name*[i] has not been defined. *Adr*[i] will then point to the first location in M of a chain of all uses of *Name* [i].

2. If *Flag*[i] = **true**, the symbol *Name*[i] has been defined. *Adr*[i] will then be its absolute address in M; i.e., *Adr*[i] contains the value of the symbol.

Also given is a routine *Search*(*arg*, *index*), which will search the symbol table for a match between *arg* and some *Name*[i]. If successful, *Search* returns **true**, and *index* contains the location in the table of the successful search. Otherwise, *Search* returns **false**, and *index* contains the next free location in the symbol table.

2.3 INPUT-OUTPUT METHODS

The storage devices in a large computer system can be ordered according to the speeds in which they may be accessed:

1. Processor storage: index registers, accumulators, instruction registers, ...

2. Main storage: core, thin film, integrated circuits, ...

3. Auxiliary storage: drum, disk, magnetic tape, ...

4. Peripheral devices: card readers, card punches, paper tape, display devices, teletypes, ...

The rate of information transfer among these devices varies by a factor of approximately 10^9 throughout this hierarchy—from one character per second in some peripherals to billions of characters per second in a central processor. Each of the above units can be viewed as *input-output* (IO) devices in some contexts; for example, information from an auxiliary storage device is often transmitted directly or indirectly to or from the central processor, other auxiliary storage devices, or peripherals.

IO operations can be divided into three main categories:

1. *Read/write.* These operations move data from one storage device to another.

2. *Control.* These are instructions sent to device controllers for activities such as positioning the access mechanism of a disk, rewinding or skipping records on a tape, or ejecting a page on a printer. Generally, control operations prepare storage devices for reading and writing.

3. *Status testing.* The status of IO devices and processors may be interrogated through these instructions; the most common example of this class is an IO busy test.

IO operations among registers of a processing unit and between a processor and main storage are scheduled and controlled automatically by hardware when machine instructions are being fetched and executed; the disparity between main storage access time and processor speed is counteracted in many computers by instruction look-ahead and interleaved storage. The IO problem in systems programming is to optimally organize, schedule, control, and perform data movement among the elements of main storage, auxiliary storage, and the peripheral devices. The ultimate aim is to achieve a maximal amount of overlap of IO operations so that the devices at each level in the storage hierarchy can be operating continuously at their rated speeds. The system attempts to accomplish this through a variety of software and hardware techniques such as IO buffering, interrupts, channels, and coroutines. We examine these techniques in the remainder of this chapter.

The IO methods and problems that are presented are not only important in their own right, but also provide examples of and insights into more general problems that occur in resource sharing and multiprogramming.

2.3.1 Direct IO

Most of the earlier computers and some of the smaller modern computers have *direct* IO instructions. By "direct," we mean that the complete IO operation is handled directly and sequentially by the central processor in its normal instruction cycle. This includes initiating the operation, controlling the IO storage areas involved, maintaining a count of the number of characters transmitted, and testing for errors; the CPU is not available until the instruction has been completely performed. The time t_p for a program p to run to completion is $t_p = t_{io} + t_c$, where t_{io} is the time required to complete the IO operations requested in p and t_c represents the compute time–the time for execution of the internal non-IO operations of p.

Hardware buffers are often used as interfaces between peripheral IO devices with fixed record lengths, such as card readers and printers, and main storage. An input (output) instruction empties (fills) the buffer into (from) main storage and activates the device to automatically refill (empty) the buffer while the program proceeds. An input (output) device is always one IO operation ahead of (behind) the program. The buffer is invisible to the programmer and allows the parallel execution of the electromechanical peripheral device and the central processing unit. If a device is busy filling or emptying a buffer when an IO call is given, the computer must *wait* until the operation finishes. The best that one can do with, say, an input-only program p and hardware buffering is approximately $t_p = \max(t_{io}, t_c) + t_b$, where t_{io} is the total time for transferring from the input device to the buffer and t_b is the total transfer time between the buffer and main storage. The programmer must space his IO operations carefully in order to avoid processor waits and achieve maximal overlap.

Considerably greater control is obtained when a program-addressable *IO busy flag* is available in the hardware. This is a one-bit register that is automatically set when an IO unit becomes busy and is reset when the unit becomes free. For a simple computer with hardware buffers *in* and *out*, an IO instruction produces the following *hardware* actions:

Input Instruction

           a: **if** *deviceflag* $= 1$ **then go to** *a* ;
               inarea $:= in$;
               deviceflag $:= 1$;
               Initiate Input Device ;

Output Instruction

           a: **if** *deviceflag* $= 1$ **then go to** *a* ;
               out $:= outarea$;
               deviceflag $:= 1$;
               Initiate Output Device ;

where *inarea* and *outarea* are storage areas for input and output records. Since the flag is addressable, the programmer may test it and branch to routines involving no IO while waiting for the unit to become free; for example,

$$\textbf{if } deviceflag = 1 \textbf{ then } Computeonly\ ;$$
$$IO\ instruction\ ;$$

It is still necessary to organize a program carefully with respect to the spacing of IO commands and compute-only sections of code if a reasonable overlap of the two is to be obtained.

2.3.2 Indirect IO

Almost all computing systems have some form of *indirect* IO so that concurrent operation of the central processor and IO devices can be achieved more easily. The central processor only initiates the IO and can then continue with the next instruction; the actual operation is controlled by an independent unit—a *channel* or *IO processor*.

A central processor IO instruction consists of a request to a channel and can be put in the form:

$$startio(channelnumber,\ channelprogramarea),$$

where *channelnumber* identifies the particular channel and *channelprogramarea* points to a main storage location containing a program or set of commands which the channel executes to perform the desired operation. For read/write operations, the channel program specifies a main storage address and an amount of data to be sent to or from that address; it will also, in general, identify a particular device controller and contain orders to the latter to select and activate the desired IO device. Both the channel and central processor compete for storage cycles during concurrent operation, with the channel normally having the highest priority; i.e., the CPU will be idle until the channel storage request has been honored. If the channel is busy when a *startio* call is issued, we shall assume that the CPU *waits* until the channel can accept the IO request.†

The status of a channel may be interrogated at any time by the central processor. A flag, either in storage or in a register, is set when the channel is busy, and reset when it is free. We shall use the Boolean variable $busy[i]$ to test the busy status of channel i; $busy[i] = \textbf{true}$ if channel i is busy and $\textbf{false}$ otherwise. Other channel, controller, and device status information, such as the occurrence of IO errors or whether a unit is busy or even connected, is also available, but that will be ignored here.

†This CPU behavior on a busy channel is not commonly found. More frequently, one always gets an immediate return from the *startio* accompanied by some status bits indicating the reason for not starting the IO.

A second method of communication between a channel and central processor is through interrupts. Here, a channel will interrupt the CPU on termination of an IO operation or on an error condition. An enabled interrupt that is set is usually serviced at the end of an instruction cycle and results in a forced transfer of control to some fixed location associated with the cause of the interrupt; the state of the machine immediately preceding the interrupt—minimally, the instruction counter contents—is automatically saved. Below is a simplified description of a hardware instruction cycle including interrupts:

M is the main storage; ic is the instruction counter; $int1$, $int2$, ..., $intn$ are fixed locations in M to which control is transferred on interrupts of types $C1$, $C2$, ..., Cn, respectively. Assume that all interrupts are enabled.

> *Next*: $w := M[ic]$;
> $ic := ic + 1$;
> *Execute*(w) ;
> **if** *Interrupt* **then**
> **begin**
>   *Store* (ic) ;
>   **if** *cause* = $C1$ **then** $ic := int1$
>   **else**
>   **if** *cause* = $C2$ **then** $ic := int2$
>   **else**
>   .
>   .
>   .
>   **else** $ic := intn$
> **end** ;
> **go to** *Next* ;

To avoid unnecessary complexities in the following discussions on buffering algorithms, we shall assume that the IO read/write commands deal with *fixed length* records and sequential devices, and we shall use *Read*(ch, loc) and *Write*(ch, loc) instead of the *startio* instruction and detailed channel program, where ch is the channel number and loc is the address of the first main storage location of the fixed block participating in the data transmission. *Read* and *Write* thus result in the *initiation* of the instruction, if possible, by the CPU and the performance of the IO by the channel; the CPU is immediately released after initiation of the channel.

2.4 SOFTWARE IO BUFFERING

In the next four subsections, a series of IO examples are worked out in detail in order to illustrate the techniques and problems of IO buffering, parallel processing between a CPU and a channel, basic interrupt handling, and storage sharing by several programs.

2.4.1   CPU Interrogates Channel

Assume that the CPU interrogates or polls a channel through the busy flag and that interrupts are not used. An extreme technique that would provide maximum overlap between the channel and CPU is represented by the statement sequence:

$$\ldots Read(ch, loc) \; ; \; Compute(loc) \; ; \ldots$$

Compute(loc) designates compute only (non-IO) operations with the storage block *loc*. The computations with the contents of the IO area, *Compute(loc)*, start immediately after the channel is initiated. The serious problem here is that the same storage area is being simultaneously changed and accessed by both the channel and the CPU. The result would generally be chaos—it is almost impossible for the CPU, when accessing a particular location in the IO area, to ascertain whether or not its contents have been changed by the *Read*. This can be rectified by changing the sequence to

```
          .
          .
          .
       Read(ch, loc);
loop:  if busy[ch] then go to loop ;
       Compute(loc) ;
          .
          .
          .
```

The time for any program to complete is then $t_p = t_{io} + t_c$ and *no* parallel operation of the CPU and channel occurs. There is no point in having a separate IO processor if this method is always used.

One obvious way to take advantage of the channel is to simulate hardware buffering. Let the input buffer be an array of n words, $Bufin[1:n]$. The following procedure *Get(Area)* has the same effect on the system as the hardware-buffered *read* presented in Sec. 2.3.1:

```
procedure Get(Area) ;
integer array Area ;
begin
  integer i ;
  procedure MoveBufin ;
    for i := 1 step 1 until n do Area[i] := Bufin[i] ;
  loop:  if busy[ch] then go to loop ;
  MoveBufin ;
  Read(ch, Bufin)
end Get
```

The system is then always reading one record ahead of its demand. The read/ compute sequence in a typical program is now of the form

$$\dots Get(loc) ; Compute(loc) ; \dots$$

Initially, *Bufin* must be loaded by executing *Read*(*ch, Bufin*). A similar procedure, *Put*(*Area*), can be written for output. The primary overhead in the *Get* and *Put* routines is the time to move the buffer contents into the desired storage location (*MoveBufin* and, say, *MoveBufout*). When maximum overlap is achieved, program completion time is approximately $\max(t_c, t_{io}) + t_b$, where t_b is the total time taken to transfer to and from the input and output software buffers and t_c is the time required to execute *Compute*(*loc*) ; $t_{io} = \max(t_{input}, t_{output})$ if separate channels are used for input and output and $t_{io} = t_{input} + t_{output}$ if one channel is shared.

To eliminate the lengthy buffer transfers, it is possible to use several buffers and work directly in the buffer areas. Let there be two buffers, *Buf*[1] and *Buf*[2], each containing n words. While a read operation is using *Buf*[1], a compute operation may reference *Buf*[2], and vice versa. The roles of the buffers are reversed at the completion of an IO. We change the *Get* routine so that, at return, its argument will contain a buffer index:

```
procedure Get(i) ;
integer i ;
begin
    Read(ch, Buf[i]) ;
    i := if i = 1 then 2 else 1
end Get
```

Then a typical program might appear:

```
        .
        .
        .
comment Initialize IO and buffer index ;
    Read(ch, Buf[1]) ; i := 2 ;
        .
        .
        .
comment Main loop ;
    loop: Get(i) ; Compute(Buf[i]) ;
        go to loop ;
        .
        .
        .
```

Note that a busy test is not required in the *Get* routine, since we have assumed that the CPU will just "wait" at an IO instruction until the referenced channel becomes free. The time to read and process one record in the above program is $\max(t_{c1}, t_{rio})$, where t_{c1} and t_{rio} are the times (assumed constant) to compute with and read one record, respectively. This is the best that we could ever hope to do for this type of program structure. The technique is termed *buffer swapping*.

Unfortunately, program structures are rarely that simple. A more frequently appearing execution sequence consists of heavy "bursts" of IO followed by much computing followed again by heavy bursts of IO and continuing in this manner. Statistical data analysis routines and language translators are often of this nature. A program skeleton of this type might be:

.
.
.

for $k : = 1$ **step** 1 **until** $n1$ **do**
begin *Get(i)* ; *Compute(Buf[i])* **end** ;
Computeonly ;
for $k : = 1$ **step** 1 **until** $n2$ **do**
begin *Get(i)* ; *Compute(Buf[i])* **end** ;
Computeonly ;
.
.

for $k := 1$ **step** 1 **until** nm **do**
begin *Get(i)* ; *Compute(Buf[i])* **end** ;
Computeonly ;
.
.
.

where the *Compute* part of the loops are relatively short and the *Computeonly* program sections are relatively long. In this case, the *Get* routines will frequently be waiting at the *Read* operation until the last read has completed. The obvious solution is to add more buffers and try to distribute the IO operations more uniformly throughout the program without disturbing the program structure by reading even farther ahead than one record.

2.4.2 Multiple Buffers and a Coroutine Program Structure[†]

Let there be a set of n buffers, $Buf[0]$, $Buf[1]$, ..., $Buf[n-1]$, $(n \geq 1)$, implicitly linked in a circular list so that $Buf[i]$ is followed by $Buf[(i+1) \bmod n]$, $i = 0, 1, \ldots, n-1$. [We shall use the notation $x +_n y$ to

[†]The treatment in this section follows approximately the model described by Knuth (1968), pp. 214–221.

denote $(x + y)$ mod n.] The main program will ask for a buffer by calling the routine *GetBuf*, then compute with the buffer returned by *GetBuf*, say *Buf*[*current*], and finally release *Buf*[*current*] by the call *ReleaseBuf*. It is assumed that the execution sequence of a main program can be put in the following form:

$$C_0 \; ; \; GetBuf \; ; \; C_1(Buf[current]) \; ; \; ReleaseBuf \; ;$$
$$C_2 \; ; \; GetBuf \; ; \; C_3(Buf[current]) \; ; \; ReleaseBuf \; ;$$
$$C_4 \; ; \ldots$$
$$\cdot$$
$$\cdot$$
$$\cdot$$
$$C_{2n-2} \; ; \; GetBuf \; ; \; C_{2n-1}(Buf[current]) \; ; \; ReleaseBuf \; ;$$
$$C_{2n} \; ; \ldots$$

where the computations C_{2i}, $i = 0, 1, \ldots$, involve no buffer references. If we are dealing with input operations *only*, *GetBuf* will retrieve the next *input-full* buffer and *ReleaseBuf* will designate *Buf*[*current*] as free (available for more input); in the output case, *GetBuf* returns an empty or free buffer and *ReleaseBuf* returns an *output-full* buffer.

Assume that *input* operations only are specified. At the same time as the main program—henceforth termed the *Compute program*—is executing, we shall try to keep the channel busy filling up buffers. This is accomplished by means of an *IO program* that drives the channel and runs in a quasiparallel manner to the *Compute* program. Two pointers to the buffers are necessary—one, *nextget*, which points to the next available buffer for the *Compute* program and the other, *nextio*, which indicates the next free buffer for the IO routine. A typical situation is illustrated in Fig. 2-6(a). Here $n = 5$ and no buffer requests have been made; the G buffers are filled with anticipated input, while the R buffers are empty and available for a read operation. Figure 2-6(b) gives the buffer status after the normal processing of a *GetBuf*; i.e., the effect is

$$current := nextget \; ; \; nextget := nextget +_5 1 \; ;$$

C designates the current buffer. A *Read* operation would normally be filling up *Buf*[*nextio*] concurrently; when the *Read* completes, a new G buffer then exists and we have

$$nextio := nextio +_5 1 \; ;$$

The release of *Buf*[*current*] by *ReleaseBuf* will change the C buffer into type R. Figure 2-6(c) contains the new buffer situation after the completion of both a *Read* and a *ReleaseBuf* call.

The two pointers will be continually "chasing" each other around the buffer circle. The algorithms must be carefully designed so that one pointer

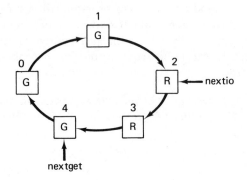

(a) No Assigned Buffer

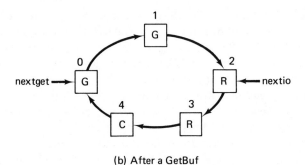

(b) After a GetBuf

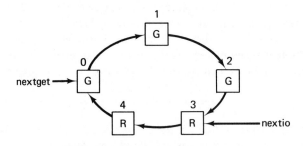

(c) After ReleaseBuf and IO Completion

Fig. 2-6   Five buffers in a circle.

does not overtake and pass the other. If *nextget* overtakes and passes *nextio*, then the buffers retrieved by *GetBuf* will no longer be input-full buffers; this can be prevented by not allowing *GetBuf* to proceed when *nextget = nextio*. A system is said to be *IO bound* if the compute program part is asking for IO faster than the IO part can produce it. Similarly, if *nextio* overtakes and passes *nextget*, the system will be overwriting input-full buffers that have not been used; i.e., there must be an empty buffer available before an IO command is issued. The system is *compute bound* if the IO program produces IO faster than the compute program can consume it.

The *Compute* and *IO* programs are designed as almost independent routines that, conceptually, run in parallel. We simulate this parallelism by means of a *coroutine* program structure. Coroutines are explained by contrasting them with more familiar subroutines. In a *subroutine* program structure, there exists an unsymmetric master/slave relationship between a calling program and its subroutine; generally, a subroutine is entered at one of a fixed number of entry points (usually 1), and all variables that are neither global nor parameters are undefined at entry. Coroutines, on the other hand, are programs that may call each other but do not have this master/slave organization; the relationship is symmetric, with each coroutine being both master and slave. On exit from a coroutine, its state is saved; the next time the coroutine is called, it *resumes* at exactly the point where it left previously with all of its internal variables unchanged; i.e., the previous state is restored. The call on a coroutine *n* will be designated "**resume** *n*" (Wegner, 1968). The arrows in the example in Fig. 2-7 show the flow of control between two coroutines *A* and *B*, where *A* is started initially. (Before a coroutine can be "resumed" for the first time, its state must, of course, be initialized.)

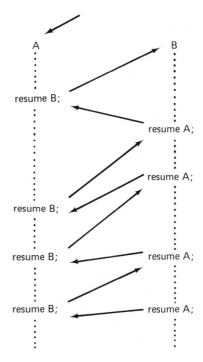

Fig. 2-7 Coroutine flow of control.

The *Compute* program, *CP*, and *IO* program, *IOP*, will each be a co-routine. To keep both the CPU and channel active, *CP* normally resumes the *IOP* if the input channel *ch* is not busy and *IOP* resumes *CP* if the channel is busy. In addition, **resume**'s are invoked if the required buffer type is not available. Let *n* be the total number of buffers and *r* be the number of *R* buffers. The two procedures *GetBuf* and *ReleaseBuf* within *CP* are

procedure *GetBuf* ;
begin
$\quad$ *c* : **if** $\neg busy[ch]$ **then resume** *IOP* ;
$\quad$ **comment** Continue only if there is an input-full buffer available ;
$\quad$ **if** $r = n$ **then go to** *c* ;
$\quad$ *current* := *nextget* ;
$\quad$ *nextget* := *nextget* $+_n$ 1
end *GetBuf*

procedure *ReleaseBuf* ;
begin
$\quad$ *r* := *r* + 1 ;
$\quad$ **if** $\neg busy[ch]$ **then resume** *IOP*
end *ReleaseBuf*

Finally, throughout the C_i, $i = 0, 1, 2, \ldots$, of *CP* we liberally intersperse the statement

$$\textbf{if } \neg busy[ch] \textbf{ then resume } IOP \ ;$$

We thus attempt to keep the channel busy whenever logically possible. The *IOP* coroutine is

$\quad$ *io*1 : $\quad$ **resume** *CP* ;
$\quad\quad\quad\quad$ **comment** Continue only if there is an empty buffer available ;
$\quad$ *io*2 : $\quad$ **if** $r = 0$ **then go to** *io*1 ;
$\quad\quad\quad\quad$ *Read*(*ch*, *Buf*[*nextio*]) ;
$\quad\quad\quad\quad$ **resume** *CP* ;
$\quad\quad\quad\quad$ *nextio* := *nextio* $+_n$ 1 ;
$\quad\quad\quad\quad$ *r* := *r* − 1 ;
$\quad\quad\quad\quad$ **go to** *io*2 ;

Initially, all buffers are set to *R* ($r = n$), and *nextget* and *nextio* are both set to the same buffer index, say 0. The same routines can be employed if we are buffering *output*: the *Read* in *IOP* is changed to a *Write*; all buffers are set to *G* ($r = 0$) initially in this case, since the *GetBuf* routine now will retrieve empty buffers and *ReleaseBuf* will return full buffers.

How large should *n*, the number of buffers, be? Let t_{ci} be the time taken for computation C_i, $i = 0, 1, \ldots$, in *CP* and let t_{rio} be the IO time for one record. If either $t_{c2i-1} + t_{c2i} < t_{rio}$ for *all i* or $t_{c2i-1} + t_{c2i} > t_{rio}$ for all *i*, then $n = 2$ will allow maximum CPU/channel overlap (execution times of *GetBuf* and *ReleaseBuf* have been ignored). This just reduces to the buffer swapping situation described earlier. In fact, $n = 1$ might be adequate if $t_{c2i-1} + t_{c2i}$ is always either *very* much less or *very* much greater than t_{rio}. It is only when the sums $t_{c2i-1} + t_{c2i}$, i.e., the times between successive *GetBuf*'s, are scattered on both sides of t_{rio} that $n > 2$ becomes beneficial.

The multiple buffering system that we have presented assumes a particular run-time execution form for the main program and also assumes a dedicated set of buffers. Although this is indeed reasonable for many programs, other organizations commonly occur. Logical records are usually *blocked* into larger physical records for more efficient use of secondary storage and IO programs. We can then view an IO operation as either filling several buffers, one logical record per buffer, or filling one buffer with several logical records. In the latter case, *GetBuf* and *ReleaseBuf* must be expanded to work both within and between buffers. A main program need not release a buffer before it requests another one—in fact, buffer requests and releases are often interleaved in arbitrary ways. Explicit links must be placed in the buffer circle to handle this possibility, since buffers would not necessarily be released in the order in which they were retrieved. Often, a "pool" of buffers is used by several almost independent compute and IO processes; an example of this is presented shortly. Finally, we should note that the simple timing analyses do *not* take into account the effects of cycle stealing during the concurrent running of the central processor and channel; this has the effect of lengthening the t_{ci}. While the above techniques based on the CPU interrogating the channel are employed in some systems and are useful for explaining the principles of buffering systems, the most common approaches take advantage of interrupts and avoid most of the resume-type calls.

EXERCISES

1. "Prove" that the *IOP* and *CP* coroutines cooperate correctly in achieving the desired buffering system for $n \geq 1$. At the minimum, it must be shown that:
   a. The system starts correctly, regardless of which coroutine is given initial control.
   b. It is impossible for either *GetBuf* or *IOP* to loop forever without obtaining a full or empty buffer, respectively.
   c. The buffers used by *GetBuf* and *IOP* are always the next input-full and next empty ones, respectively.
   (For a survey of techniques for proving the correctness and termination of programs, see Elspas, *et al.*, 1972.)

2. Consider the replacement of the two statements of *GetBuf* starting at the label c by:

$$\text{if } r = n \ \theta \ \neg busy[ch] \text{ then resume } IOP \ ;$$

   where either $\theta = \vee$ or $\theta = \wedge$.

Will either of these changes result in a correct program? If the first two statements of *IOP* are replaced by

$$io2: \quad \textbf{if } r = 0 \textbf{ then resume } CP ;$$

will *IOP* still work?

3. Rewrite the *IOP* and *CP* coroutines to eliminate all labels and **go to** statements. Assume that Algol has been extended to include a "while" statement of the form

$$\textbf{while } BE \textbf{ do } S ;$$

where *BE* is a Boolean expression and *S* is a statement; this new statement is equivalent to the code

$$w: \quad \textbf{if } BE \textbf{ then begin } S ; \textbf{ go to } w \textbf{ end } ;$$

where *w* is a unique local label.

4. Let each physical record consist of *m* logical records and the buffers be designated by $Buf[i, j]$, $i = 0, \dots, n - 1$; $j = 0, \dots, m - 1$ $(m, n \geq 1)$. Assume that the operation $Read(ch, Buf[i, *])$ will read a physical record into $Buf[i, 0]$, $Buf[i, 1], \dots, Buf[i, m - 1]$. Make the necessary changes to the main and *IOP* coroutines to handle this blocked record situation; i.e., *GetBuf* and *ReleaseBuf* are still to return *logical* records.

2.4.3 Channel Interrupts CPU

It is assumed that a channel will interrupt the CPU at the termination of an IO operation; possible interrupts from other causes will not be considered. Interrupts allow much greater control over CPU and IO concurrency and almost eliminate the need for channel busy tests. We assume again that the execution sequence of a main program can be put in the same form as that given at the beginning of the last section and employ the same multiple buffer data structure. The case of *input* operations only is first treated.

The main program procedures *GetBuf* and *ReleaseBuf* then become

```
procedure GetBuf ;
begin
  loop:  if r = n then go to loop ;
         current := nextget ;
         nextget := nextget +ₙ 1
end

procedure ReleaseBuf ;
begin
  r := r + 1 ;
  if ¬busy[ch] then Read(ch, Buf[nextio])
end
```

The $\neg busy[ch]$ test is *necessary* here, since r could be zero before a *ReleaseBuf* call.

On an IO completion interrupt, the following code (IR) is executed:

$$nextio := nextio +_n 1 ;$$
$$r := r - 1 ;$$
$$\textbf{if } r \neq 0 \textbf{ then } Read(ch, Buf[nextio]) ;$$
$$Restore \text{ } state ;$$

When the interrupt occurs, it is assumed that the state of the interrupted program is saved by hardware; *Restore state* changes the computer state back to that of the interrupted process. We initialize the system with

$$r := n ;$$
$$nextget := nextio := 0 ;$$
$$Read(ch, Buf[nextio]) ;$$

The main program and interrupt routine (IR) are independent. Note that the IO operations are initiated automatically *whenever* it is is logically possible to do so.

What is wrong with the above set of programs? A new problem arises because of the asynchronous nature of an interrupt—one can occur at *any* point during the execution of the main program. Suppose that there is an interrupt sometime during the execution of the statement "$r := r + 1$;" in *ReleaseBuf*. A reasonable compilation of this statement for a single accumulator single address machine would be the three instructions:

(1)   *LD r*

$\longleftarrow I_1$

(2)   *ADD* "1"

$\longleftarrow I_2$

(3)   *STO r*

An interrupt at I_1 would have the following effect, if we assume that $r = 5$ at (1):

1. Instruction (1) sets $AC = 5$ (AC is the accumulator).

2. The second instruction in IR sets $r = 4$.

3. The state of the main program is restored ($AC = 5$).

4. Instructions (2) and (3) set $r = 5 + 1 = 6$.

We then have $r = 6$ *instead* of $r = 5$. The same error results if the main program were interrupted at I_2. This is an example of a frequent problem that occurs when more than one process is allowed to access and change a common data area (in this case, the variable r) simultaneously. In a general setting, we must make the affected section of code effectively indivisible.† (The next chapter discusses this problem in greater detail).

One technique for preventing the above "race" conditions is to communicate between *ReleaseBuf* and *IR*. *ReleaseBuf* will let *IR* know if the interrupt has occurred during the *critical section* "$r := r + 1$;" and *IR* will similarly signal to *ReleaseBuf*. Let b and *flag* be Boolean variables, with initial values **false**. Replace "$r := r + 1$;" in *ReleaseBuf* by the statements

b := **true** ;
$r := r + 1$;
b := **false** ;
if *flag* then $r := r - 1$;
flag := **false** ;

Replace "$r := r - 1$; if $r \neq 0$ then *Read(ch, Buf[nextio])* ;" in *IR* by

if b **then** *flag* := **true**
else
begin
    $r := r - 1$;
    if $r \neq 0$ **then** *Read(ch, Buf[nextio])*
end ;

If *ReleaseBuf* is interrupted in its critical section, b will be **true** and the *IR* will neither decrement r nor read but set *flag*; *ReleaseBuf* then tests the flag and does the decrementing for *IR* if *flag* was **true**. An interrupt outside of this critical section finds $b =$ **false** and the normal expected processing takes place. It is assumed that b may be set in one machine operation.

Note that our solution will allow at most one interrupt in the critical section. If the IO operations are extremely fast or, more realistically, if the main program can be preempted from the CPU for long periods of time by other processes, then it may be desirable to permit several interrupts to occur at this point.

EXERCISE

Why can only one interrupt at most occur in the *ReleaseBuf* critical section when *ReleaseBuf* and *IR* have been modified as above? Change the algorithms so that a new *IO* operation is always initiated in *IR* as long as a buffer is available.

---

†The example we have chosen is almost too simple, since some machines have single (indivisible) instructions that increment a storage cell; the use of such an instruction for implementing "$r := r + 1$;" would eliminate the problem here. However, our purpose is to illustrate the problem in the simplest possible setting.

2.4.4   Buffer Pooling for Input and Output

Let us use a set of $n \geq 2$ equal-size buffers as a *pool* or shared resource to satisfy requests for empty, input-full, and output-full buffers. The main program will now be permitted both input and output requests. The advantage of sharing the buffers as opposed to using separate buffer areas for input and output is conservation of main storage; with reasonably spaced buffer requests, n shared buffers can be as effective as using separate areas of n buffers each. (In more general systems, buffer pooling is convenient for handling disk or terminal IO.)

For input, the main program will get the next input-full buffer, *curin*, by the call *Gbufin* and release the buffer by *Rbufin*; an output sequence will consist of a *Gbufout* call to retrieve an empty buffer, *curout*, followed at some later time by an *Rbufout* call that returns an output-full buffer to the pool for printing by an output process. The execution time flow of the main program is assumed to be

$$C_0 \; ; \; Gbufx_1 \; ; \; C_1(Buf[y_1]) \; ; \; Rbufx_1 \; ; \; C_2; \; Gbufx_2 \; ; \; C_3(Buf[y_2]) \; ;$$
$$Rbufx_2 \; ; \; C_4 \; ; \ldots ; \; Gbufx_n \; ; \; C_{2n-1}(Buf[y_n]) \; ; \; Rbufx_n \; ; \ldots$$

where (1) x_i is either "*in*" or "*out.*"

      (2) If $x_i = $ "*in*" then $y_i = $ "*curin*" ;
           if $x_i = $ "*out*" then $y_i = $ "*curout.*"

      (3) The C_i have the same interpretation as the last two sections.

The IO programs are logically running in parallel with the main program and are normally activated by IO termination interrupts. An input process will get an empty buffer, *inio*, from the pool and return it as input-full; the output process will retrieve the next output-full buffer, *outio*, from the pool and return it as empty after the output operation has completed (Fig. 2-8). Input and output will occur on separated dedicated channels, *ch*1 and *ch*2, respectively.

It is necessary to identify the three different types of buffers that may be in the pool—*empty*, *input-full*, and *output-full*. Since the three processes get

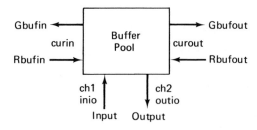

Fig. 2-8 Sharing buffers for input and output.

and return buffers in an almost asynchronous manner, a linked list data structure is most convenient; each buffer type in the pool is linked in a chain. Let $F[em]$, $F[in]$, and $F[out]$ point to the first buffer of type empty, input-full, and output-full, respectively, in the pool and let $L[em]$, $L[in]$, and $L[out]$ be pointers to the last buffer of each type, respectively. For each of the n buffers, we associate a forward pointer $F[i]$ that links buffer i to the next buffer in the chain of the same type as i. A buffer is returned to the pool by adding to the *end* of the appropriate list and retrieved by removing from the *front* of the list; i.e., the lists are first-in first-out (FIFO) queues. Figure 2-9 illustrates a typical buffer pool ($n = 8$) during program execution at some point in $C_{2k-1}(Buf[curout])$. C_{2k-1} is filling $Buf[7]$ for later output, channel 1 is filling $Buf[3]$ with input, and channel 2 is emptying $Buf[5]$. Two buffers (4 and 2) are empty, three are on the input-full list (6, 0, and 1), and the output-full list is empty.

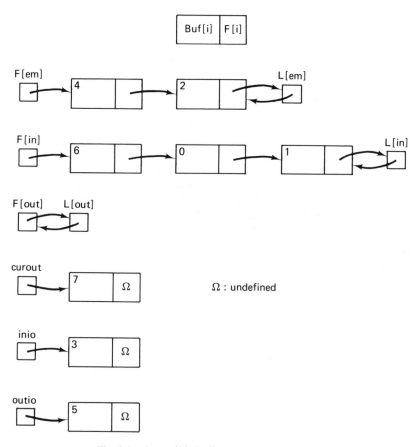

Fig. 2-9 A possible buffer pool configuration.

Buffer manipulation is accomplished by two general routines, *AddBuf* (*type, number*) and *TakeBuf*(*type*), where *type* $\in$ {*em, in, out*} and $0 \leq$ *number* $\leq n - 1$. *AddBuf* adds *Buf*[*number*] to the end of the list of class *type* while the function, *TakeBuf*, removes the first buffer on the list and returns its index as the function value. The *AddBuf* routine is

> **procedure** *AddBuf*(*type, number*) ;
> **value** *type, number* ; **integer** *type, number* ;
> **begin**
>   **integer** *oldlast* ;
>   *oldlast* := *L*[*type*] ;
>   *F*[*oldlast*] := *number* ;
>   *F*[*number*] := *type* ;
>   *L*[*type*] := *number*
> **end** *AddBuf*

Let $|x|$ be the number of buffers on the list of type x; let $|em| = eb$ (empty buffers), $|in| = ifb$ (input full buffers), and $|out| = ofb$ (output full buffers). Initially, $eb = n$ and $ifb = ofb = 0$. This completes the specification of all the variables that we shall use; Table 2-1 lists each variable and its meaning for reference purposes.

Variable	Meaning
n	Number of buffers; $n \geq 2$
Buf[i]	ith buffer in pool
curin	Current input buffer is *Buf*[*curin*]
curout	Current output buffer is *Buf*[*curout*]
inio	Buffer used by input operation is *Buf*[*inio*]
outio	Buffer used by output operation is *Buf*[*outio*]
em	Empty buffer class designation
in	Input-full buffer class designation
out	Output-full buffer class designation
F[t]	Pointer to first buffer of class t, $t \in$ {*em, in, out*}
L[t]	Pointer to last buffer of class t, $t \in$ {*em, in, out*}
eb	Number of empty buffers
ifb	Number of input-full buffers
ofb	Number of output-full buffers

Table 2-1   Variables Used In Buffer Pooling Programs

The procedures called by the main program are

```
procedure Gbufin ;
begin
while ifb = 0 do
    if ¬busy[ch1] then startin ;†
    ifb := ifb − 1 ;
    curin := TakeBuf(in)
end Gbufin
```

```
procedure Rbufin ;
begin
    eb := eb + 1 ;
    AddBuf(em, curin) ;
    if ¬busy[ch1] then startin
end Rbufin
```

```
procedure Gbufout ;
begin
    while eb = 0 do
        if ¬busy[ch2] then startout ;
    eb := eb − 1 ;
    curout := TakeBuf(em)
end Gbufout
```

```
procedure Rbufout ;
begin
    ofb := ofb + 1 ;
    AddBuf(out, curout) ;
    if ¬busy[ch2] then startout
end Rbufout
```

The auxiliary procedures *startin* and *startout* initiate the IO operations:

```
procedure startin ;
if eb ≠ 0 then
begin
    eb := eb − 1 ;
    inio := TakeBuf(em) ;
    Read(ch1, Buf[inio])
end startin
```

```
procedure startout ;
if ofb ≠ 0 then
begin
    ofb := ofb − 1 ;
    outio := TakeBuf(out) ;
    Write(ch2, Buf[outio])
end startout
```

†See Exercise 3 at end of Sec. 2.4.2 for the definition of this form of **while** statement.

Interrupts at input and output termination transfer control to the routines:

*ch*1 *Interrupt* (*input*) (*IR*1)

$$ifb := ifb + 1 \; ;$$
$$AddBuf(in, inio) \; ;$$
$$startin \; ;$$
$$Restore\ state \; ;$$

*ch*2 *Interrupt* (*output*) (*IR*2)

$$eb := eb + 1 \; ;$$
$$AddBuf(em, outio) \; ;$$
$$startout \; ;$$
if ¬*busy*[*ch*1] **then** *startin* ;
$$Restore\ state \; ;$$

The critical section problem discussed in the last section is more severe here but has been ignored for simplicity. A careful study of the above programs reveals yet another problem that occurs often in resource-sharing systems. What happens if all the buffers (the shared resource) are input-full when a *Gbufout* call is given? $eb = ofb = 0$, and the first statement in *Gbufout* loops forever! *Gbufout* needs an empty buffer before it can continue, but the empty buffer producers, *Rbufin* and *IR*2, can not be invoked unless *Gbufout* continues; we are at an impasse. This type of situation is commonly termed *deadlock* or, more vividly, "a deadly embrace." A general discussion of this problem is given in Chapter 8 (but see Exercise 3).

Should input (output) interrupts be inhibited during execution of *IR*2 (*IR*1)? As long as one is careful about critical sections and stacks states so that "*Restore state*" refers to the correct machine state, interrupts within interrupt handling routines are tolerable. However, the conventional approach, especially for short routines, is to mask off other interrupts and thus avoid these complexities.

We conclude with a somewhat negative remark concerning the clarity of the straightforward and common program organizations presented in these last two sections. It is extremely difficult to trace the logic of these programs and convince oneself of their correctness because of the parallel execution of the CPU and channel processes and the asynchronous nature of the IO interrupts; for example, is the IO busy test in *Gbufout* necessary? (Is it?)

Discussion

It is easy for the reader to become mired in the details of our programs, and to lose sight of the main points. In addition to presenting some viable techniques for handling IO and buffers, the preceding examples represent concrete instances of several more general concepts and problems in operating systems.

Logical and physical parallelism among processes is a basic characteristic of modern systems. Virtually all systems have hardware processors that can operate concurrently; the most common example is the CPU and channels. The parallel activity of programs on these processors can be controlled by either polling methods, for example, when a CPU program interrogates a channel, or, more commonly, through interrupts. It is also frequently useful to view the execution of several programs as logically parallel activities, even though they may actually be run sequentially on a single processor in a time-multiplexed fashion. This type of parallelism can be totally simulated by software using coroutines, as illustrated in Sec. 2.4.2; alternatively, hardware interrupts may be employed to initiate or resume a logically concurrent process, such as the *IR* routine of Sec. 2.4.3.

Parallel processes often need to share the same set of resources, such as the buffers in our examples. It then becomes necessary to carefully regulate and synchronize this sharing for correct operation; the critical section and deadlock problems introduced in the last two examples illustrate some of the complexities and pitfalls of sharing. The buffer pooling programs, in particular, show the need for a better way to *describe* parallel activities and their interactions.

We shall be treating all of these issues in greater detail. The IO buffering algorithms of this chapter will be occasionally used as examples in later chapters.

EXERCISES

1. Write the Algol integer procedure *TakeBuf(type)* that returns the index of the first buffer on the *type* list and updates the buffer data structure to reflect this removal.

2. Modify the buffer pooling algorithms to ensure correct handling of all critical sections. The simultaneous manipulation of linked lists by several processes must also be considered in this context.

3. Modify the buffer pooling algorithms to prevent the deadlock situation with respect to the empty buffer resource. Can this be prevented if the number of buffers $n = 1$?

4. *Input-Output Buffering in a text formatting application:* The purpose of this programming exercise is to apply buffer pooling and coroutine techniques to an input-compute-output situation where the CPU interrogates the channels. Design and implement a program that accepts free format text interspersed with editing symbols from cards and produces corresponding formatted text on a line printer. Expanded versions of this type of program can often simplify the writing of books, theses, papers and letters.

The program should consist of three coroutines: an input coroutine, which fills buffers with unformatted text; a formatting coroutine, which produces output buffers of formatted text; and an output coroutine, which controls the printing.

A common storage pool of n ($n \geq 2$) buffers, each of size 80 bytes, is used by all routines for the three different buffer types. [Fig. 2-10(a)].

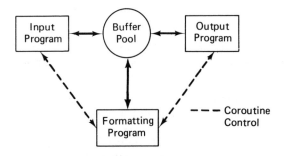

(a) Program and Data Paths

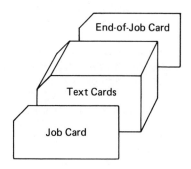

(b) Format of Job Deck

Fig. 2-10   Exercise 4.

The input to the system is a *set* of *jobs* organized as follows [Fig. 2-10(b)]: A job card heads each job and has the entries

|FORMAT   cc 1-7
⟨ job id ⟩   cc 10-20 job identifier

The last card of each job is an end-of-job indicator:

|FINISHED   cc 1-9

The data part of each job consists of a number of text cards, containing symbols from the set $S \cup \{b\} \cup \{\#, \$, *\}$, where $S = \{A, B, \ldots, Z, ., ;, ?, :, ,, ''\}$, and b indicates a blank.

The formatting program should edit the input according to the rules:

Let x be the current input symbol.

(1) If $x \in S$, then x is the next output character (except as noted in 6 below).

(2) If $x = \#$, then start a new output line.

(3) If $x = \$$, then start a new output paragraph.

(4) If $x = *$, then the following string of blanks is not collapsed.

(5) Strings of the form $x_1 b b^n x_2$ where $x_1 \notin \{b, *, \#, \$, ''\}$, $x_2 \neq b$, and $n \geq 1$, are collapsed to $x_1 b x_2$, i.e., excess blanks are removed. If $x_1 \in \{\#, \$\}$, the blanks are eliminated after x_1 has been obeyed.

(6) Any input string of the form $b x_1 x_2 \cdots x_n b$, $x_i \in S$, must be edited so that $x_1 x_2 \cdots x_n$ appears on only *one* line of output; it cannot cross line boundaries.

Job card processing consists of printing the card and initializing a job timer. An end-of-job card is printed directly, followed by the elapsed time for the job. At the completion of a run, your program should print time totals for total elapsed time (CPU time), input time, and output time. Vary the number of buffers n from 2 to 10 and note the effect on total elapsed time. The program should be tested with a realistic amount of data (say, 50 jobs and more than 400 text cards).

If a computer system that permits a user to easily interrogate a channel and timer is not available, then these features may be simulated by using the following specifications. Let the input and output operations occur on separate dedicated channels; each operation deals with fixed-length records of 80 bytes. Assume that the time (simulated) for each task is:

Task	Units of Time	
Read a card	2	(IO)
Print a line	2	(IO)
Process a job card	1	(CPU)
Process an end-of-job card	1	(CPU)
Interpret $ in text card	1	(CPU)
Interpret # in text card	1	(CPU)
Interpret * in text card	1	(CPU)
Process a text card (in addition to the above)	1	(CPU)
End-of-line processing	1	(CPU)

The IO busy tests in the compute program should be placed after the completion of all tasks except the first two, in addition to where they are logically necessary. Increment a simulated hardware timer at these IO busy tests to reflect the task completions.

2.5 THE IO SUPERVISOR

The largest part of a job-at-a-time batch system is devoted to the super-
vision and performance of IO; this component is called the *input-output
control system* (IOCS) or *IO supervisor*. An important by-product of this
central control was the introduction of *symbolic* IO units. Instead of specifying
an absolute physical device address in an IO operation, a user refers to an IO
unit symbolically; an IO operation could be of the form

$$\langle operation\ name\rangle\ (\langle symbolic\ device\ name\rangle, \langle other\ information\rangle)$$

where the $\langle operation\ name\rangle$ may be, say, *READ, WRITE, CONTROL*, or
TEST; for example, *READ(CARDREADER, INPUTAREA)*. A table mapping symbolic to physical IO units is kept in storage. The system can now
make and change the physical device assignments to reflect a particular
installation configuration, to gracefully recover from temporary hardware
breakdowns, or to improve efficiency. For example, *CARDREADER* above
could be a card reader at one installation, a tape unit at another (when off-
line card-to-tape conversion is used), or a disk unit (if all peripheral IO is
passed through disk storage).

The IOCS will perform the following services:

1. *Buffer administration.* IOCS will provide common and private buffer
storage and dynamically keep track of all assignments. This includes on an
expanded scale, the buffer routines described earlier (e.g., the different versions of *Rbuf* and *Gbuf*).

2. *Translation of IO requests.* Symbolic device names are mapped to real
addresses, and the appropriate sequence of channel program code is produced.

3. *Scheduling of IO.* Several requests for a channel or a device may be
simultaneously outstanding. This can occur if a channel is dedicated to a
single device, if one channel is shared by several devices, if several channels
may share devices, or if channel/CPU main storage interference dictates a
limit on the number of concurrent IO operations. Requests must be queued,
and a channel scheduling program determines the next IO operation to initiate.

4. *Interrupt handling.* Interrupts caused by IO completions and IO
errors are serviced. This usually involves updating buffer data structures and
calling the channel scheduler to initiate the next IO operation, as illustrated
in the simpler setting of our previous examples.

3 INTERACTING PROCESSES

A channel process performing an IO operation in parallel with the execution of a compute-only process by a CPU is one real example of parallel activity in a computing system. Both *hardware parallelism*—the parallel operation of several hardware processing units—and *logical parallelism*—the conceptual parallelism imposed by a human regardless of whether processing occurs sequentially or in parallel—appear frequently and naturally. A multiprogrammed operating system, including the user jobs executing within it, can be logically described as a set of *sequential* processes that operate almost independently of one another, *cooperate* by sending messages and synchronization signals to each other, and *compete* for resources. In this chapter, we examine mechanisms for describing the parallelism, communication, and competition among sequential processes, and give examples illustrating their application. The basic concepts of interacting processes were first developed by Dijkstra and appeared in his pioneering monograph, "Cooperating Sequential Processes" (Dijkstra, 1965a; 1968b).

3.1 PARALLEL PROGRAMMING

3.1.1 Applications

Increases in effective computer speeds can be achieved by improvements in either component technology or machine architecture. Given a fixed technology, parallel execution of hardware units can, in principle, dramatically improve system performance as compared with sequential operation. Several independent processors are often connected to common storage and control circuitry; these include central processors, IO processors, such as data channels, and special purpose processors, such as arithmetic units. More than one program and parts of a single program can then execute in parallel and send messages to each other. In situations of minimal hardware parallelism, it is frequently advantageous to time-share a single processing unit among several processes; a useful abstraction is to consider these processes as running in parallel. We shall initially explore the "natural" parallelism that exists in several very simple algorithms and ignore the problem of communicating among processes. Our main purpose is to introduce, through simple and familiar examples, some elementary notions of parallel programming.

Figure 3-1 illustrates the kinds of precedence constraints that are possible among processes, if we assume that a system has a common start and finish point. The execution of a process p_i is represented by a directed edge of a

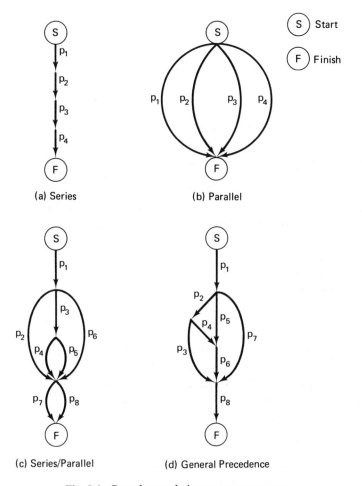

(a) Series   (b) Parallel

(c) Series/Parallel   (d) General Precedence

Fig. 3-1   Precedence relations among processes.

graph. Each graph in the figure denotes an execution-time trace of a set of processes, and the graph connectivity describes the start and finish precedence constraints on the processes. For convenience, these graphs will be called *process flow graphs*. All components in the series/parallel example are properly nested. Let $S(a, b)$ denote the series connection of process a followed by process b and let $P(a, b)$ denote the parallel connection of processes a and b. Then a process flow graph is *properly nested* if it can be described by the functions S and P, and only function composition.†

Examples

The first three graphs in the figure can be described:

$$S(p_1, S(p_2, S(p_3, p_4))),$$
$$P(p_1, P(p_2, P(p_3, p_4))),$$

and

$$S(p_1, S(P(p_2, P(S(p_3, P(p_4, p_5)), p_6)), P(p_7, p_8))),$$

respectively.

The general precedence graph (d) in the figure is *not* properly nested. We prove this by first observing that any description by function composition must include at the most interior level an expression either of the form $S(p_i, p_j)$ or $P(p_i, p_j)$ for $p_i, p_j \in \{p_k | k = 1, \ldots, 8\}$. $P(p_i, p_j)$ cannot appear, since Fig. 3-1(d) does not contain any subgraph of this form. All serially connected p_i and p_j have at least one other process p_k that starts or finishes at the node ij, say, between p_i and p_j; but ij becomes unavailable for further use if $S(p_i, p_j)$ appears, and the connection of p_k could then not be described. Therefore, $S(p_i, p_j)$ cannot be used either, and a properly nested description is not possible.

The following three examples of parallelism give rise to properly nested process flow graphs:

1. *Evaluation of arithmetic expressions.* If side effects or numerical accuracy do not dictate a fixed sequential evaluation, the subexpressions of arithmetic expressions can be evaluated in parallel; the amount of parallelism that can occur is limited by the depth of the expression tree (Fig. 3-2; edges are labelled by the code executed by the corresponding process). Many problems in which the primary data structure is a tree can be logically described in terms of parallel computations.

2. *Sorting.* During the ith pass in a standard two-way merge sort, pairs

---

†This property is very similar to the "proper nesting" of block structure in programming languages and of parentheses within expressions.

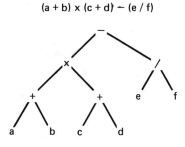

Expression Tree

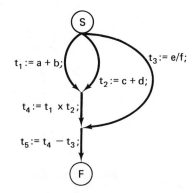

Fig. 3-2 Arithmetic expression evaluation.

Process Flow Graph

of sorted lists of length 2^{i-1} are merged into lists of length 2^i; each of the merges can be performed in parallel within a pass (Fig. 3-3).

3. *Matrix multiplication.* On performing the matrix multiplication, $A = B \times C$, all elements of A can be computed simultaneously.

EXERCISE

Consider arithmetic expressions E containing only simple variables and the binary operator $+$, i.e.,

$$E ::= v \mid E + v$$
$$v ::= a_1 \mid a_2 \mid a_3 \mid \ldots$$

Suppose that *any* number of addition operations can be done in parallel and that each such operation takes one time unit including fetching the two operands and storing the result. What is the minimum time required to evaluate a given expression $a_1 + a_2 + \ldots + a_n, n \geq 1$, as a function of n? Prove your result.

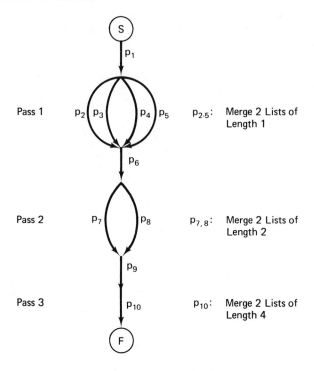

Fig. 3-3 Merge sort of a list of eight elements.

3.1.2 Some Programming Constructs for Parallelism

The "and" Notation

Wirth (1966b) suggested a simple addition to Algol that would allow a programmer to indicate the possible parallel execution of statements. Parallel execution is specified by replacing the semicolon separating the statements by the symbol **and**. For example, program statements for evaluating the expression of Fig. 3-2 are

> **begin**
> $t1 := a + b$ **and** $t2 := c + d$;
> $t4 := t1 \times t2$
> **end**
> **and** $t3 := e / f$; $t5 := t4 - t3$;

Parallel computations can be created conditionally and dynamically, as illustrated by the following program, which computes in parallel each element of the matrix product $A = B \times C$ (Wirth, 1966b):

```
integer array A[1:m, 1:n], B[1:m, 1:p], C[1:p, 1:n] ;
procedure product(i, j) ;
value i, j ; integer i, j ;
begin
    integer k ; real s ;
    s := 0 ;
    for k := 1 step 1 until p do
        s := s + B[i, k] × C[k, j] ;
    A[i, j] := s
end product ;

procedure column(i, j) ;
value i, j ; integer i, j ;
product(i, j) and
    if j > 1 then column(i, j − 1) ;

procedure row(i) ;
value i ; integer i ;
column (i, n) and
    if i > 1 then row(i − 1) ;

row(m)
```

The creation of parallel processes is graphically traced in Fig. 3-4 for the case $m = n = p = 2$.

Let a process p_i in a process flow graph be described by the sequence of program statements S_i. Then, any properly nested flow graph can be described linearly with the **and** notation: $S(p_i, p_j)$ maps into "**begin** S_i ; S_j **end**"; $P(p_i, p_j)$ maps into "**begin** S_i **and** S_j **end**". However, **and** is not sufficient to describe any process flow graph.

Fork, Join, and Quit

The primitives **fork**, **join**, and **quit** (Conway, 1963; Dennis and Van Horn, 1966) provide a more general means for linearly describing parallel activity in a program.

Execution by a process p of the instruction "**fork** w" causes a new process q to start executing at the instruction labelled w; p and q then execute simultaneously. If a process p executes the instruction "**quit**", p terminates. The instruction "**join** t, w" has the following effect:

```
-----------------
t := t − 1 ;
if t = 0 then go to w ;
-----------------
```

The area enclosed by the dotted line is considered an *indivisible* operation.

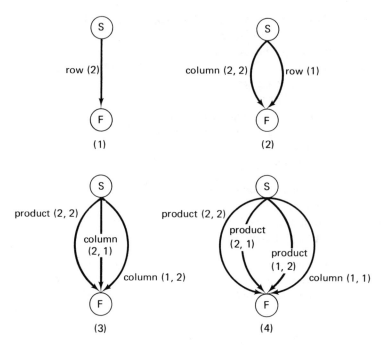

Fig. 3-4 Creation of parallel processes in matrix multiplication ($m = n = p = 2$).

A program segment for evaluating the expression of Fig. 3-2 is

```
        n := 2 ;
        fork p3 ;
        m := 2 ;
        fork p2 ;
        t1 := a + b ; join m, p4 ; quit ;
 p2:    t2 := c + d ; join m, p4 ; quit ;
 p4:    t4 := t1 × t2 ; join n, p5 ; quit ;
 p3:    t3 := e / f ; join n, p5 ; quit ;
 p5:    t5 := t4 − t3 ;
```

This is certainly less transparent than the program of the last section. However, iterations can be described more clearly, as illustrated by the following example from picture processing.

We are given an array $A[0: n + 1, 0: n + 1]$ consisting of 0's and 1's representing a digitized picture. It is desired to "smooth" the picture by replacing each interior point $A[i, j]$ by 1 if the majority of $A[i, j]$ and its immediate 8 neighbors are 1, and by 0 otherwise. This process is called *local averaging* and is logically a parallel computation. We assume that the smoothed picture is stored in a new array.

procedure *Localaverage*(*A*, *B*, *n*) ;
value *n* ; **integer array** *A*, *B* ; **integer** *n* ;
begin
  integer *t*, *i*, *j* ; **private** *i*, *j* ;
  $t := n \uparrow 2$;
  for *i* := 1 **step** 1 **until** *n* **do**
  for *j* := 1 **step** 1 **until** *n* **do**
    fork *e* ;
  quit ;
  e: $B[i,j] :=$ **if** $A[i-1, j-1] + A[i-1, j] + A[i-1, j+1]$
              $+ A[i, j-1] + A[i, j] + A[i, j+1] + A[i+1, j-1]$
              $+ A[i+1, j] + A[i+1, j+1] \geq 5$ **then** 1 **else** 0 ;
  join *t*, *r* ;
  quit ;
  r: **end** *Localaverage*

In order to create private copies of variables within parallel processes, variables may be declared as "private" to a process by the declaration "**private** $x_1, x_2, \ldots, x_n$." The variables $x_1, x_2, \ldots, x_n$ then only exist for the process "executing" the private declarations; in addition, any new process created by the latter (using a **fork**) will receive a private copy of the private variables of the father process. As a further example, the three statements starting at label *e* in the *Localaverage* program could be replaced by

      e: **begin private integer** *u*, *v*, *x* ;
          $x := 0$;
          for $u := -1$ **step** 1 **until** 1 **do**
          for $v := -1$ **step** 1 **until** 1 **do**
            $x := x + A[i+u, j+v]$;
          $B[i,j] :=$ **if** $x \geq 5$ **then** 1 **else** 0 ;
          join *t*, *r* ;
          quit ;
        end ;

The statements **fork, join,** and **quit** suffice to describe any process flow graph. Below is a program for the graph of Fig. 3-1(d), where S_i denotes the program statements for process p_i:

        $t6 := 2$; $t8 := 3$;
        *S*1 ; **fork** *w*2 ; **fork** *w*5 ; **fork** *w*7; **quit** ;
    *w*2: *S*2 ; **fork** *w*3 ; **fork** *w*4 ; **quit** ;
    *w*5: *S*5 ; **join** *t*6, *w*6 ; **quit** ;
    *w*7: *S*7 ; **join** *t*8, *w*8 ; **quit** ;
    *w*3: *S*3 ; **join** *t*8, *w*8 ; **quit** ;
    *w*4: *S*4 ; **join** *t*6, *w*6 ; **quit** ;
    *w*6: *S*6 ; **join** *t*8, *w*8 ; **quit** ;
    *w*8: *S*8 ; **quit** ;

The parallel computations in the examples of this section are too small to be of practical concern in operating systems. However, the programming constructs introduced are useful for describing the parallel activities in an OS and will be applied in subsequent sections.

EXERCISES

1. Show that the general precedence graph in Fig. 3-1 cannot be described with the **and** notation.

2. Write an Algol procedure using **and** to compute the dot product $\sum_{i=1}^{n} a_i b_i$ of two vectors in parallel.

3. Let the set T of simple arithmetic expression trees be defined as follows:
   (a) $x \in T$ for any simple variable or constant x.
   (b) if $t_1 \in T$ and $t_2 \in T$, then $\begin{array}{c} \theta \\ \diagup \diagdown \\ t_1 \quad t_2 \end{array} \in T$,

   for any *binary* operator $\theta \in \{+, -, \times, /\}$.
   Operators have their usual interpretation. Write an Algol procedure, using **and** to evaluate the expression represented by any $t \in T$. (Select a suitable computer representation for t.)

4. Why must most of the **join** operation be indivisible?

5. Write a program for parallel matrix multiplication, using **fork, join, quit**, and **private**.

6. Use **fork, join, quit**, and **private** to program a two-way merge sort with parallel merging at each pass.

3.2 THE CONCEPT OF A PROCESS

We have been using the term "process" in a rather loose manner, relying on the reader's intuition to grasp its meaning. A generally accepted, but informal definition is:

A sequential process (sometimes called "task") is the activity resulting from the execution of a program with its data by a sequential processor.

Logically, each process has its own processor and program. In reality, two different processes might be sharing the same program or the same processor. For example, in the matrix multiplication program in Sec. 3.1.2, n^2 processes use the same code, $product(i, j)$. Thus, a process is *not* equivalent to a program, nor is it the same as a processor; it is a $\langle processor, program \rangle$ pair in execution.

The execution of a process can be described as a sequence of *statevectors* $s_0, s_1, \ldots, s_i, \ldots$, where each statevector s_i contains a pointer to the next program instruction to be executed as well as the values of all intermediate and defined variables of the program. From another point of view, a state-vector of a process p is that amount of information required by a processor in order to run p. The statevector of p can be changed either by the execution of p *or* by the execution of other processes that *share* some statevector components with p.

Communications among processes and control over their operation will occur by setting common variables and by special process primitive operations to be defined later. If we examine a process at any point in time, it will be either *running* or *blocked*. A process p is (logically) running if it is either executing on a processor or could be executing if a processor were available; in the latter case, we shall often say that the process is in *ready* status. A process p is blocked if it may not run until it receives a signal, message, or resource from some other process.

[More precise and formal definitions of the process notion are sometimes used. At one extreme, an attempt is made to broaden the domain to encompass a variety of common hardware processes, such as a timer, a CPU, or a mechanical card reader, and perhaps even human processes, for example, a machine operator following a set of written rules for controlling a system. Another approach is to formalize the definition in order to simplify a theoretical analysis of some restricted aspect of interacting processes. Examples are the general definitions of Horning and Randell (1973) and the model of Holt (1971a) described in Chapter 8.]

By examining the logic of processes and ignoring the number of physical processors available, we can provide processor-independent solutions to a number of systems problems; that is, the solutions will ensure that a system of processes cooperate correctly, regardless of whether or not they share physical processors. The process concept has several other important applications in operating systems. It has permitted the isolation and specification of many primitive OS tasks, has simplified the study of the organization and dynamics of an OS, and has led to the development of useful design methodologies. Interacting processes are one of our main themes, and all of the above points are discussed further in later sections and chapters. Processes will be specified by their programs, and the **and** notation will be used to describe parallelism.

3.3 THE CRITICAL SECTION PROBLEM

3.3.1 The Problem

When several processes may asynchronously change the contents of a common data area, it is necessary to protect the data from simultaneous access and change by two or more processes. The updated area may not, in general, contain the intended changes if this protection is not provided. This situation was illustrated in some of the IO buffering examples in the last chapter. The common data shared by several processes most often describes a *resource*; updating the data corresponds to allocating or freeing elements of the resource.

Consider two processes p_1 and p_2, both asynchronously incrementing a common variable x representing the number of units of a resource:

$$p_1 : \ldots x := x + 1 \; ; \ldots$$
$$p_2 ; \ldots x := x + 1 \; ; \ldots$$

Let C_1 and C_2 be central processors with internal registers $R1$ and $R2$, respectively, and sharing main storage. If p_1 were executing on C_1 and p_2 on C_2, then either of the following two execution sequences could occur over time:

(1) $p_1 : R1 := x \; ; R1 := R1 + 1 \; ; x := R1 \; ; \ldots \ldots$
   $p_2 : \ldots \ldots \ldots R2 := x \qquad ; R2 := R2 + 1 \; ; x := R2 \; ;$
   $\mid t_0 \longrightarrow$ time $\mid t_n$
(2) $p_1 : R1 := x \; ; R1 := R1 + 1 \; ; x := R1 \; ; \ldots \ldots \ldots \ldots$
   $p_2 : \ldots \ldots \ldots \ldots \ldots \ldots \ldots \ldots R2 := x \; ; R2 := R2 + 1 \; ; x := R2 \; ;$

Let x contain the value v at time t_0. At t_n, x would contain $v + 1$ if the execution on processors C_1 and C_2 followed (1) and $v + 2$ if it followed sequence (2). Both values of x could also be realized if p_1 and p_2 were time-sharing a single processor with control switching between the processes by means of interrupts. If p_1 and p_2 were invoked as part of an airlines reservation system and x represented the number of available seats on a particular flight, customers and management would be very unhappy if x contained $v + 1$ instead of $v + 2$. Similarly, if x contained the number of blocks of memory allocated to user jobs in an MS, the above possibilities would be intolerable. Clearly, *each* increment of x should count. The solution is to allow only one process at a time into the *critical section* (CS) "$x := x + 1 \; ;$". In general, the critical section could consist of any number of statements, for example, the buffer manipulations in Sec. 2.4.4.

The problem and its environment can now be stated more precisely. We are given several sequential processors, which can communicate with each other through a common data store. The programs executed by the processors each contain a critical section in which access to the common data is made; these programs are considered to be cyclic. The problem is to program the processors so that, at any moment, only *one* of the processors is in its critical section; once a processor, say C, enters its CS, no other processor may do the same until C has left its CS. The following assumptions are made about the system:

1. Writing into and reading from the common data store are each un-

dividable operations; simultaneous reference (loads or stores) to the same location by more than one processor will result in sequential references in an unknown order.

2. Critical sections may not have priorities associated with them.

3. The relative speeds of the processors are unknown.

4. A program may halt outside of its CS.

The problem can also be formulated in terms of several processes asynchronously time-sharing a single processor. It is convenient to forget about the number of physical processors and think only about a set of (almost) independent *processes*, each of which has a CS.

The system of cyclic processes for the CS problem is assumed to have the following program forms:

> **begin**
> $P1$:　**begin** $L1$:　$CS1$; *program*1 ; **go to** $L1$ **end**
> 　　　　　**and**
> $P2$:　**begin** $L2$:　$CS2$; *program*2 ; **go to** $L2$ **end**
> 　　　　　**and**
> 　　　　　·
> 　　　　　·
> 　　　　　·
> 　　　　　**and**
> Pn:　**begin** Ln:　CSn ; *programn* ; **go to** Ln **end**
> **end** ;

where CSi is the CS for process i, the statement on each line Pi is the code for process Pi, and $n \geq 2$.

3.3.2　Software Solution (Dijkstra, 1965a, 1968b)

The problem will be initially restricted to two processes (Fig. 3-5). Our primary aim is to prevent $P1$ and $P2$ from being in their respective CS's

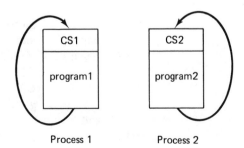

Fig. 3-5 Two processes with critical sections.

Process 1　　　　　Process 2

together (*mutual exclusion*). At the same time, two possible types of *blocking* must be avoided:

1. A process operating well outside its CS cannot be blocking another process from entering its CS.

2. Two processes about to enter their CS's cannot, by an "after you"–"after you" type of intercommunication, postpone indefinitely the decision on which one actually enters.

We shall now try to develop solutions to the problem and illustrate some of the pitfalls that exist.

The problem is easily solved if we insist that *P*1 and *P*2 enter their CS's alternately; one common variable can keep track of whose turn it is:

> **begin integer** *turn* ; *turn* := 2 ;
>   *P*1: **begin** *L*1: **if** *turn* = 2 **then go to** *L*1 ;
>   *CS*1 ; *turn* := 2 ;
>   *program*1 ; **go to** *L*1
>   **end**   **and**
>   *P*2: **begin** *L*2: **if** *turn* = 1 **then go to** *L*2 ;
>   *CS*2 ; *turn* := 1 ;
>   *program*2 ; **go to** *L*2
>   **end**
>   **end** ;

However, if *P*1 were run on a much faster processor than *P*2, or if *program*1 were much longer than *program*2, or if *P*1 halted in *program*1, this would hardly be satisfactory. One process well outside its CS can prevent the other from entering its CS.

An attempt is made to avoid this possible blocking by using two common variables, *C*1 and *C*2, as a flag to indicate whether a process is inside or outside of its CS.

> **begin Boolean** *C*1, *C*2 ; *C*1 := *C*2 := **true** ;
>   *P*1: **begin** *L*1: **if** ¬*C*2 **then go to** *L*1 ;
>   *C*1 := **false** ; *CS*1 ;
>   *C*1 := **true** ; *program*1 ;
>   **go to** *L*1
>   **end**   **and**
>   *P*2: **begin** *L*2: **if** ¬*C*1 **then go to** *L*2 ;
>   *C*2 := **false** ; *CS*2 ;
>   *C*2 := **true** ; *program*2 ;
>   **go to** *L*2
>   **end**
>   **end** ;

When $C1$ or $C2$ is **false** (**true**), the corresponding process is inside (outside) its critical section. Mutual blocking is now not possible, but both processes may enter their CS's together; the latter can occur since both programs may arrive at $L1$ and $L2$ together with $C1 = C2 =$ **true**.

The mutual execution of the last example is avoided by setting $C1$ and $C2$ **false** at $L1$ and $L2$, respectively:

> **begin Boolean** $C1$, $C2$; $C1 := C2 :=$ **true** ;
> $\quad$ $P1$: $\quad$ **begin** $A1$: $\quad$ $C1 :=$ **false** ;
> $\qquad\qquad\qquad$ $L1$: $\quad$ **if** $\neg C2$ **then go to** $L1$;
> $\qquad\qquad\qquad$ $CS1$; $C1 :=$ **true** ;
> $\qquad\qquad\qquad$ $program1$; **go to** $A1$
> $\qquad\qquad$ **end** $\qquad$ **and**
> $\quad$ $P2$:.. (similar to $P1$)
> **end** ;

The last difficulty has been resolved, but mutual blocking is now possible again. $C1$ may be set **false** at $A1$ at the same time that $C2$ is set **false** at $A2$; in this case, both $P1$ and $P2$ will loop indefinitely at $L1$ and $L2$. The obvious way to rectify this is to set $C1$ and $C2$ **true** after testing whether they are **false** at $L1$ and $L2$:

> **begin Boolean** $C1$, $C2$; $C1 := C2 :=$ **true** ;
> $\quad$ $P1$: $\quad$ **begin** $L1$: $\quad$ $C1 :=$ **false** ;
> $\qquad\qquad\qquad$ **if** $\neg C2$ **then begin** $C1 :=$ **true** ;
> $\qquad\qquad\qquad\qquad\qquad\qquad\quad$ **go to** $L1$
> $\qquad\qquad\qquad\qquad\qquad$ **end** ;
> $\qquad\qquad\qquad$ $CS1$; $C1 :=$ **true** ;
> $\qquad\qquad\qquad$ $program1$; **go to** $L1$
> $\qquad\qquad$ **end** $\qquad$ **and**
> $\quad$ $P2$: $\quad$ ...
> **end** ;

Unfortunately, this solution may still lead to the same type of blocking as in the last example; if both processes are exactly in step at $L1$ and $L2$ and their speeds are exactly the same for each succeeding instruction, the same loop as before will develop around $L1$ and $L2$.

The above attempts illustrate some of the subtleties underlying this problem. The following solution was first proposed by the mathematician T. Dekker:

```
begin integer turn ; Boolean C1, C2 ;
    C1 := C2 := true ; turn := 1 ;
    P1:  begin A1:   C1 := false ;
                L1:   if ¬C2 then
                        begin  if turn = 1 then go to L1 ;
                               C1 := true ;
                        B1:    if turn = 2 then go to B1 ;
                               go to A1
                        end
                      CS1 ; turn := 2 ;
                      C1 := true ; program1 ;
                      go to A1
           end     and
    P2:  begin A2:   C2 := false ;
                L2:   if ¬C1 then
                        begin if turn = 2 then go to L2 ;
                              C2 := true ;
                        B2 :  if turn = 1 then go to B2 ;
                              go to A2
                        end
                      CS2 ; turn := 1 ;
                      C2 := true ; program2 ;
                      go to A2
           end
    end ;
```

$C1$ and $C2$ ensure that mutual execution does not occur; *turn* ensures that mutual blocking does not occur. Mutual execution is impossible, since any Ci ($i = 1$ or 2) is always **false** when Pi asks permission to enter its CS at label Li. Mutual blocking is impossible, since the variable *turn* does not change value during the decision-making code preceding the CS's. Suppose, for example, that $turn = 1$ and both processes are attempting to enter their CS's. Then, $P1$ can only cycle at the first two statements at $L1$ with $C1$ remaining constant at **false**; similarly, $P2$ can only loop at $B2$ with $C2$ constant at **true**. But the latter implies that $P1$ will get permission to enter at $L1$. Since no other looping is possible in this case, the solution prevents mutual blocking. If $P1$ and $P2$ were running on the same processor, the solution is still correct as long as the processor is guaranteed to switch control between $P1$ and $P2$ after a finite amount of time.

EXERCISES

1. The following program was proposed as a solution to the critical section problem. Does it prevent mutual execution and blocking?

```
begin integer ask, inuse ;
    ask := inuse := 0 ;
P1:   begin L1:   if ask ≠ 0 then go to L1 ;
                  ask := 1 ;
                  if ask ≠ 1 then go to L1 ;
                  if inuse ≠ 0 then go to L1 ;
                    inuse := 1 ;
                  if ask ≠ 1 then go to L1 ;
                  CS1 ; ask := inuse := 0 ;
                  program1 ; go to L1
      end         and
P2:   begin L2:   if ask ≠ 0 then go to L2 ;
                  ask := 2 ;
                  if ask ≠ 2 then go to L2 ;
                  if inuse ≠ 0 then go to L2
                    inuse := 1 ;
                  if ask ≠ 2 then go to L2 ;
                  CS2 ; ask := inuse := 0 ;
                  program2 ; go to L2
      end
end ;
```

2. Dekker's CS solution prevents mutual execution and mutual blocking. But is it possible that one of the processes could be blocked forever, looping through Ai, Li, and Bi, while the other process continually executes its CS? (Remember that the relative processing speeds of $P1$ and $P2$ are unknown; hence any speed is possible for each process.)

3. Derive a program solution for the critical section problem for n processes ($n \geq 2$) operating in parallel (Dijkstra, 1965b; Eisenberg and McGuire, 1972).

3.4 SEMAPHORE PRIMITIVES

3.4.1 The P and V Operations

There are two unappealing features of the software solution to the critical section problem:

1. The solution is mystifying and unclear; a simple conceptual requirement, mutual exclusion in CS's, results in complex and awkward additions to programs.

2. During the time when one process is in its CS, another process may be continually looping, and accessing and testing common variables. To do this, the waiting processor must "steal" memory cycles from the active one; if the processes are sharing a single processor, then the waiting process is consuming valuable CPU time without really accomplishing anything. The result is a general slowing down of the system by processes that are not doing any useful work.

Dijkstra (1965a) introduced two new primitive operations that considerably simplified the communication and synchronization of processes. In their abstract form, these primitives, designated P and V, operate on *nonnegative integer variables* called *semaphores*. Let S be such a semaphore variable. The operations are defined as follows:

1. $V(S)$: S is increased by 1 in a single *indivisible* action; the fetch, increment, and store cannot be interrupted, and S can not be accessed by another process during the operation.

2. $P(S)$: Decrement S by 1, if possible. If $S = 0$, then it is not possible to decrement S and remain in the domain of nonnegative integers; the process invoking the P operation then *waits* until it is possible. The successful testing and decrementing of S is also an indivisible operation. (We defer until Sec. 3.5 any discussion of how the waiting occurs when $S = 0$.)

If several processes simultaneously call for P or V operations on the same semaphore, these operations will occur sequentially in an arbitrary order; similarly, if more than one process is waiting on a P operation and the affected semaphore becomes positive, the particular waiting process that is selected to complete the operation is arbitrary and unknown.

It is the semaphore variables that are used to synchronize processes. The P primitive includes a potential wait of the calling process, whereas the V primitive may possibly activate some waiting process. The indivisibility of P and V assures the integrity of the values of the semaphores.

3.4.2   Mutual Exclusion Using Semaphore Operations

Semaphore operations allow a simple and straightforward solution to the critical section problem. Let *mutex* be a semaphore variable; *mutex* is used below to protect the CS's. A program solution for n processes operating in parallel is

```
begin semaphore mutex ;
        mutex := 1 ;
 P1:   begin . . . end and
 P2:   . . .
        .
        .
        .
 Pi:   begin Li:   P(mutex) ; CSi ; V(mutex) ;
                    programi ; go to Li
        end and
        .
        .
        .
 Pn: . . .
end ;
```

The value of *mutex* is 0 when any process is in its CS; otherwise *mutex* = 1. The semaphore has the function of a simple lock. Mutual exclusion is guaranteed, since only one process can decrement *mutex* to zero with the *P* operation; all other processes attempting to enter their CS's while *mutex* is zero will be forced to wait by *P(mutex)*. Mutual blocking is not possible, because simultaneous attempts to enter CS's when *mutex* = 1 must, by our definition in Sec. 3.4.1, translate into *sequential P* operations. When a semaphore can take only the values 0 or 1, it will be called a *binary* semaphore.

3.4.3 Semaphores as Resource Counters and Synchronizers in Producer Consumer Problems

Each process in a computer system can be characterized by the number and type of resources it *consumes* (uses) and *produces* (releases). These could be "hard" resources, such as main storage, tape drives, or processors, or "soft" resources, such as full buffers, critical sections, messages, or jobs. Semaphores can be used to maintain resource counts and to synchronize processes, as well as locking out critical sections. For example, a process can block itself by a *P* operation on a semaphore *S* and can be awakened by another process executing *V(S)*:

```
begin semaphore S ; S := 0 ;
    P1:  begin . . .
              comment Wait for signal from P2 ;
              P(S) ; . . .
          end      and
    P2:  begin . . .
              comment Send wakeup signal to P1 ;
              V(S) ; . . .
          end
  end ;
```

*P*1 can also be viewed as consuming the resource designated *S* through the instruction *P(S)* while *P*2 produces units of *S* through *V(S)*. In this section, we illustrate the use of semaphores in typical resource producer-consumer applications.

Example 1: Two Processes Communicating through Buffer Storage (Dijkstra, 1965a, 1968)

A producer process produces information and then adds it to buffer storage; in parallel with this, a consumer process removes information from buffer storage and then processes it. This is an abstraction of the situation where, for example, a main process will produce an output record and then transfer it to the next available buffer while, asynchronously, an output process removes a record from buffer storage and then prints it. Let buffer storage consist of N equal-sized buffers, each buffer capable of holding one record. We shall use two semaphores as resource counters:

$$e = \text{number of empty buffers,}$$

and

$$f = \text{number of full buffers.}$$

Assume that adding to or taking from a buffer constitutes critical sections; let b be a binary semaphore used for mutual exclusion. The processes may then be described:

> **begin semaphore** e, f, b ; $e := N$; $f := 0$; $b := 1$;
>   *producer*: **begin** Lp: *produce next record* ; $P(e)$;
> $P(b)$; *add to buffer* ; $V(b)$; $V(f)$; **go to** Lp
>   **end**   **and**
>   *consumer*: **begin** Lc: $P(f)$; $P(b)$; *take from buffer* ; $V(b)$;
> $V(e)$; *process record* ; **go to** Lc
>   **end**
> **end** ;

Incrementing and decrementing e and f must be indivisible, or their values could be in error; one could alternately treat the changes to e and f as critical sections, but some additional logic must be included to take care of the possible waits on the P operations (see the end of this section for more details). Mutual exclusion around the buffer manipulation might not be necessary above; however, if linked lists of buffers are employed or the program is generalized to m producers and n consumers ($m, n \geq 1$), mutual exclusion is necessary.

Example 2: Outline of an Input Spooler

Instead of allocating a card reader and printer to each noninteractive job executing in a multiprogrammed system, "virtual" card readers and printers are usually provided on auxiliary storage. Jobs are collected on auxiliary storage prior to their execution, and their output is written on auxiliary storage during processing. Multiprogramming can then be done much more efficiently. The job scheduler has more freedom in selecting jobs; (virtual) input-output operations are faster, thus decreasing the amount of time a job occupies main storage; and the load on card readers and printers can be spread uniformly across jobs. That part of a system that (a) reads jobs onto auxiliary storage and (b) prints job output from auxiliary storage is called a *spooler*.† We shall look at a skeleton of the input part of a hypothetical spool-

†The acronym "SPOOL" stands for *S*imultaneous *P*eripheral *O*perations *OnL*ine; it was first used on the IBM 7070 computer system.

ing subsystem [task (a) above] for the simple computer configuration of Fig. 3-6. (Channels 1 and 3 are usually subchannels of a multiplexor channel but can be considered independent for the present example).

The input spooler can be organized according to Fig. 3-7, where the five processes are assumed to operate in parallel. A buffer pool of n buffers ($n \geq 2$), each of length 80 bytes (1 card image), will hold *empty* (*em*), *input-full* (*in*), and *output-full* buffers (*out*). The data structure of the buffer pool, the buffer manipulation routines, and some of the variable names are taken from Sec. 2.4.4. For convenient reference, the program variables and their meaning are summarized in Table 3-1; they will be explained further as we develop the code for the five processes.

The producer-consumer relationship among the three CPU processes, *I*, *M*, and *O*, are given in Table 3-2 with respect to the buffer resources. The main CPU process *M* will take input-full buffers; compute with the latter,

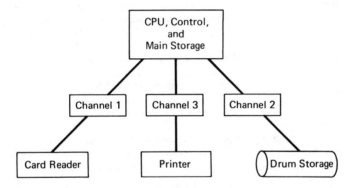

Fig. 3-6   Simple computer configuration.

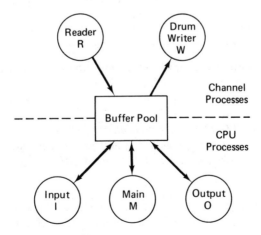

Fig. 3-7   Input spooler.

Table 3-1 Variables Used In Spooler Programs

Variable	Meaning
n	Number of buffers; $n \geq 2$
$Buf[i]$	ith buffer in pool
curin	Current input buffer is $Buf[curin]$
curout	Current output buffer is $Buf[curout]$
inio	Buffer used by R is $Buf[inio]$
outio	Buffer used by W is $Buf[outio]$
em	Empty buffer class designation
in	Input-full buffer class designation
out	Output-full buffer class designation
$F[t]$	Pointer to first buffer of class t, $t \in \{em, in, out\}$
$L[t]$	Pointer to last buffer of class t, $t \in \{em, in, out\}$
cem	Buffer counting semaphores: empty buffers
cin	input-full buffers
cout	output-full buffers
mem	Mutual exclusion semaphores: empty buffers
min	input-full buffers
mout	output-full buffers
sR	Startio semaphores: Card Reader
sW	Drum
xR	Interrupt semaphores: Card Reader
xW	Drum

Table 3-2 Producer-Consumers of Buffer Resources

Resource	Processes	
	Producer	Consumer
em	M, O	M, I
in	I	M
out	M	O

for example, reformat the input, set up job tables, and add jobs to queues; and produce output-full buffers for the drum. Zero or more output records may be produced for each input record. Let M have the following form:

M: **begin** LM: $GetNextInputFullBuffer$; $Compute$;
$(GetEmptyBuffer$; $Compute$; $ReleaseOutputFullBuffer$;)*
$ReleaseEmptyBuffer$; **go to** LM
end ;

where (s)* designates zero or more occurrences of the string s at execution time. Let cem, cin, and cout be semaphores that count available buffer resources of type em, in, and out. To ensure the integrity of the buffer data structure, we use three binary semaphores, *mem*, *min*, and *mout*, for mutual exclusion of buffer manipulations. Then the buffer routines in M are

GetNextInputFullBuffer: $P(cin)$; $P(min)$; *curin* := *TakeBuf*(*in*) ; $V(min)$;

ReleaseEmptyBuffer: $P(mem)$; *AddBuf*(*em*, *curin*) ; $V(mem)$; $V(cem)$;

GetEmptyBuffer: $P(cem)$; $P(mem)$; *curout* := *TakeBuf*(*em*) ;
$V(mem)$;

ReleaseOutputFullBuffer: $P(mout)$; *AddBuf*(*out*, *curout*) ; $V(mout)$;
$V(cout)$;

The purpose of the I process is to provide empty buffers for the reader process (R), initiate R, and add input-full buffers to the pool when R terminates. For each channel process i, associate two binary semaphores si and xi, which will simulate hardware *startio* signals and *interrupt* signals. A CPU process will issue a $V(si)$ to initiate the channel process i while a channel process will interrupt a CPU at IO termination by a $V(xi)$. Conversely, a channel process will be waiting for a "fire-up" signal on a $P(si)$ and an IO interrupt handler will be waiting at $P(xi)$ for activation. I and R then follow:

I: **begin** LI: $P(cem)$; $P(mem)$; *apd* ; *inio* := *TakeBuf*(*em*) ; $V(mem)$;
$V(sR)$; $P(xR)$;
$P(min)$; *AddBuf*(*in*, *inio*) ; $V(min)$;
$V(cin)$; **go to** LI
    end ;

R: **begin** LR: $P(sR)$; *RealRead*(*chl*, *Buf*[*inio*]) ;
$V(xR)$; **go to** LR
    end ;

RealRead indicates that R will perform the entire read operation before proceeding to the next instruction. The *apd* statement in I means "avoid possible deadlock" and refers to the situation described earlier in Sec. 2.4.4; it is possible that an empty buffer request by M can never be honored, because process R has consumed all of them and there exist no output-full buffers that can be emptied. This problem can be avoided by inserting for *apd* the instructions:

> **comment** Return to start of I if this is the last empty buffer ;
> **if** $F[em] = L[em]$ **then**
> **begin** $V(cem)$; $V(mem)$; **go to** LI **end** ;

This assures that at least one empty buffer is always available at a *GetEmpty-*

Buffer in *M*. (A more complete test would require an empty buffer only if there were no output-full buffers or no output activity.)

Similar routines can be easily constructed for *O* and *W*. In these, we ignore the important problem of drum storage allocation and assume that a start location *d* on the drum has somehow been furnished to *W* at each write. The command "*RealWrite*(*ch2*, (*Buf*[*outio*], *d*)) ;" can be used by *W*. Figure 3-8 portrays the interactions of the *O* and *W* processes.

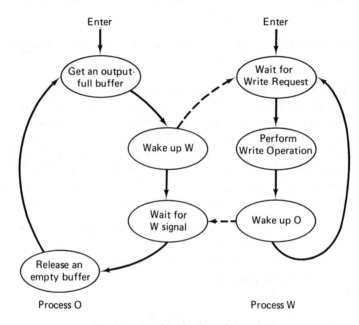

Fig. 3-8   Synchronization of *O* and *W*.

The system of processes is then described:

> **begin semaphore** *mem, min, mout, cem, cin, cout, sR, xR, sW,*
>   *xW* ;
> *mem := min := mout := 1 ; cem := n ;*
> *cin := cout := sR := xR := sW := xW := 0 ;*
> *M* **and** *I* **and** *O* **and** *R* **and** *W*
> **end** ;

Each of the five processes would normally be continuously active in the system (either running or waiting for a wake-up signal), so it is natural to make them cyclic processes.

This outline of a hypothetical input spooler omits many details. It does, however, illustrate how a set of cooperating sequential processes may be *logically* described, using semaphores for mutual exclusion within resource allocation routines, resource counting, and synchronizing processes. "Permission to enter a critical section" and synchronizing signals can also be viewed as resources in a producer-consumer environment. In this case, all the semaphores can be considered as "soft" resources.

Example 3: Message Communications Between Internal Processes and a Terminal

Consider a system where a number of internal processes $P_1, P_2, \ldots$, P_n communicate with a human operator or an interactive user U at a typewriter console. We wish to allow both the P_i and the terminal user to originate one-way and two-way messages. The four possible types of communication and examples of their application are:

1. *Process-to-User (PU)*. A process P_i sends a one-way message (no reply required) to U. A typical message might contain some systems or process statistics, for example, the number of jobs run during the last hour or a notice that a divide overflow has just occurred.

2. *Process-to-User-to-Process (PUP)*. A process P_i initiates a two-way message to the console user; the latter must respond with a reply to the originating P_i. We permit U to delay his answer; he notifies the system of the delay by immediately sending a dummy answer, say "WILCO." At some later time, the appropriate reply is then sent. An immediate response could be made to a message requesting today's date; a typical situation calling for a delayed answer is a request by P_i for the operator to mount a tape. In either case, some immediate reply, dummy or otherwise, is required.

3. *User-to-Process (UP)*. This is a one-way message from U to some P_i, for example, to announce the availability of some peripheral that had previously been taken off-line for repair or to turn on a debugging switch inside a program.

4. *User-to-Process-to-User (UPU)*. The user queries a process and waits for its answer. Example queries might be "How much auxiliary storage is being used for spooled jobs?" or "Type the names of the routines in my private program library."

Transmission from the computer to the console will occur over a half-duplex line—data can be sent in either direction, but only one transmission at a time is possible. The line could be a standard channel or a communications line to a remote terminal; we shall not be concerned with the particular type. It is assumed that U has the highest priority relative to the P_i in initiating messages and that he indicates this desire by pressing an "attention" button, which sets an internal flag a. The flag a can be set at anytime, even during transmission of output across the line.

The internal processes will be divided into two disjoint sets for simplicity:

$$\mathcal{P}_1 = \{P_i \text{ that involve only } PU \text{ and } PUP \text{ transmissions}\}$$
$$\mathcal{P}_2 = \{P_i \text{ that handle only } UP \text{ or } UPU \text{ messages}\}.$$

Processes in $\mathcal{P}_1$ initiate conversations with the console user, while those in $\mathcal{P}_2$ handle conversations initiated by the user. Direct communication between the terminal and the internal processes is difficult because of the need to route terminal messages to the correct P_i. We therefore use a message interpreter process MI for this task as well as for error checking and initiating the actual input-output operations. The system is illustrated in Fig. 3-9. This example

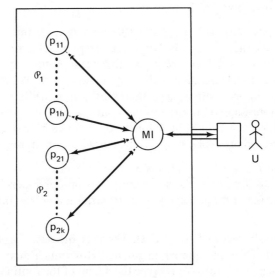

Fig. 3-9   Internal processes communicating with a terminal.

describes a set of appropriate data structures and the code required to synchronize and perform the message sending and receiving functions.

Let each message consist of a triple, (p, t, m), where p is the name of the internal process involved, $t \in \{up, upu, pu, pup\}$ designates the type of message, and m contains the message text; the first two entries permit the operator and MI to identify the message. A buffer pool is used to hold each message; each buffer b is of the form

$$Buf[b] = (pr[b], ty[b], text[b]),$$

where the three components correspond to the above message entries. Two queues are maintained in the pool:

1. A list of *empty* buffers.
2. A list of *full* buffers of type *pu* or *pup*.

Buffer retrieval and release occurs through the familiar routines *TakeBuf*(x) and *AddBuf*($x, index$) where $x \in \{empty, full\}$ (see Sec. 2.4.4). Associated with each $P_i \in \mathcal{P}_2$ is a variable $B[i]$ which used to contain a buffer index during *up* or *upu* processing. Finally, several semaphores are employed for mutual exclusion, synchronization, and resource counting. Table 3-3 summarizes the meaning of each variable referenced in the programs.

A process $P_i \in \mathcal{P}_1$ has the code skeleton:

```
Pi:   begin  Li:
             .
             .
             .

             comment Send PU message ;
       PU:   b := Dequeue(ce, me, empty) ;
             Buf[b] := (i, pu, m) ;
             Queue(cf, mf, b, full) ;
             .
             .
             .

             comment Start PUP transmission ;
       PUP:  b := Dequeue(ce, me, empty) ;
             Buf[b] := (i, pup, m) ;
             Queue(cf, mf, b, full) ;
             comment Wait for reply ;
             P(s[i]) ;
             m := text[b] ;
             Queue(ce, me, b, empty) ;
             .
             .
             .

       go to Li
       end ;
```

The auxiliary procedures of P_i are defined:

Table 3-3   Variables Used In Message Communications Programs

Variable	Meaning
a	Attention flag
up	Message class designation: user-to-process
upu	user-to-process-to-user
pu	process-to-user
pup	process-to-user-to-process
$Buf[b]=$	bth buffer in pool:
$(pr[b],$	process name
$ty[b],$	type of message
$text[b])$	message text
$empty$	Empty buffer class designation
$full$	Full buffer class designation
ce	Buffer counting semaphores: empty buffers
cf	full buffers
me	Mutual exclusion semaphores: empty buffers
mf	full buffers
$s[i]$	Synchronization semaphore for process i
ans	Synchronization semaphore for up/upu messages

integer procedure $Dequeue(s1, m1, t)$;
semaphore $s1, m1$;
begin $P(s1)$; $P(m1)$; $Dequeue := TakeBuf(t)$; $V(m1)$ **end**

procedure $Queue(s1, m1, index, t)$;
semaphore $s1, m1$;
begin $P(m1)$; $AddBuf(t, index)$; $V(m1)$; $V(s1)$ **end**

A process $P_j \in \mathcal{P}_2$ has the form:

P_j: **begin** Lj:
        UP/UPU: $P(s[j])$; **comment** Wait for message ;
        $b := B[j]$; $m := text[b]$; $t := ty[b]$;
        if $t = upu$ **then**
        begin
          Find the appropriate reply ;
          $text[b] := reply$
        end ;
        comment Wake up MI ;
        $V(ans)$;
       go to L_j
      end ;

The message interpreter is more complex:

```
MI:   begin LMI:
            if a then
            begin
               comment U requests attention. Read his message when he
                   types it ;
               Receive(p, t, m) ;
               a := false ; comment Reset the attention flag ;
               if t = up ∨ t = upu then
               begin comment Enter message in buffer ;
                   b := B[p] := Dequeue(ce, me, empty) ;
                   Buf[b] := (p, t, m) ;
                   comment Wake up p ; V(s[p]) ;
                   comment Wait until message is received or reply is
                       returned ; P(ans) ;
                   if t = upu then Send(Buf[b]) ;
                   comment Reply is typed if upu ;
                   comment Now release the buffer to the pool ;
                   Queue(ce, me, b, empty)
               end
               else if t = pup then
               begin comment This is a delayed response to a pup ;
                       text[B[p]] := m ; V(s[p])
               end
            end
            else
            begin comment Process pu or pup if full queue has entries ;
               if F[full] ≠ full then
               begin
                   b := Dequeue(cf, mf, full) ;
                   Send(Buf[b]) ;
                   comment check for pup ;
                   if ty[b] = pup then
                   begin Receive(p, t, m) ;
                       comment Is this a dummy response ;
                       if m = "WILCO" then B[p] := b
                       else
                       begin text[b] := m ; V(s[p]) end
                   end
               end
            end ;
            go to LMI
      end ;
```

The semaphores $s[i]$, $i = 1, \ldots, n$, are used to ensure that the P_i are synchronized with MI and the U for PUP, UP, and UPU messages. The semaphore ans keeps MI synchronized with the $P_i \in \mathcal{P}_2$. The remaining semaphores serve the same functions as in Example 2. An alternate approach for $\mathcal{P}_2$ processes might be to queue up the UP messages and insist that MI wait only for UPU replies. Note that no error checking exists in MI; this must certainly be included in any real system. The example is another illustration of the application (and necessity) of synchronization primitives in an environment where several processes may coexist, communicate, and share resources.

Binary and General Semaphores

The behavior of a general semaphore can always be simulated by using only binary semaphores. Each general semaphore S can be replaced by an integer variable N_S and two binary semaphores, $mutex_S$ and $delay_S$. For each operation $P(S)$, we use

(1) $P(mutex_S)$; $N_S := N_S - 1$; **if** $N_S \leq -1$ **then**
                              begin $V(mutex_S)$; $P(delay_S)$ **end** ;
                    $V(mutex_S)$;

Each $V(S)$ is replaced by

(2) $P(mutex_S)$; $N_S := N_S + 1$; **if** $N_S \leq 0$ **then** $V(delay_S)$; **else** $V(mutex_S)$;

Initially, $mutex_S = 1$, $delay_S = 0$, and N_S is set to the initial value of S. A process that would be blocked on a $P(S)$ is also blocked on (1), since $N_S \leq -1$ and $P(delay_S)$ would be invoked; similarly, if a $V(S)$ could cause a process to continue, (2) would also do this through the $V(delay_S)$.

EXERCISES

1. What is the effect of interchanging
    (a) $P(b)$ and $P(e)$ or
    (b) $V(b)$ and $V(f)$ in the producer process of Example 1?

2. Write programs for the O and W processes in the input spooler (Example 2).

3. Suppose that the best size for a drum record is 320 bytes (i.e., 1 drum record = 4 buffer records). Let a drum write operation be designated:

    $$RealWrite(ch2, ((b_1, b_2, b_3, b_4), d)) ;$$

    where the b_i are buffer pointers and d is the drum record address. Change processes M, O, and W, and any semaphores you wish in Example 2, to reflect this new output record length. Assume the number of buffers $n \geq 5$.

4. Consider four sequential processes, *prod*1, *con*1, *con*2, and *prod*2, which access

a common buffer pool of n buffers ($n \geq 1$). *prod*1 is a compute process that fills buffers; *con*1 is an output process that writes (empties) the buffers filled by *prod*1. *prod*2 is an input process that reads data into buffers; *con*2 is a compute process that computes with the data produced by *prod*2. Each process is organized in the following manner:

(1) Get an appropriate buffer, say i, from the common pool.

(2) Compute (*Compute* (*Buf*[i])) or perform an IO operation (*Read*(*Buf*[i]) or *Write*(*Buf*[i])) with the selected buffer.

(3) Release *Buf*[i] to the pool.

(4) Go to step (1).

Assume that the *Read* and *Write* operations are *direct* IO instructions. Write Algol programs with semaphore operations to describe the four processes. The system of processes is organized:

> **begin semaphore** . . .
>   *prod*1 **and** *con*1 **and** *prod*2 **and** *con*2
> **end** ;

5. Consider the possible parallel activities in a compiler depicted in Fig. 3-10. Each of the four processes $P1$, $P2$, $P3$, and $P4$ is cyclic and communicates with one or more other processes through the common data areas AL, ILC, and OM. Process $P1$ will add atom pointers to AL that are consumed by $P2$. $P2$ also produces intermediate language code for ILC that is consumed by $P3$. $P1$, $P2$, and $P3$ produce output messages in OM that are consumed by $P4$. Let the com-

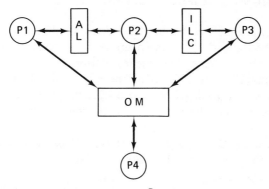

Data:

AL: Atom List
ILC: Intermediate Language
       Code
OM: Output Messages

Processes:

P1:   Scan
P2:   Syntax and Semantics
P3:   Code Generation
P4:   Output

Fig. 3-10   Parallel processes in a compiler.

mon data areas be arrays:

$$AL[0: al\text{-}1],\ ILC[0: ilc\text{-}1],\quad \text{and}\quad OM[0: om\text{-}1]\ (al,\ ilc,\ om \geq 1)$$

which are organized as cyclic buffers. Assume that each data area request or release involves only one element of an array. Write the relevant code for each process for adding and removing elements of common storage and for assuring their correct synchronization. The global form is

> **begin semaphore** . . .
>   *P*1 **and** *P*2 **and** *P*3 **and** *P*4
> **end** ;

6. Insert the appropriate code in the process *MI* of Example 3 to test for and react reasonably to operator errors.

7. What should be done to avoid a possible deadlock when one is using the buffer pool resource in Example 3?

8. Design a message interpreter and the internal processes so that each P_i in Example 3 handles transmissions of all four types (*PU, PUP, UP, UPU*).

9. Redo Example 1, using only binary semaphores.

10. Are the binary semaphore simulations presented at the end of this section still correct if $V(mutex_S)$ is moved to precede the N_S test in either (1) or (2)?

11. Use semaphores to describe the synchronization of the eight processes in the general precedence case of Fig. 3-1(d).

3.5 IMPLEMENTING SEMAPHORE OPERATIONS

No currently available computers have direct hardware instructions corresponding to the *P* and *V* semaphore operations. However, software versions of *P* and *V* have been used as the synchronization primitives in at least two operating systems (Dijkstra, 1968; Bétourné et al., 1969). It is not difficult to program the logical equivalents of these operations on a computer that can both *test* and *set* a storage location in *one* (*indivisible*) operation. Let our version of such an instruction be designated $TS(X)$, where the storage location X can contain either an "O" (**false**) or a "1" (**true**); we shall treat X as a Boolean variable. Then $TS(X)$ performs the following actions:

$$\text{test: } R := X\ ;$$
$$\text{set: } X := \textbf{true}\ ;$$

where R is a program-addressable register of the machine executing the *TS*. (Assume that R can hold either of the values **true** or **false**.)

To simplify the algorithms in the following sections, we shall ignore the register R and treat $TS(X)$ as an *indivisible* Boolean procedure that returns the value previously assigned to R:

> **Boolean procedure** $TS(X)$;
> **Boolean** X ;
> **begin**
> $TS := X$;
> $X :=$ **true**
> **end** TS

3.5.1 Implementation with a Busy Wait

A critical section CSi can be protected in the process Pi with the code

> Li: **if** $TS(mutex)$ **then go to** Li ;
> CSi ; $mutex :=$ **false** ;

It is assumed that a single instruction, for example, a *store immediate*, is sufficient to set *mutex* to **false** at the end of the *CS*. *mutex* = **true** when a process is in its *CS* and **false** otherwise. If Pi attempts to enter CSi when *mutex* is **true**, it will do a busy wait, looping around Li and consuming storage cycles and processor time. The effect of a binary semaphore S can then be achieved:

> $P(S)$ *is equivalent to:* L: **if** $TS(S)$ **then go to** L ;
> $V(S)$ *is equivalent to:* $S :=$ **false** ;

The logical equivalence of general and binary semaphores presented at the end of the last section can be employed to simulate a *general* semaphore S; we use a simple variable N_S for counting, a binary semaphore m_S for mutual exclusion, and a binary semaphore d_S for delay:

(1) $P(S)$ can be simulated with the code

> $L1$: **if** $TS(m_S)$ **then go to** $L1$; $N_S := N_S - 1$;
>   **if** $N_S \leq -1$ **then**
>   **begin** $m_S :=$ **false** ;
> $L2$: **if** $TS(d_S)$ **then go to** $L2$
>   **end** ; $m_S :=$ **false** ;

(2) $V(S)$ is implemented in a similar manner.

Busy waits for CS's may not be inefficient if they are "short" waits. Frequently, CS's may be executed relatively quickly. (They should be planned to have this property if at all possible.) It may then be possible to *inhibit interrupts* during CS execution so that permission to enter a CS is guaranteed to be granted to someone within a small time interval. In an environment involving more general CS's and synchronizations where, for example, a process may be blocked waiting for an IO operation to be completed, or a hardware resource to become available, or a message from another process that can arrive at any arbitrary time, lengthy busy waits may be unsatisfactory. They can degenerate a multiprogrammed system into a uniprogrammed one, as well as increase the response time for real-time events to intolerable levels.

EXERCISES

1. Give the code for implementing $V(S)$ for a general semaphore S.

2. Redo Example 1 of the last section (Sec. 3.4.2), using TS and a busy wait.

3. Consider the instruction $TSB(X, L)$ which performs a test, set, and branch as one operation as follows:

if X **then go to** L **else** $X := $ **true ;**

Code the P and V operations on binary semaphores, using TSB. (Some machines have a primitive TSB where the instruction counter is incremented by either 1 or 2, depending on the results of the test.)

3.5.2 Avoiding the Busy Wait

A busy wait is avoided by providing for possible suspension (*blocking*) of processes on P operations and possible activation of processes on V operations. A process p that cannot proceed on a $P(S)$ will be blocked by saving p's statevector, releasing the processor executing p, and inserting p on a *blocked list* L_S associated with the semaphore S. If L_S is not empty, a $V(S)$ will activate some process, say p, on L_S by removing p from L_S and inserting p on a global *ready list RL*. The P and V operations will also conditionally attempt to allocate a free processor to a process on RL. A process executing a P or V is protected from processor preemption during these operations. A TS is used to prevent processors, other than the one executing the operation, from simultaneously accessing the semaphore, blocked lists, and RL; interrupts are inhibited during the operations to ensure that P and V go to completion before the processor is released. Under reasonable assumptions, lengthy busy waits will not occur.

The P and V operations are then defined:

1. $P(S)$:

> *Inhibit interrupts* ;
> L: **if** $TS(mutex)$ **then go to** L ;
> $S := S - 1$;
> **if** $S \leq -1$ **then**
> **begin** *Block process invoking* P;
> $p := RemovefromRL$;
> $mutex :=$ **false** ;
>   *Transfer control to p with interrupts enabled*
> **end**
> **else**
> **begin** $mutex :=$ **false** ; *Enable interrupts* **end** ;

It is assumed that *RemovefromRL* always returns a process name from RL;†
at this point, we are not concerned with the particular process selected from
RL. Note that $P(S)$ must be considered an indivisible machine operation.
Thus if a process q is blocked on invoking $P(S)$, the location counter part of
its saved statevector will point to the next instruction of q following $P(S)$.

2. $V(S)$:

> *Inhibit interrupts* ;
> L: **if** $TS(mutex)$ **then go to** L ;
> $S := S + 1$;
> **if** $S \leq 0$ **then**
> **begin** $p := RemovefromL_s$;
>   **if** *freeprocessors* **then**
>   *Start executing p on a free processor*
>   **else** *Add p to RL*
> **end** ;
> $mutex :=$ **false** ;
> *Enable interrupts* ;

We have allowed the semaphore to have negative values in this imple-
mentation. If a semaphore S is negative, then its absolute value $|S|$ gives the
number of blocked processes on L_S. Since interrupts are inhibited and a
busy wait exists at L, it is important that the above code be short and efficient for the same reasons discussed in the last section. It is still possible to

---

†It is convenient to maintain one "idle" or "dummy" process on RL for each processor;
in this way, RL will never be empty when a real working process becomes blocked. An idle
process is selected by *RemovefromRL only* when RL contains no working processes.

have long, even infinite, busy waits in a multiprocessor system. Suppose that a single cyclic process were constantly executing P and V on one processor and that each of the remaining processors were looping on a TS. Timing conditions could be such that the first process always entered the CS and left the others looping forever. This situation can be prevented by expanding the CS entry mechanism so that it grants entry on a round robin basis.

The contents and organization of process data structures, the various lists, and process schedulers are given in Chapter 7. We have also omitted several error checks that must be included in a real implementation; for example, what happens in $V(S)$ if $S \leq -1$ on entry and L_S is empty?

EXERCISE

Modify the P and V implementations of this section so that infinite busy waits are impossible.

3.6 OTHER SYNCHRONIZATION PRIMITIVES

Other synchronization primitives that serve the same functions as P and V have been suggested and implemented in operating systems. The actions of *all* primitives discussed below are assumed to be *indivisible*. It is convenient to distinguish between those used strictly for critical section protection and those employed for more general message communication.

Dennis and Van Horn (1966) proposed a very straightforward CS lockout mechanism. CS's are enclosed within a **lock** w–**unlock** w pair, where w is an arbitrary one-bit lock variable. The primitives are defined:

> **lock** w: L: **if** $w = 1$ **then go to** L
> else $w := 1$;
> **unlock** w: $w := 0$;

The lock command is the same as a $TSB(w, *)$ instruction (* indicates self-reference; see Exercise 3, Sec. 3.5.1). Our earlier discussions on the problems of the busy wait apply here also. The ENQ (*enqueue*) and DEQ (*dequeue*) macro-instructions available in the IBM operating system/360 (OS/360) (IBM, 1967) are used for CS protection; they avoid the busy wait and provide for process blocking and resumption. ENQ is used to gain control of a resource, while DEQ releases the resource; a process cannot release a resource (DEQ) unless it controls it (a previous ENQ). In their simplest form, ENQ and DEQ have a single parameter, a resource name. Their execution has the following effect:

$ENQ(r)$:   **if** *inuse*[r] **then**
            begin *Insert p on r-queue; Block p* **end**
            else *inuse*[r] := **true** ;

$DEQ(r)$: p := *Removefromr-queue* ;
            if $p \neq \Omega$ **then** *Activate p*
            else *inuse*[r] := **false** ;

The resource r ("permission to enter a CS") has a queue of processes (r-*queue*) waiting for its availability. The process invoking ENQ is assumed to be named p in the above. In DEQ, if $p = \Omega$, the r-*queue* is empty; "*Activate p*" would generally result in putting p on a ready list and calling a process scheduler.†

OS/360 has general facilities for process synchronization in the form of $WAIT$ and $POST$ macro-instructions. In their simplest form, they have one parameter that represents an event; the event parameter essentially designates a storage area for the synchronization signal and simple messages. Only *one* process may $WAIT$ for a given event to occur (be $POST$ed) but any number of processes may $POST$ the same event. The basic actions of these macros are

$WAIT(e)$:   **if** ¬*posted*[e] **then**
            begin *wait*[e] := **true** ; *process*[e] := p ; *Block p* **end**
            else *posted*[e] := **false** ;

$POST(e)$:   **if** ¬*posted*[e] **then**
            begin if *wait*[e] **then**
                 begin *wait*[e] := **false**;
                        Activate process[e]
                 end
            else *posted*[e] := **true**

            end ;

It is again assumed that p is the name of the process invoking the $WAIT$. In this version,‡ the $WAIT$ is similar to an ENQ with a maximum queue length of 1.

A set of processes must *cooperate* with one another in using all the primitives discussed so far in this chapter. A more basic (lower-level) set of primitives that may also be employed in some instances with uncooperative

---

†This is a highly simplified interpretation of ENQ and DEQ. They also allow conditional requests for control and release of a resource, requests for several resources simultaneously, and sharing of resources (nonexclusive control).

‡Again we have taken some liberties with the IBM definitions. The more general $WAIT$ and $POST$ allow waiting for several events or some subset of events and provide for limited message passing; also, $WAIT$ does not reset the *posted*[e] flag.

processes is *Block* and *Wakeup* (Saltzer, 1966; Lampson, 1968). A wakeup-waiting switch *wws[i]*, associated with each process *i*, is used in much the same way as *wait[e]* in *WAIT* and *POST* to prevent blocking when a *Block* is preceded in time by a *Wakeup*. *Block* and *Wakeup* operate on processes in the following way:

$$Block(i): \quad \textbf{if } \neg wws[i] \textbf{ then } Block \textit{ process } i$$
$$\textbf{else } wws[i] := \textbf{false} ;$$

$$Wakeup(i): \quad \textbf{if } ready(i) \textbf{ then } wws[i] := \textbf{true}$$
$$\textbf{else } Activate \textit{ process } i ;$$

The test *ready(i)* returns **true** if *i* is running or ready, and **false** otherwise. A command such as *Block(*)* can be used for a possible self-block. *Block* and *Wakeup* thus explicitly operate on processes rather than sending signals to *anyone* ready to receive them.

Process communication basically involves the transmission of messages among processes. In this context, we can view a semaphore as defining a queue of null messages and *P* and *V* as low-level message transmission operations (Wirth, 1969). A *V* operation adds a message to the queue, whereas a *P* operation removes one from the queue if possible. The value of the semaphore is the number of such messages in the queue, if we retain our original restriction to nonnegative integers. An interesting and elegant set of *message transmission primitives* was devised for a multiprogramming system for the RC 4000 computer (Brinch Hansen, 1970); the primitives were used for communications among internal processes as well as for transmitting peripheral IO records. The main data structures are a common pool of buffers used for message transmission and a message queue, say *mq[i]*, associated with each process *i*. We shall use the following variables in the descriptions below:

r: intended receiver of a message
m: contents of the message
b: buffer to hold a message
s: a message sender; s_b: original sender of message in buffer *b*
a: answer or reply to a message
t: type of answer, dummy or real
p: name of process invoking a primitive

Boldface parameters below are set on return from the operations; otherwise, parameters are set on input. Brinch Hansen's synchronizing primitives are

1. *Sendmessage (r, m, **b**)* ;
   Obtain a buffer *b* from the pool. Copy *m*, *p*, and *r* into *b* and enqueue *b* on *mq[r]*. Activate *r* if it is waiting for a message.

2. *Waitmessage* (**s**, **m**, **b**) ;
   If $mq[p]$ is empty, block process p; otherwise, remove a queue element b. Return the message of b in m and the sender in s.

3. *Sendanswer* (t, a, b) ;
   Copy t, a, and p into b and enqueue b in $mq[s_b]$. Activate s_b if it is waiting for an answer.

4. *Waitanswer* (**t**, **a**, b) ;
   Block p until an answer arrives in b. Put answer in a and type in t. Return buffer b to the pool.

The normal message protocol requires the use of all four primitives: The sender emits a *Sendmessage* followed at some point by a *Waitanswer*, while the receiver issues a *Waitmessage* and subsequently, a *Sendanswer*. A type "Dummy" answer is inserted by the system when the addressed message receiver process does not exist. The sender and receiver of a message are stored in the buffer to permit the system to verify the identity of processes on a *Sendanswer* or *Waitanswer*. Uncooperative processes that purposely or inadvertently try to interfere with a conversation are then exposed.

All of the primitives discussed in this chapter potentially involve the logical blocking and/or activation of processes. Potential blocking and activation of processes occur however, when "resources" of *any* kind are requested or released; for example, as a result of requesting or releasing blocks of main storage. We examine this more general case in detail in Chapter 7 after some other facets of multiprogramming systems have been developed.

EXERCISES

1. Implement the general semaphore operations P and V in terms of the IBM OS/360 macros *ENQ, DEQ, WAIT,* and *POST*.

2. Use **lock, unlock,** *Block*, and *Wakeup* to describe the producer-consumer communications in Example 1, Sec. 3.4.3.

3. Repeat Exercise 2, using the Brinch Hansen primitives for producer-consumer communication.

4. Use the Brinch Hansen primitives instead of P and V in Example 3, Sec. 3.4.3.

4 INTRODUCTION TO MULTIPROGRAMMING SYSTEMS

4.1 RATIONALE FOR MULTIPROGRAMMING

A classical batch processing operation in which one job at a time flows through the system in a strictly sequential manner is inherently inefficient in computers that have independent IO processors or channels. Consider first the utilization of processor resources. With careful planning, it is sometimes possible to achieve maximum overlap of central and IO processor execution. (This is a difficult task, which is rarely accomplished.) Job optimization in this sense, nevertheless, still results in idle IO or central processors for compute-bound or IO-bound programs, respectively. Even when processors are kept busy most of the time, the utilization of other computer resources is often poor; for example, any main storage not occupied by the current job (and some minimal part of the operating system) is essentially a wasted resource. If more than one program were simultaneously active, not only would the amount of idle resources decrease, but also, more significantly, job throughput and turnaround time would improve. This was the original reasoning underlying the development of multiprogrammed systems. In the absence of independent hardware IO processors, multiprogramming may still be beneficial, however. For example, by sequentially sharing processor time, several interactive users may be permitted to run small jobs at their terminals; the computer is systematically allocated to each terminal for a short period of time so that a user is given the illusion of his own computer.

The basic idea is to *maintain more than one independent program or job in an active state in main storage.*† A particularly good choice would be an IO-bound job A (e.g., updating a large data file) and a compute-bound job B

---

†More correctly, we should speak in terms of the *process(es)* associated with a job.

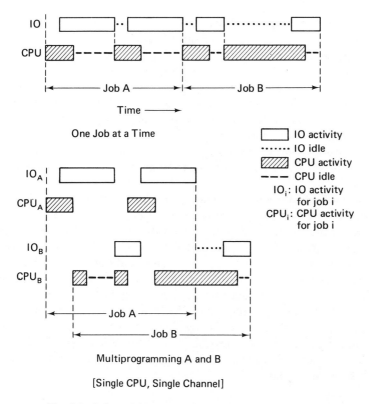

Fig. 4-1 Job-at-a-time processing and multiprogramming.

(e.g., solving a set of partial differential equations). While A is waiting for IO, B can compute; on an IO completion, control is switched back to A. Figure 4-1 illustrates the execution of two such jobs in both a job-at-a-time and a multiprogrammed environment; during the multiprogrammed execution, A and B are both assumed to be resident in main storage and they share the CPU and channel. The time saved by multiprogramming is evident in this simple example. Note that multiprogramming involves the sharing of *time* on processors and the sharing of *space* in main storage, as well as the potential sharing of other resources.

There are several other benefits derived from a multiprogrammed organization. In order to get jobs into and out of the system, there must also be systems processes sharing time and space with user processes. It then becomes feasible to handle more than one job entry station and interactive computing from many individual consoles. An additional space-saving benefit accrues from the ability to share code. If several active processes require the same language translator or request the same system service, a single copy of these routines may be shared asynchronously, provided that they are written as "pure" programs (programs that do not modify themselves). The system and users also have more control over the scheduling of jobs. The resource requirements and priorities of a set of waiting jobs—say, waiting on auxiliary storage—can be used by schedulers to optimize systems resource usage and to ensure adequate response for high-priority jobs. Similarly, the software and hardware mechanisms for switching among processes allow high-priority tasks to dynamically take precedence over or even preempt lower-priority ones. The economic and technical success of hardware and software resource-sharing through multiprogramming benefits users in one other—perhaps the most important—way; it makes it feasible to provide a wide variety of services.

Currently, most medium- and large-scale batch, interactive, real-time, and general-purpose operating systems are multiprogrammed. However, the advantages of this mode of operation are not gained without a price. Extensive software facilities as well as additional hardware are required, and-time and space overhead caused by the system is significant during execution.

The purpose of Chapter 4 is to present a global view of multiprogramming systems. This view is developed by first examining the hardware and software requirements for multiprogramming. We then outline the two extreme levels of virtual machine that appear in any OS—the user interface represented by a command and control language and the first-level software interface to the machine called the MS nucleus. The last section outlines some general approaches to MS design.

4.2 SYSTEMS COMPONENTS

4.2.1 Hardware Features

We shall be concerned with a family of computing systems, each member of which has the following basic elements: p central processing unit(s) P_i, m module(s) of main (executable) storage M_i, c data channel(s) or IO processor(s) C_i, k IO device controller(s) K_i, d auxiliary storage device(s) D_i, and io input and output peripheral(s) and terminal(s) IO_i, where $p, m, c, k, d, io \geq 1$. Figure 4-2 presents a typical organization of these components; this is just an expanded version of our minimal machine of Chapter 1.

Any modern computing system can be represented as a member of this family. The P_i may be symmetrically organized with respect to one another or may be related on a master/slave basis. Similarly, the M_i can be of different types and have different hierarchical relationships to one another. We could include transmission control units as a possibility for the K_i; in that case, the communication lines connect the K_i to remote devices (α_i or β_i in the figure) which then may be general computing systems as well as I or O.

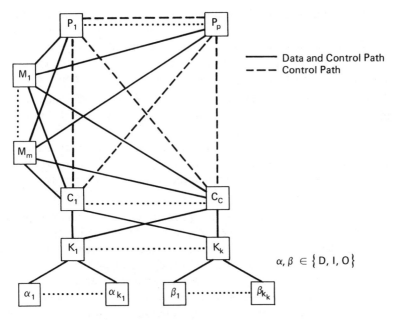

Fig. 4-2   Hardware configuration for a general computing system.

Within the above organization, there are a number of hardware features that either simplify or are necessary for a multiprogrammed operation:

1. *Priority interrupt facilities.* Switching of CPU control from one process to another usually occurs as a result of hardware interrupts generated either externally through IO channels and other devices or internally by program errors, deliberate traps (e.g., "supervisor" call instructions), timers, and hardware malfunctions.† Interrupts generally arrive at unpredictable times, and several different interrupt-causing events may occur simultaneously. Software and hardware priorities on interrupts are necessary because of the relative importance to the system of the processes waiting for interrupt signals to awaken them and because of the existence of timing constraints between an interrupt-causing event and its processing. For example, a machine error must normally be treated immediately; an "input-available" signal from an on-line data acquisition device may require service within a short period of time or data could be lost; and an IO completion interrupt signal at the termination of a magnetic tape write could be handled at some indefinite time in the future, depending on the priority of the particular tape-writing process. A built-in set of hardware priorities for broad classes of interrupts plus the

†See the footnote comments in Sec. 1.5 on systems that use polling techniques rather than interrupts.

ability to inhibit and enable interrupts by program permits the system dynamically to establish precedence relationships among interrupt-causing events. When an interrupt occurs, the hardware should quickly save the state of the current process, determine the cause of the interrupt, and change the CPU state to initiate an appropriate interrupt-handling routine.

2. *Storage and instruction protection.* In order to efficiently prevent erratic or malicious processes from destroying or invading the privacy of other processes, including systems processes, it is important to have hardware facilities for protecting areas of main storage and for restricting the set of machine instructions available to a particular process. For example, it is not generally desirable for a user program directly to inhibit interrupts.

3. *Dynamic address relocation.* Hardware which dynamically computes instruction and data addresses during program execution makes it possible to move a program or parts of a program in and around main storage without performing a lengthy static relocation of addresses. In systems with extensive facilities of this type, programs need not occupy contiguous areas of storage, may be easily swapped in and out of storage, can be contracted and expanded at run time, and may only partially reside in main storage. Dynamic address relocation is not necessary for multiprogramming but is certainly convenient.

4. *Timer.* A program-controllable timer that can produce an interrupt after counting an arbitrary number of small time increments must be included in the CPU in order to control the sharing of time among several processes. This is necessary for both a noninteractive batch system and for interactive time-sharing.

5. *Base registers.* Program sharing among several processes requires that the program address data indirectly through registers that will contain the base addresses of data areas associated with a process using the program. The shared program and its permanent data may then remain read-only.

6. *Direct access auxiliary storage.* Large rapidly accessible auxiliary storage is necessary for storing user jobs, library and systems programs, and output streams. This gives the system flexibility in selecting jobs to load, allows the primary input and output peripheral devices to be kept almost continuously active, and reduces the delays in getting information into and out of main storage.

In later chapters we shall discuss these hardware features in more detail, since they influence the design and organization of any operating system.

4.2.2 Basic Software

The software requirements for multiprogramming can be motivated and inferred by examining a user job as it flows through a typical system. Con-

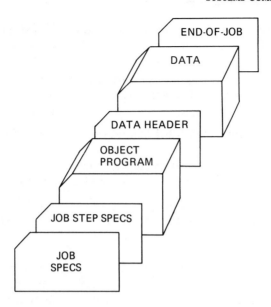

Fig. 4-3 Job *J*.

sider first a simple noninteractive job *J*, involving the execution of an object
language program obtained from a previous compilation. We assume that *J*
is submitted through a batch input station and has the form of Fig. 4-3.

1. *J* is read into main storage and placed on auxiliary storage (input
spooling). At this time, information for scheduling *J* is extracted from the job
and job step specifications. This information includes job priority, classifica-
tion (e.g., IO-bound), and general resource requirements (e.g., main storage,
estimate of CPU-time, tape drives, etc.). *J* becomes known to the system by
storing its characteristics in a resident-job list.

2. Eventually, *J* is selected for processing. This decision is based on the
properties and states of the current processes in the system and the characteristics of *J* relative to other jobs on the resident-job list. Main storage is
allocated and the object program part of it is loaded; this could also include
the loading and linking of library programs. After loading, the input program
is no longer considered as data but defines the program for a new input process, say *j*, which is created. Process *j*, with its initial state, is inserted on a list
of ready processes. Auxiliary storage space used for the object deck can now
be released.

3. Process *j* is eventually allocated a CPU and starts executing. If a higher-
priority process enters the system or is awakened, *j* may be preempted from
its CPU and revert to the ready list; the preempting process could be an independent process or a dependent one, such as the process responsible for

buffering input for *j*. Input and output occur through virtual card readers and printers on auxiliary storage. Whenever *j* has to wait for the completion of an IO operation, it will enter *blocked* status and release the CPU. In general, *j* will experience many changes of status through ready, running, and blocked; these changes are interrupt-driven. (The linking-loading process in 2 will also move through these status types.)

4. Process *j* is terminated either naturally or as a result of an error condition. Main storage is deallocated, auxiliary storage containing the input data is released, completion messages and charging information for *J* are added to the output file of *J*, and *J* is inserted on a completed-jobs list.

5. An output routine (output spooling) will finally print *J*'s output on a peripheral printer. A systems log is updated with the vital statistics of the job. *J* is then completely removed from the system.

A time-sharing job involving interactive user communication through a typewriter or graphics terminal does not pass through the spooling phase, but otherwise has a similar flow. The user interface with the system—job and job specifications—is an on-line command language rather than job control cards as above. Programs to be run are loaded on request or created in real-time by the user. The process or processes resulting from this job change status often as they request and receive resources from the system and communicate with the user at his terminal. The necessity of a rapid system response to user commands dictates different scheduling policies than for batched jobs.

We can infer the following execution-time characteristics of systems from the job flow just described:

1. Processes are created and destroyed, and often change status; e.g., process *j*.

2. Processes generally need to communicate with each other; e.g., the spooling operations (see also Example 2 of Sec. 3.4.3 again).

3. Resources are dynamically acquired and released; e.g., main and auxiliary storage.

4. Much input-output and file processing is necessary; e.g., creation and manipulation of resident-job files.

A cross-section of a multiprogramming system taken during its operation will reveal a number of user and systems processes in ready, running, or blocked status. The ready processes are waiting for the availability of CPU's, while the blocked ones are generally blocked on requests for resources. In addition to the CPU processes, there will exist "external" IO processes associated with data channels, peripherals, and auxiliary storage. Figure 4-4(a)

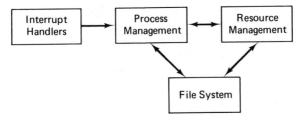

(a) Basic Software Components

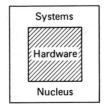

(b) The Extended Machine

Fig. 4-4   Basic multiprogramming software.

contains the most basic software components necessary to control such an operation.

The central task is that of *process management*—the creation, removal, communication, control, and scheduling of processes. The system may be very sensitive to the scheduling strategies employed; i.e., the algorithms that decide which of many competing processes may make progress by being assigned a processor. Competition for all the other resources is arbitrated by a *resource management* system, which administrates and allocates such key resources as main and auxiliary storage space; systems performance is determined in large measure by the selected resource allocation policies. The third component is a *file system;* this subsystem is responsible for creating, destroying, modifying, and retrieving information on auxiliary storage and peripherals. The file system represents an expanded version of the IOCS of earlier batch systems. The three components are highly interrelated and communicate with one another; for example, processes for resource management are required by the file system in order to control the disposition of secondary storage or to obtain buffers. Finally, these components are generally invoked through a set of basic interrupt-handling routines, e.g., the creation, termination, blocking, and waking up of a process normally occur through interrupts. Note that a particular system may not explicitly have this organization, but the functions of each block can be distributed through other system modules.

The operating system can be interpreted as an extension of the computer hardware, i.e., a virtual machine, providing additional and more convenient facilities for specifying and controlling a computation. That part of the system which permanently resides in main storage has historically been called the system *nucleus* [Fig. 4-4(b)]. The nucleus will usually consist of a minimal set of primitives and processes for the management of processes, resources, and input-output.

At a higher level than the above basic software are the processes and program modules responsible for administrating the flow of jobs through the system, responding to user requests for services, and controlling the OS itself. We include in this category the input and output spooling subsystem, the interpreter of the user job control or command language and the associated processes created to manage each phase of a job, and processes to communicate with the machine operator and allow him to control the OS operation and configuration. Elements of the basic software components are used to implement these higher-level functions.

4.3 OPERATING SYSTEM NUCLEUS

The OS *nucleus* is a basic set of primitive *operations* and *processes* from which the remainder of the system is constructed. This nucleus has always been implemented by conventional software but, in future systems, may be expected to appear either directly in hardware or as microprograms.

The distinction between a process and a primitive operation deserves some explanation. When a primitive operation is invoked by a process, it takes the form of a subroutine call or in-line code (a macro expansion) and is part of the calling process, often a *critical section* within the latter. On the other hand, a process requesting a service from another process sends a request message to that process and, frequently, blocks itself until the service has been rendered; i.e., the two processes are thought of as almost independent activities running in *parallel*. The service process, say a member of the nucleus, can be written to remain in blocked status until it receives a request, or it could be continually *polling* the system for work. In the first case, one could also treat the process as an operation, the difference being one of conceptual convenience. A practical consideration here is that a process call is more complicated, and consumes more time and space. One often thinks of nucleus operations as processes, regardless of the implementation method, because a process requesting a systems service does not normally have the capability (resources) to perform that service for itself; if it wishes to do so, some other process must grant the requesting one the required resources. One example is a "supervisor" call instruction, which causes a hardware process to change the state of the machine to make additional resources available (e.g., the ability to execute channel initiation instructions).

The set of nucleus routines can be divided into four subsets according to their function: process management, resource allocation, input-output, and interrupt handling. This section introduces some possibilities for the primitives required in each subset.

Primitives For Process Control and Communication

Processes are continually entering and leaving a MS; the obvious examples are those defined in user jobs. Primitives are therefore necessary for *creating* a process and for *deleting* one. Creation involves initializing a state vector, allocating enough resources for the process to run when it is given a processor, and identifying the process to the system, for example, by entering its name in a global list. When a process is destroyed (terminated), its resources must be released and its identification purged from any systems data structures. Process status could be implicitly set to *ready* on creation, or it could be inactive initially; in the latter case, a separate operation is required to put it in ready status, i.e., to "start" the process.

The parallel programming notations described in Sec. 3.1.2 implicitly included these two operations. "**fork** *e*;" creates a new process. The initial state vector would contain at least the state elements: *instruction counter* $= e$ and *status* $=$ "*ready*"; the process could be given, as a shared resource, the storage area containing the code starting at label *e*. Conversely, the **quit** operation destroys the invoking process. In a less transparent way, the **and** notation also implies process creation and termination. A reasonable interpretation of

$$S_0; S_1 \text{ and } S_2; S_3$$

is provided by the equivalent code:

$$S_0; t := 2; \textbf{fork } s_2; S_1; \textbf{join } t, s_3; \textbf{quit};$$
$$s_2: S_2; \textbf{join } t, s_3; \textbf{quit};$$
$$s_3: S_3;$$

Communication and synchronization primitives are the second requirement. We want basic facilities for transmitting messages among processes, including, either directly or indirectly, block and wake-up signals. External hardware interrupts provide this service at the lowest level among interrupt handling processes on different processors. The previous chapter discussed several possible candidates for more general software primitives—the semaphore P and V operations; *Block* and *Wakeup*; *WAIT* and *POST;* and the Brinch Hansen communication routines. Underlying each of these operations must be some mechanism for storing state vectors and moving processes among ready and blocked lists.

The nucleus can often be organized so that *process schedulers*, i.e., processor allocators, are embedded within the above process primitives and are called indirectly *only* through these operations. A scheduler for a given set of processors can allocate on some priority basis; it might, therefore, be invoked on any change of priorities of processes in the system as well as within the other primitives. A *change process priority* operation might then be included as part of the nucleus. If we assume that messages are just another class of resources, then the communications primitives can be subsumed by the resource operations, as discussed below.

Primitives for Resource Management

The major hardware resources requiring explicit management routines are central processors, IO processors, main storage, auxiliary storage, and peripheral devices. Associated with each class of resources are procedures for *allocating* and *freeing* one or more elements of the class. A general form for these primitives might be

$$x := allocate(resourceclass, requestdetails) ;$$
$$free(resourceclass, identificationdetails) ;$$

The parameter *requestdetails* would include items such as the number of units desired and whether the request is "critical" or not, i.e., whether the process invoking *allocate* can proceed if the resource cannot be granted immediately. When a resource is allocated, the routine typically returns a pointer identifying the particular member of the class.

Example

A request for 3000 words of main storage could be made by the call

$$FIRSTADDRESS := allocate(MAINSTORE, WORDS = 3000) ;$$

Similarly, four blocks of main store could be released by

$$free(MAINSTORE, BLOCKS = (13, 8, 21, 75)) ;$$

Note that a process invoking an *allocate* command with a critical request must be placed in blocked status if the request cannot be granted immediately. Consequently, calls on process management primitives may be embedded in the resource routines. The *free* routine similarly implies a possible awakening of processes waiting for the availability of the resource. Resource management for hardware units becomes particularly complex when a process can acquire resources *dynamically* as opposed to *static* acquisition at the time of creation.

Software resources, such as shared data, full buffers, messages, and even critical sections, can also be treated here. This becomes more apparent if we replace the names *allocate* and *free* by *request* and *release*, respectively; resources of all types can be "requested" and "released." A uniform resource management mechanism based on general *request* and *release* operations has been investigated and developed by Weiderman (1971); we pursue this approach further in Chapter 7.

The techniques for dealing with different classes of resources vary considerably and are the subject of several later chapters. In most OS's, each resource class has a separate set of primitives. However, the interaction of resource requests must be considered in order to detect, prevent, and dispose of deadlock situations (Sec. 2.4.4 and Chapter 8), as well as to optimize systems behavior.

Input-Output Operations

The IO nucleus is similar to the job-at-a-time batch processing IOCS discussed in Sec. 2.5 but is complicated by the requirements of multiprogramming. The essential primitives are *read*, *write*, and *control* operations for communicating between main storage and the various IO devices; also included is a basic facility for transmitting messages between the computer and one or more operator consoles.

At the lowest nucleus level, an IO operation might be

$$executeIO(channel, channelprogram) ;$$

This would call a channel scheduler to initiate the operation; using semaphores, we may describe the effect within the nucleus as follows:

$$P(channelfree[channel]) ;$$
$$startio(channel, channelprogram) ;$$
$$P(iocomplete[channel]) ;$$
$$V(channelfree[channel]) ;$$

The first P operation in the sequence has a potential call on the channel allocator, while the second P operation essentially waits for an IO completion interrupt. Alternatively, the *executeIO* or a different low-level primitive could just insert the IO request on the appropriate channel scheduler queue, and immediately return to the calling program, which can then continue in parallel with the IO; the calling program must explicity test for IO completion at some later time.

At the highest level, an IO request, such as *READ(CARDREADER, INPUTAREA)*, would generally invoke elements of a file system (Chapter 9) for searching directories for file locations, "opening" a file (i.e., making it available for use), buffering, generating commands for both physically positioning the file and for performing the operation, and scheduling the resultant sequence of operations. All of these functions could be implemented in an elaborate IO nucleus. The primitives for process and resource management would be employed throughout the above tasks.

Interrupt Handling Routines

External interrupts and some internal ones can be interpreted as hardware wakeup signals directed to blocked CPU processes. Both types of interrupts signal one or more of the following events (Watson, 1970):

1. A process has been completed. Examples are the termination of hardware channel processes or the termination of an internal software process; the latter could be triggered by the *quit* operation.

2. A service has been requested. A machine operator might, for example, generate an "attention" interrupt from the operator's console in order to initiate some directives to the OS; in computers with master and slave modes of operation, slave mode user programs request the services of protected systems routines, such as resource allocators, through internal interrupts.

3. An error has occurred. Errors on IO operations, and internal addressing and underflow/overflow errors are typical of this class of events.

A software interrupt handler must complete the state saving of the interrupted process (generally, existing hardware does not save enough state components), determine which process is to be awakened or which routine is to be called by interpreting the message associated with the interrupt, and wakeup or invoke the selected process or routine, respectively. This implies that the interrupt handler is given enough information to find the latter. In the simplest case, the first instruction of the selected process or routine is just that location to which control is transferred on the interrupt. However, this is rarely possible, since current hardware does not permit the specification of a different location for *each* interrupt-causing event.

Example

On many computers, a user process requests IO service by means of a supervisor call instruction (*SVC*) which results in an internal trap to an *SVC* interrupt handler. The latter will call, wakeup, or send a message to (e.g., by insertion on a queue) the required IO routine or process; the details of the request must be passed from the user process to the *SVC* interrupt handler in order for it to find the correct IO routine, and to the IO routine so that the correct IO instruction can be specified. The IO routine, in turn, must transmit its identity, say by placing it in some agreed-upon location, to the IO interrupt handler. The external interrupt signalling the completion of the IO operation will invoke the IO interrupt handler, which then determines the

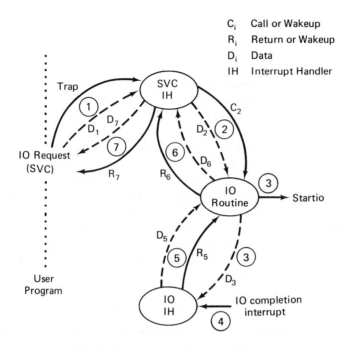

C_i Call or Wakeup
R_i Return or Wakeup
D_i Data
IH   Interrupt Handler

Fig. 4-5   Interrupt handling in an IO sequence.

correct IO process (routine) to wakeup (call). The IO routine might return or send a wakeup signal to the *SVC* interrupt handler, which, finally, transfers control back to the original requesting process. Figure 4-5 illustrates the possible sequence of events; the order is indicated by circled numbers. The *SVC* interrupt handler, IO routine, and IO interrupt handler can be treated either as separate processes or as part of their invoking process.

One of the most difficult issues in designing interrupt handlers and the first-level routines they awaken or call is the question of interrupt *priorities*. For a particular interrupt handler process, what interrupt-causing events, if any, should be allowed to preempt the process, and at what point(s) during its execution? In other words, where should interrupts of various types be enabled, disabled, and inhibited and, if software control of priorities is available, what should these priorities be at any given time?

A common procedure is to arrange the interrupts and their routines in a hierarchical priority fashion such that routines at level i can be preempted only by interrupts associated with any level $j, j > i$. This often implies hardware or software stacking and unstacking of interrupts and state vectors as one moves through the hierarchy. An alternative solution is to treat the interrupt handlers as critical sections, with interrupts inhibited within them.

4.4 THE USER INTERFACE

4.4.1 Command and Control Languages

Components of an operating system are continually invoked by running programs, through requests for services, such as IO or resource allocation, and in response to interrupts and errors. At a higher level, declarative and imperative information *about* programs and files, including those belonging to the system, are communicated via *command and control* languages—CCL's (also called *command* languages, *control* languages, or *job control* languages). System users employ these languages to transmit specifications and requests concerning their jobs, resources, and files; and machine operators use similar languages to control and interrogate the disposition of hardware and software resources, and to respond to systems messages and errors.

Often, the same basic syntax can be provided for both users and machine operators, and for both batch and interactive users. The most rudimentary and "traditional" statement form in a CCL is

$$\langle command \rangle \qquad \langle parameter\ list \rangle$$

where $\langle command \rangle$ gives the name of a command or declaration to be processed and $\langle parameter\ list \rangle$ contains a list of parameters or arguments associated with the command. It is common to precede the command field by one or more special characters, such as /, \$, !, or #; the purpose of these symbols is to uniquely identify the statement as belonging to the CCL, as opposed to any other type of data records that may also appear in an input stream. In some of the more elaborate languages, CCL statements may also be labelled to permit future reference by other statements and the system. Finally, arbitrary comments are usually permitted at the end of each statement. Thus, the typical command language is similar in appearance to a sophisticated macro-assembly language.

Since the CCL is the primary and common interface for *all* users with the computer system, it is important that human engineering considerations be emphasized in its design. The main reason for mentioning this (perhaps very obvious) point is that these languages have been and still are extremely and unnecessarily clumsy. They are not easy to learn and use; requests for simple services require complex sequences of obscure code and parameters; and statements are too rigid and inflexible in their syntax.

Example

When most users submit a FORTRAN program, they envisage a virtual FORTRAN machine that directly interprets that program—and computer people quite correctly encourage them to do so; they are *not* normally concerned with the fact that the program will be compiled, linked, loaded, and run, or with the many substeps associated with these four operations. Consequently, it seems most reasonable to provide a simple statement such as

(1) $RUN FORTRAN

to express this simple common request, rather than forcing the use of a more complicated sequence, say

(2) $EXECUTE FORTRAN(OPTIMIZED,VERSION=10),INPUT=
     CARDRDR,OUTPUT=(DISK,NAME=FORTOBJ)
     $LINKANDLOAD FORTOBJ,FORTRANRUNTIME,NAME=
     MYPROG
     $RUN MYPROG,INPUT=CARDRDR,OUTPUT=PRINTER

At the same time, more detailed control facilities, such as that illustrated in (2) but with a more readable syntax, should be available to the sophisticated user.

A CCL "program" is rarely, if ever, compiled but is *interpreted* at the statement level by the operating system. Thus, another component of any OS is the CCL interpreter that essentially analyzes each statement and invokes the appropriate system module. From another point of view, the CCL defines a virtual machine for a user; as far as he is concerned, the operating system is just a machine with a two-step cycle:

1. *Get next CCL statement S.*

2. *Interpret S.*

In fact, the highest-level process associated with a user job is often a complicated version of the above cycle. Similarly, there is a process responsible for reading and interpreting control commands issued from an operator's console.

4.4.2 Job Control

The first statement of any interactive or batch job is a CCL command that identifies the user and job, and "logs" him into the system. Information items that may appear as arguments to this initial "sign-on" include user's name, job name, account number, priority, resource limits (e.g., maximum amount of CPU time, maximum number of lines to be printed), and resource reservations (e.g., memory, peripherals). Similarly, a job and/or console session is terminated via an explicit or implicit CCL "sign-off" command; an implicit termination occurs, for example, when a user "hangs up" the communications line (e.g., telephone) at a terminal, when the system ends a job due to error conditions, or when a sign-on command is processed—implicitly terminating the preceding job.

The fundamental task performed by the virtual machine represented by the operating system is the execution of user programs. Thus any CCL will contain commands directing the OS to load and execute user programs and language processors (e.g., assemblers, compilers). Some CCL's distinguish between user programs, and manufacturer-provided language processors and other programs, while others treat the two uniformly. Typical commands for this program management activity are ones to execute a given program, load a program, link several programs together, or invoke a language processor. Associated with these commands, as parameters and/or separate statements, may be resource reservation and limit data, similar to that used for the sign-on statement; arguments specific to the particular program invoked, such as the names of the files to be used by the program; and debugging services requested, such as traces and dumps.

The third major set of CCL statements relates to file processing. These serve such basic functions as identifying the primary input and output files to be used by programs, requesting allocation of IO devices, and describing the files referenced by user programs. Depending on the level of control exercised by the user, there are a potentially staggering number of detailed parameters corresponding to the file commands. Examples are

1. Disposition of the file, e.g., temporary or permanent.

2. Protection (access control) data for a new file.

3. Buffering and blocking parameters.

4. Space reservations on secondary storage.

5. IO devices to be employed.

6. File organization, e.g., sequential or direct access.

Facilities for file editing, such as merging, copying, and modifying files, may also be invoked through the CCL. This may be a separate system with its own language, or the individual editing operations could all be contained in the CCL.

In addition to the above basic commands for job, program, and file processing, several other types of statements may be present, especially in a highly interactive environment. For example, there are often commands that permit a user to suspend, examine, change, and resume some running process; and statements that permit a programmer to define a number of default parameters for all his jobs. Most larger systems also provide some type of CCL macro or procedure definitions so that a group of CCL statements can be briefly invoked as a group. In the example at the beginning of Sec. 4.4, statement (1) might be a macro call that automatically translates into the sequence given by (2).

Examples

1. *IBM OS/360* (IBM, 1965). The job control language for IBM OS/360 has a relatively simple set of commands with a great deal of complexity in the command parameters. There are essentially only three basic commands:

(a) A job statement (*JOB*) delimits the beginning of a job.

(b) An execute command (*EXEC*) indicates the beginning of a job step and specifies either a program to be executed or a "catalogued" procedure, which, in turn, contains a series of control statements defining several steps.

(c) A data definition statement (*DD*) describes the files for each job step and requests resources for file processing.

Most of the complexity in this language lies in the parameters for the *DD* statement.

2. *MULTICS* (1967). This system is oriented chiefly towards interactive use. Each CCL command translates into a procedure call and, as such, may return a value; because of this clean uniform interpretation, users can extend the language by adding their own commands and corresponding procedures. The command arguments are "evaluated" by the system before the associated procedure is invoked. CCL commands may be nested in the argument field so that argument evaluation can also result in the calling of command procedures to return a value. The following classes of commands are available:

(a) Job and process control.
(b) Language processor execution.
(c) File editing and creation.
(d) File directory and access control.
(e) Procedure linking and peripheral IO of files.
(f) Debugging.
(g) User IO calls that bypass the standard systems defaults.
(h) Resource reservation.
(i) Accounting.

We have presented only a very brief outline of command and control languages, omitting much of their detailed complexity. At the present time, they differ greatly from system to system, and a completely coherent and model design for such languages has not yet appeared (Boettner, 1969). One current approach is to combine the CCL with a standard higher-level programming language so that the user expresses both the operating systems control and his computational needs in the same language. Much work remains to be done in this area.

4.5 ELEMENTS OF A DESIGN METHODOLOGY

The main functions of an operating system are to provide services to users and to control and allocate resources efficiently. To implement these functions, an MS is viewed as a dynamic set of interacting processes that communicate through common data structures and perform process, resource, and file management for users and itself. The basic tasks in the design of an MS are to describe the user services—i.e., the virtual machine of the user—and to specify the processes (and their intercommunication) for realizing this virtual machine.

There exist many approaches to MS design, but we are aware of only two that are *systematic* and *manageable* and at the same time have been *validated* by producing real working operating systems. These are the hierarchical abstract machine approach developed by Dijkstra (1968a) and the nucleus methods of Brinch Hansen (1971). After outlining the principal ideas of the two methods, we present a design methodology that is, in effect, a combination of them.

The Dijkstra approach arranges the OS processes in an hierarchy, where each level defines a successively more abstract virtual machine. By "more abstract," we mean that as one moves up the hierarchy, more resource management tasks are performed; thus, processes at one level can assume the availability of resources handled by processes at lower levels or, in other words, certain classes of resources may be ignored at each level. For example, if dynamic allocation of main storage is performed at level i, then processes at level $j, j > i$, can essentially ignore storage problems in the most general case.

This technique was applied to the design of the "THE" operating system at the Technological University in Eindhoven (Dijkstra, 1968a). The "THE" MS has the following process hierarchy:

Level	Tasks of Processes at Each Level
0	processor allocation
1	main and auxiliary storage management ("segment controller")
2	communication between internal processes and operator console ("message interpreter")
3	IO buffering and handling of peripherals
4	user programs
5	the operator

Processes above level 0 need not be concerned with the number of physical processors available; processes above level 1 deal only in "segments" of information, independently of their location in main or auxiliary storage;

processes above level 2 assume their own private conversational console, even though only one console exists in the system. Synchronization is achieved by hardware interrupts and software semaphore operations. For example, the timer interrupt is associated with level 0, and an interrupt from an auxiliary storage IO operation acts as one of the wakeup signals for processes at level 1.

The hierarchical abstract machine methodology is very appealing. By isolating OS functions on an hierarchical level basis and establishing clean and well-defined channels of communication between and within levels, the complexity of design and debugging is considerably reduced; in fact, the claim is made that the system can be "proven" logically correct before implementation and that the actual code can be exhaustively and completely debugged (Dijkstra, 1968a). The creative, and difficult, design task is to specify the level structure and the functions of each level.

The nucleus-based methodology was developed and used for the MS on the RC4000 computer (Brinch Hansen, 1971). The philosophy is to concentrate on the design of an MS nucleus that is sufficiently general to permit the construction and modification of a variety of OS's. The argument for this philosphy is that the organization and resource allocation strategies of systems continually have to be extended and modified in response to changing loads, and demands for new services and new modes of operation. Brinch Hansen was the first to develop, implement, and validate the "bottom-up" nucleus approach, and the nucleus and basic MS for the RC4000 is one of the most elegant existing systems. We do not discuss any details here, since Chapter 7 is concerned with the specifications of a comprehensive nucleus.

The principles developed by Dijkstra and Brinch Hansen, as well as the experiences of other workers, suggest a number of guide lines for MS design. We present these, not as a precise and rigid formula that can be mechanically followed, but as a rational framework for approaching a complex task that, at present, is part art, part engineering, part science, and part management. Our elements of a design methodology can be formulated as a sequence of general steps that a designer should follow:

1. Specify the virtual machine of the user. The external job control or command language L is defined, and the services performed by each command in L are described.

2. Describe the "paths" of user jobs and processes through the hardware and MS. (It is logical to describe *what* a system is to do before determining *how* it does it.)

3. Determine the processes necessary to perform the tasks implied by steps 1 and 2. Specify the function of each process, and how it interacts with other processes, and the data structures required for communication. Arrange the processes in a Dijkstra-like hierarchy, if possible.

4. Define the components of the system nucleus and their data structures. Resource allocation strategies are specified, at least in skeleton form, in steps 3 and 4.†

5. Using simulation and analytical techniques, "prove" the correctness of the design and predict the behavior of the MS.

Procedures for system maintenance and recovery from failure *must* be designed at the same time; these can be treated as "special" types of user jobs and processes generated by "special" users, and can be included as such in the above steps. The steps are performed in a highly iterative manner, with the results of one step generating design changes at other steps. When the design is satisfactory, actual coding and implementation may proceed.

At present, step 5 is extremely difficult to accomplish, and most current systems bypass the correction and prediction phases entirely. A realistic simulation requires almost as much effort—and much of the same code—as an actual implementation of the system being simulated. One promising technique currently under investigation is to combine the design, simulation, and implementation so that both design changes and the actual implementation follow easily from simulations. The basic idea is to make a simulation *evolve* into the real operating system, in much the same way as one designs a program from the top down in terms of a set of general blocks or procedure calls that eventually become completely specified as elementary statements (Zurcher and Randell, 1968; Weiderman, 1971).

†Steps 3 and 4 are so interrelated that they could be done in parallel or in the reverse order.

5 MAIN STORAGE MANAGEMENT

Main storage, the memory that may be directly accessed as data or instructions by a central processor, is often the critical and limiting resource in a computer system. In this chapter, we examine the principal software techniques and hardware aids for the allocation and administration of main memory.

5.1 STATIC AND DYNAMIC RELOCATION

Section 2.2 discussed the origin and fundamentals of static address relocation. This *relocation* method usually forces a static storage *allocation* policy: All main memory for a user's program and data is assigned and all addresses are relocated to reflect this assignment *before* execution of a program commences. Addresses are said to be *dynamically* relocated when relocation occurs at run time *immediately* preceding *each* storage reference. In this case, the "*effective*" addresses of all instructions and data—the result of adding the contents of any designated index and/or base registers to address fields—are relocatable; addresses are "bound" to the real machine at the last possible moment. Dynamic relocation allows the dynamic *allocation* of storage; that is, it becomes practical to assign and release storage for parts of a program and its data during the execution of the program.

5.1.1 Hardware Address Relocation

Dynamic relocation is normally accomplished by hardware† and is invisible to all users except some systems programmers. To illustrate the concept,

†It could, of course, be done interpretively by software, but this is too inefficient to be practical in most cases.

we consider the instruction cycle of a simple one-address machine both with and without dynamic relocation. Let $M[0:m]$ represent main storage, *reg* be a general-purpose register, *ic* be the instruction counter, *Address(w)* compute the effective address of the instruction *w*, and *Operator(w)* select the operation code *oc* from *w*, where $oc = 1$ indicates addition, $oc = 2$ is a store register operation, and $oc = 3$ designates an unconditional transfer. Without dynamic relocation, the basic hardware instruction cycle for such a machine is typically

$$
\begin{aligned}
Next: \quad & w := M[ic] ; \\
& oc := Operator(w) ; \\
& adr := Address(w) ; \\
& ic := ic + 1 ; \\
plus: \quad & \textbf{if } oc = 1 \textbf{ then } reg := reg + M[adr] \\
& \textbf{else} \\
store: \quad & \textbf{if } oc = 2 \textbf{ then } M[adr] := reg \\
& \textbf{else} \\
xfer: \quad & \textbf{if } oc = 3 \textbf{ then } ic := adr \\
& \textbf{else} \\
& \quad . \\
& \quad . \\
& \quad . \\
& \textbf{go to } Next ;
\end{aligned}
$$

With dynamic relocation hardware, the addresses *ic* and *adr* are treated as relocatable addresses and *mapped* into real storage addresses at the time of reference. We designate the mapping function as *NLmap*, for *N*ame *L*ocation *map* (Dennis, 1965):

NLmap: {relocatable effective addresses} ⟶ {real storage addresses}.

The basic instruction cycle algorithm has the following two changes to make it describe a similar machine with dynamic relocation:

1. $M[ic]$ is replaced by $M[NLmap(ic)]$ in the statement labelled *Next*.

2. $M[adr]$ is replaced by $M[NLmap(adr)]$ in both the statements *plus* and *store*.

NLmap can be viewed as a hardware box placed between the CPU and main storage and through which all storage addresses must pass. Figure 5-1 illustrates the hardware mapping; a memory access consists of two steps after effective address computation—first, the address is dynamically relocated by *NLmap* and, second, the actual read or write operation is performed. During the mapping, *NLmap* may reference main storage for tables and the CPU for special registers.

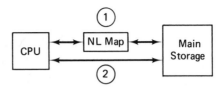

Fig. 5-1 Storage reference with dynamic relocation.

(1) : Dynamic Address Relocation

(2) : Read or Write

The storage system seen by the typical user, the space of relocatable effective addresses, is called *name* space or *virtual* storage. The real address space is sometimes termed *location* space. Note that if programs or data are relocated in main storage only the *NLmap* need be changed; name space addresses remain invariant to location space assignments.

Static and dynamic relocation each have their limitations and advantages for MS. These are discussed next.

5.1.2 Arguments for Static and Dynamic Relocation

Many commercial MS's run on machines without relocation hardware and employ static relocation techniques. Linking, relocation, storage allocation, and often loading of entire programs are done before processes enter ready status, when execution may logically commence. The relative virtues of this mode of operation are the ability to use conventional and economical hardware addressing, the simplicity of the linking loader and its interactions with other systems components, and the existence of much practical experience in engineering such systems. However, these systems have several features that prevent the efficient utilization of resources and that are often inconvenient for users.

The most common storage allocation policy under a system with static relocation is to assign a large *contiguous* area of memory to each user for his job or job step;† users must generally cooperate by specifying in advance their storage needs. One possible result of contiguous allocation in a multiprogramming environment is fragmentation of main storage; i.e., storage may become a checkerboard of unused (and often unusable) "holes." Figure 5-2 illustrates this situation in a simple case. In the figure, H_i represents a hole, and $|X|$ is the quantity of storage occupied by program or hole X. Suppose program B finishes, creating a hole between A and C; if program D is now ready to be loaded, there is not enough contiguous storage available,

---

†The exception to this contiguity is the operating system, which is often allocated to a separate area and *shared* by all users.

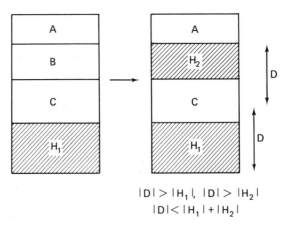

$$|D| > |H_1|, \ |D| > |H_2|$$
$$|D| < |H_1| + |H_2|$$

Fig. 5-2 Storage fragmentation.

even though the total amount of unused memory is ample. Theoretically, contiguous assignment is not necessary, and individual procedure and data areas may be allocated separately; this, however, complicates the storage management and protection procedures considerably. (Fragmentation occurs in different forms and with different degrees of severity, regardless of the allocation policy; we shall return to this problem in the succeeding pages.)

A typical MS will offer *overlay* facilities that permit a user to reduce his memory utilization while running jobs with large storage requirements. The basic idea is to statically allocate the same area of storage to more than one routine or part of a program, and initially load only a first overlay segment. When control is transferred to an overlay routine, the new routine overwrites some currently resident code; the actual loading of absolute code ("core images") occurs dynamically during execution. The user programmer must plan and specify the identity and storage of his overlays, and include this information as part of his job control data; this implies that the user knows *a priori*, at least globally, the run time flow of control of his programs. In summary, the user must perform most of the storage management himself. User-specified overlays represent one attempt to conserve main storage, and their widespread use reflects both the large memory needs of many programs and the fact that most processes will only use a small percentage of their code during a given time interval; for example, a program often contains a high density of error routines that are rarely used but which nevertheless can consume valuable storage space.

In the overlay scheme, programs are *swapped* in and out of storage, but a given program will always be swapped into the *same* memory space during a single run. Linking and relocation occur only once, at the beginning of the run. One could envisage a more flexible scheme in which a given program could be swapped into different areas as execution progresses; linking and relocation are then necessary on each swap. This would also require that

(1) programs not modify themselves

(2) no absolute storage addresses appear in data

(3) the invariant programs be strictly separated from their variable data.

(5-1)

In time-sharing systems with static relocation, programs are usually swapped into the same areas because of the above complexities.

Static relocation also makes it difficult (but not impossible) for users to share the same main storage copy of procedures (why?); a separate copy for each user is normally allocated. Thus, if several users are simultaneously performing a FORTRAN compilation, there might be several copies of the same FORTRAN compiler in memory. Special cases of sharing, the most obvious being parts of the operating system and perhaps resident compilers, can still be implemented, but *each* case is usually incorporated explicitly in the original MS design, as a later modification to the MS, or within a complete independent subsystem.

The chief arguments for dynamic relocation are that, in principle, it permits a flexible and efficient use of main storage and, at the same time, allows a convenient virtual memory interface to users. With the more sophisticated relocation hardware, storage allocation can be performed dynamically *on demand* rather than statically before execution; that is, the system has the option of delaying the storage assignments up to the time of the first address reference to a block of code or data. Consequently, linking and loading of a particular procedure is similarly delayed, and storage that has not been referenced in the recent past can be released if necessary. Checkerboarding of storage *may* decrease because a contiguous allocation policy for each user is not necessary and the units of allocation may be small. (This feature holds for either a static or dynamic *allocation* policy.) During a single run, a procedure may easily be swapped in and out of different areas of memory. With dynamic relocation, it is also easier for several processes to share a single copy of a procedure. Finally, it is possible to present to the user a large contiguous virtual storage space and to relieve him of any management tasks related to overlaying and estimation. In this case, the system has almost complete responsibility for storage management and, hopefully, can perform this function more efficiently than individual users. (The above arguments do not hold if only the simplest type of relocation hardware is available—for example, a single relocation register; the main virtue of this rather primitive type is the ability to move a user's space to different areas of main storage easily.)

These advantages must be weighed against the additional costs and complexity of both hardware and software. In fact, it is possible to degrade an MS considerably unless dynamic relocation policies are carefully selected and tested. The above points will be developed further in this chapter.

EXERCISE

Why are the conditions in list (5-1) of this section necessary?

5.1.3 Virtual Memories

The organization of virtual memory (VM) or name space is dependent on the mapping hardware, *NLmap*, that performs the translation to location space. However, it is convenient to describe the two principal VM organizations before we consider their implementation.†

The simplest and most obvious form of VM is a contiguous linear space corresponding to our conventional view of storage. VM is a large, linearly addressed sequence of cells (words, bytes, . . .) with addresses typically sequenced: $0, 1, 2, \ldots, n - 1$, where $n = 2^k$. We call this a *single segment* name space.

A *multiple segmented* VM divides name space into a set of segments S_i, where each S_i is a contiguous linear space. A *segment* is a user-defined entity that can be treated as a logical and independent unit, for example, a procedure, an Algol block, or an array of data. One may also view a program segment as that code which becomes or is a relocatable object module. Addresses can be put in the form of a pair $[s, w]$, where s represents a segment identifier and w is a word identifier (name or number).

Examples of VM addresses

1. [5, 927] : word 927 in segment 5. This could be the result of an effective address computation immediately prior to dynamic relocation.

2. [*MATRIX*, 315] : the 315th word in the segment named *MATRIX*. The addresses in relocatable object code normally take this form.

3. [*COMPILER*, *ENTRYPOINT*3] : This is a typical reference to an external segment and may appear in a relocatable procedure or data segment prior to static or dynamic linking.

It is sometimes possible to manipulate segment names in the same way as

†Randell and Kuehner (1968) survey the organizations and issues discussed in this section.

conventional addresses; thus, some function f might be applied to a segment name S_i to yield another name S_j; e.g., if S_i is an integer, f could be some arithmetic operation involving S_i. This violates the independence of segments to some extent, and the more desirable systems do not allow computations with segment names.

The organization of VM as a set of logical segments is appealing for a number of reasons. First, what constitutes a segment is usually determined by a user when he defines his program and data areas; they are thus the natural units by which a user refers to his information. As a consequence, operating systems can conveniently access user information on a segment basis. Information sharing (that is, sharing of programs and data), protection against invalid access and addressing errors, storage allocation, and language translation may all be treated by the system in units of segments. Because segments are approximately independent of one another, it is often possible in dynamic storage systems to permit them to grow and shrink as execution progresses, provided VM is large enough.

In order to implement a VM, there are three main storage management decisions that must be resolved. Randell and Kuehner (1968) refer to these as the *fetch, placement,* and *replacement* strategies.

The *fetch* strategy defines the policy of *when* to load VM and *how much* of VM to load at a time. At one extreme, a static linking loader loads all of VM prior to execution; a policy at the other extreme is to load at the last possible moment, i.e., at the time of reference to a segment or part of a segment. In this latter case of *demand* loading, the "how much" decision has to be made. The disadvantages of static loading are the possible waste of main storage and IO time when only a small part of VM is accessed within a given time interval or run. On the other hand, demand loading can incur much system overhead and consume an inordinate amount of IO time, especially in a nearly saturated situation, where the same code may be loaded and replaced many times during a single run.

The *placement* strategy determines *where* in executable storage to load all or part of VM. For example, one could either assign the first "hole" that fits or the smallest hole that fits. If there are several levels of executable storage, e.g., fast and slow core, to which level should a given piece of code be allocated?

The third problem, *replacement*, appears in systems that employ dynamic memory allocation policies. Here we must decide *what* to remove or swap from executable storage when there is not enough room available for a set of information that must be loaded; the intuitive solution is to select that area of storage with the least likelihood of being referenced in the near future. We will consider various solutions to these problems in the context of specific dynamic relocation hardware.

5.2 PRINCIPLES OF SEGMENTATION AND PAGING

5.2.1 Single Segment Name Space

5.2.1.1 Contiguous Storage Allocation

In one of the earliest methods for dynamic relocation, a single segment name space is mapped into a contiguous region of main storage. This can be accomplished through a relocation register, say RR, which always contains the location space base address for the process currently running on the CPU. The mapping, $NLmap$, is simply a run time version of the basic static relocation described in Sec. 2.2.1:†

> **integer procedure** $NLmap(ea)$;
> **comment** ea is an effective address ;
> $NLmap := ea + RR$;

Location spaces (or portions thereof) for several different processes may reside concurrently in main storage for multiprogramming purposes. The state vector of each process p must minimally contain:

1. The virtual storage instruction counter ic_p.

2. The base address ba_p of p's real memory (location space).

A switch from process p_1 to p_2 then includes the following actions:

> $ic_{p1} := ic$;   (Store state of p_1)
> $ic := ic_{p_2}; RR := ba_{p_2};$ (Load state of p_2)

where ic is the machine instruction counter (Fig. 5-3).

Each name space must be less than or equal to main storage in size. The fragmentation example of Sec. 5.1.2 is therefore applicable here also. In fact, fragmentation appears in some form in almost all static and dynamic storage systems. The main advantage of the simple relocation register is that programs may be swapped in and out of different areas of memory easily; only the base address of location space need be changed. Programs and data are still statically linked and relocated in VM prior to initial loading. As one example, the IBM 7090, a popular second-generation single-address machine, was modified for the MIT Project MAC time-sharing system to perform dynamic relocation with a single relocation register (IBM, 1963).

If there is more than one relocation register, the contiguous location space

---

†We ignore the problem of storage protection during the mapping until Sec. 5.3.

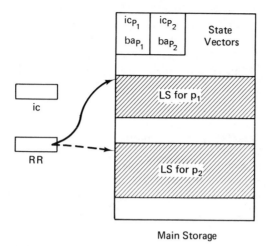

Main Storage

LS: Location Space

Fig. 5-3 Process switching.

requirement is no longer necessary and more general segmented VM organizations can be implemented. Note that the relocation registers, as part of the *NLmap*, must *not* be accessible to the normal user program. (Why not?)

EXERCISE

Many computers store base addresses in registers that participate in effective address computation. By just changing one's point of view, the base registers can be interpreted as relocation registers. If it is desired to use these registers for dynamic relocation to permit, for example, different storage allocations for the same code during a run, what restrictions must be imposed on user programs? How can they be enforced? Present your answer in terms of some particular machine, for example, the IBM/360.

5.2.1.2 Paging

The term *paging* is used to describe a particular implementation of virtual memory and organization of main storage. The latter is divided into a number of equal-sized contiguous *blocks* or frames $b_0, b_1, \ldots, b_{B-1}$; block size is typically 512 or 1024 words. An absolute memory address a is considered a pair (b, l), where b is a block number and l is a word number. For example, if block size is 2^m, then, usually, $b = integerpartof(a/2^m)$ and $l = a - b \times 2^m$. Similarly, a name space segment is divided into a number of equal-sized contiguous *pages* $p_0, p_1, \ldots, p_{P-1}$, where page size is identical to block size. (This statement is not precisely correct; VM is first increased in size so that $|VM|$, the name space size, is equal to a multiple of block size.) An effective address *ea*, i.e., an address *ea* in VM, is treated as a pair (p, l), where p is a page number and l is a line or word number; the correspondence between *ea* and (p, l) is obtained in the same manner as that between a and (b, l) above. The *NLmap* then associates a VM page with a real memory block, as illustrated in Fig. 5-4.

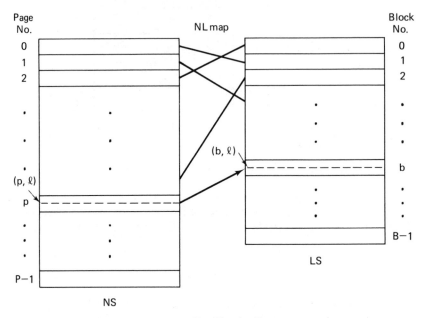

$$NLmap\ ((p, l)) := (b, l);$$

Fig. 5-4   Paging.

In a paging system, the basic unit of storage allocation is a block. Programs and data need not occupy a contiguous area of memory but can be scattered through it on a page basis. Thus, if a demand for k blocks of storage is made and there are at least k free blocks, the placement decision is very simple—any block may be allocated for any page. One might conclude erroneously that paging eliminates the fragmentation problem. It is certainly true that the specific difficulty illustrated in Fig. 5-2 cannot occur. However, because the size of VM information units are rarely multiples of block size, there generally exist many blocks that are only partially allocated with VM information. Thus, we now have an "internal" fragmentation problem (we analyze this problem in Sec. 5.5). Most implementations of paging include protection mechanisms that signal a "missing page" when reference is made to a page not resident in main storage. With this feature, an operating system can provide facilities for large virtual memory spaces for users; it is possible for a name space to be *much* larger than main storage. Dynamic storage allocation can be implemented by loading pages at their first reference rather than statically. This policy is called *demand paging*.

The *NLmap* translates a VM address (p, l) into a real address $(b, l) = b \times 2^m + l$, where block size is 2^m. One approach for implementing *NLmap* is to maintain a table of length B that gives the correspondence between every block and page. Let this table be an array $pn[0 : B - 1]$, where $pn[b]$ contains either the number of the page stored in block b for the current process or some indication that block b is not allocated to the current process. Assuming that each addressed page is in main storage, the *NLmap* can be written as follows:

```
integer procedure NLmap((p, l)) ;
begin
    for b := 0 step 1 until B − 1 do
        if pn[b] = p then go to adr ;
    adr: NLmap := b × 2 ↑ m + l
end
```

A sequential search such as the above is extremely inefficient, even if accomplished through hardware, since the *NLmap* must make $B / 2$ comparisons on the average at *every* storage reference. To make this approach practical, the table is stored in an associative memory, and the search is effectively performed in parallel.

An associative memory is one in which cells are referenced by their *content* rather than their address. A familiar example will clarify this concept. Each entry in a telephone book is addressed by a triple: (*page, column, line*). To find a phone number for an individual, it is necessary to search the directory for a (*last name, first name*) match; this task is not difficult *only* because the entries have been sorted in alphabetic order by name. If, however, one starts with a phone number and desires the name or address of the party with that number, the task is hopelessly time-consuming. Storing the telephone book in a general associative memory would permit access of any entry using either a name or an address or a phone number as the search key; that is, any field in an entry can be used and the search occurs by content. Sorting is then not required. Hardware implementations of associative memories are not quite this general and normally only provide one search field for each entry. The standard software technique for simulating such a memory is hash coding (Morris, 1968).

Paging can be credited to the designers of the ATLAS computer, who employed an associative memory for the *NLmap* (Kilburn, *et al.*, 1962). The effective address (p, l) is an $n + m$ bit number where the high-order n bits correspond to page number and the low-order m bits to line number. The

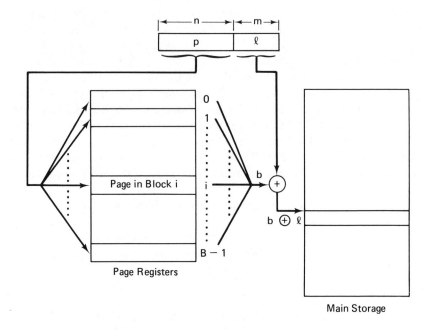

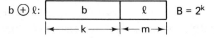

Fig. 5-5   ATLAS address mapping.

page number is transformed by a parallel hardware search through an associative memory of B page registers into a block number b. The concatenation of b onto l yields the physical storage address (Fig. 5-5). For the ATLAS computer, $m = 9$ (512 word page/block size), $n = 11$, and $B = 32$; thus a 2^{20}-word virtual memory was provided for a 2^{14}-word (16 K) machine. The original ATLAS operating system employed paging solely as a means of implementing a large VM; multiprogramming of user processes was not attempted initially. In either case, the state vector of a process must include the contents of the page register.

The more recent schemes maintain a *page table* in main storage for *each* process. The ith entry in each page table identifies the block, if any, that contains page number i for that process. A page table register (*PTR*) will contain the base address of the page table corresponding to the process currently executing on the CPU. The address computation performed by the *NLmap* is

$$NLmap((p, l)) := M[PTR + p] \times 2 \uparrow m + l,$$

where M represents main storage. Figure 5-6 presents the mapping in graph-

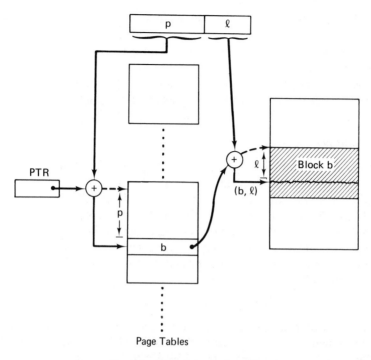

Fig. 5-6 *NLmap* for pure paging.

ical form. For example, suppose that the page table for the current process were located starting at address 1000 with the contents

$$1000: 21, \quad 1001: 40, \quad 1002: 3, \quad 1003: 15, \ldots,$$

and block size were 1024 words; then the *PTR* would contain 1000, and an effective address (2, 100) would dynamically map into $M[1000 + 2] \times 1024 + 100 = 3 \times 1024 + 100 = 3172$. Note that at least *two* memory accesses must be made in order to read or write any storage word during a virtual memory operation—one access to the page table and the second for the read/write. To avoid the first access most of the time, it is common to use either an associative memory or a set of registers for all or part of the page table of the current process. A process state vector must, of course, include the page table address.

Example

The XDS 940 computer (XDS, 1969) is a paged machine with a maximum name space of 16K words and memory size of 64K words. Thus, it does not have a large virtual memory but uses the paging for noncontiguous storage allocation and easy swapping and replacement of pages in main storage.

Block size is 2K words. The eight block number entries in a user page table are loaded into fast registers prior to execution; the dynamic relocation mapping occurs through these registers rather than main storage. A *PTR* register is not necessary. The paging hardware available on the XDS Sigma 7 computer permits a large virtual memory of up to 132K words for each user. It has 256 fast registers that implement the mapping in a similar manner to that in the XDS 940; page size is 512 words in the Sigma 7.

5.2.2 Multiple Segment Name Space

There are two different approaches to implementing a multiple segment VM. The first treats the segment as the basic unit for storage allocation and assumes that storage can be dynamically allocated and relocated in variable-size blocks. The second employs paging. A VM address [s, w] is considered a triple (s, p, l), where the word number w has been broken into a (*page, line*) pair. Storage is organized on a fixed-block basis with block size equal to page size. At this point in time, it is not evident which, if any, of these two techniques is preferable.

5.2.2.1 Contiguous Allocation Per Segment

Storage is allocated and addresses are relocated on a segment basis. The most prominent example of this method is found in the Burroughs B5500 and B6500 computers (Burroughs, 1964, 1967). These are stack machines oriented towards the efficient compilation and execution of block-structured languages. Segments correspond to natural source language units such as Algol blocks, procedures, and arrays.

A *segment table*—the Burroughs group calls it a program reference table— is maintained in main storage for each active user process. Each entry in the table contains the base location of the code or data and protection information. A segment table register (*STR*) points to the segment table for the process currently running in the CPU; the *STR* is similar to the *PTR* described in the last section. An effective address [s, w] is mapped to a real storage address as follows:

$$NLmap([s, w]) := M[STR + s] + w,$$

where we have assumed that segments are numbered sequentially and the ith entry in the segment table $i = 0, 1, \ldots$ corresponds to segment number i. The segment table itself is treated as a segment by the system. The mapping is performed more efficiently most of the time by keeping $M[STR + s]$ in the hardware stack for the current segment s.

The main objections to this organization as compared with paging are the possibilities of much unused memory (external fragmentation) because the unit of allocation is variable in size, and because of the complexity of the placement policy (Denning, 1970). On the other hand, paged systems are often subject to serious internal fragmentation and, in the demand paging case, to excessive IO. Experiences with the Burroughs systems indicate that efficient performance can be obtained; the paging systems using dynamic allocation policies do not seem to be any more efficient.†

5.2.2.2 Paging With Segmentation

Paging in a segmented system has been used primarily for large general-purpose time-sharing systems. The GE 645 (MULTICS, 1967), IBM 360/67 (Comfort, 1965), and RCA Spectra 70/46 (Oppenheimer and Weizer, 1968) computers are examples of the first "generation" employing this organization.

Storage is organized in fixed-size blocks that are allocated to program and data pages as before. One more level of indirectness in the dynamic mapping is introduced. A segment table register *STR* points to a segment table for the current process; the segment table entries point to page tables which, in turn, point to storage blocks. All tables are stored in main memory. The *NLmap* for an effective address $ea = [s, w] = (s, p, l)$ is

$$NLmap((s, p, l)) := M[M[STR + s] + p] \times 2 \uparrow m + l \; ;$$

as illustrated in Fig. 5-7.

In these systems, each segment and page table is considered to be a page. Each process has its own private segment table and may or may not have private page tables. Sharing can be accomplished relatively easily by sharing page tables and program/data pages. Demand paging is attractive under this organization; in principle, it permits an efficient use of storage and allows dynamic changes in segment size. The disadvantages of paging within segmentation are the extra storage required for the tables, the overhead of administrating storage in such a complex system, and the inefficiency of two storage references at each mapping.

Examples

Effective addresses are divided into (s, p, l) triples for the three machines illustrated. From the number of bits in each field, we can easily compute the block size, and the maximum number of segments and pages per segment for each virtual space:

ea	s	p	l
GE 645 (word addressing)	18	8	10 bits
IBM 360/67 (byte addressing)	4 or 12	8	12
RCA Spectra 70/46 (byte addressing)	5	6	12

†The reader should be aware that this is a controversial issue about which much has been said, but little quantitative comparative information is available.

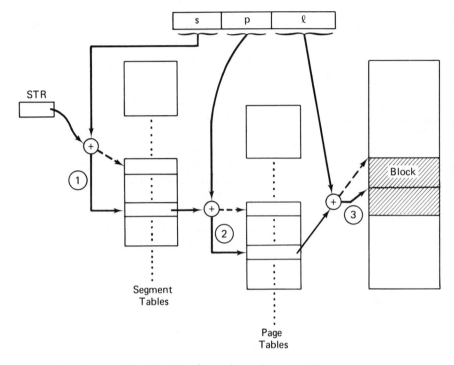

Fig. 5-7   Map for paging and segmentation.

Mapping efficiency is obtained by the use of a small number of associative registers (in the GE and IBM case) or by storing the entire VM-real memory correspondence of the current process in a fast "translation" memory (RCA). The associative registers contain entries of the form: (*segment number, page number, block number*), where the *block number* identifies the storage block corresponding to the segment and page. The normal mapping occurs only if the (*segment, page*) is not in an associative register; in this case, a hardware exchange of the contents of one of the registers with the current mapping occurs so that future references will go through the associative register. In the RCA implementation, separate page and segment tables are not used; instead, a complete set of (*segment, page, block*) entries are kept for each process and loaded into a special translation memory when control is switched to the process.

5.3   REAL AND VIRTUAL STORAGE PROTECTION

Storage protection facilities are required both to control a process's access to its own instructions and data, and to prevent a process from access- ing (e.g., reading, writing, or executing) the information associated with other processes; that is, processes must be protected from themselves and from others. An obvious example is the protection of the operating system from overwriting or erroneous execution by user programs. Other examples occur naturally in sharing situations, when one is dealing with proprietary information, and in program debugging.

Several different modes of protection are possible. The most basic kind is an "all or nothing" type. Information within a process's allocated (virtual or real) storage area may be accessed for any purpose; addressing outside of this area is prohibited and causes an interrupt leading to a systems routine. This can be implemented with *bounds* registers that specify the upper and lower addresses of a contiguous storage area, *length* indicators containing the size of a storage area, *presence* bits to indicate whether a particular segment or page is in main store, identification *keys* associated with storage blocks, or some combination of these. Specific examples are presented shortly. More detailed access protection for a storage area S usually consists of Boolean combinations of the following:

1. *Read (R)*. S may be read. Instructions that load information from S into a register or into some other storage area, or that compare elements of S are permitted; storing into S or executing from S—for example, by transferring control to some address in S—is illegal if access is R-only.

2. *Write (W)*. Storing from a register or some other area of memory into S is permitted.

3. *Execute (X)*. S may be executed as a program; internal reads for constants are usually also allowed.

Often the R protection is interpreted to include X as well. In terms of these basic modes, the most common forms of access restrictions are

$\neg(R \lor W \lor X)$:	No access is permitted.
$R \land \neg(W \lor X)$:	Read-only. A table of constants or part of a data file, for example, a historical file on student grades, might be given this designation.
$(R \lor W) \land \neg X$:	This protects a read-write data area, for example, an array in a scientific computation, from attempts at execution by an incorrect program.
$\neg(R \lor W) \land X$:	Execute-only. The security of program instructions in systems programs and proprietary programs is possible with this combination. S cannot be treated as data.
$R \lor X \land \neg W$:	Writing is not permitted.
$R \lor X \lor W$:	Unrestricted access is provided.

The protection information can be attached to the storage system in any of three ways. The obvious and, perhaps, simplest approach is to associate it directly with physical storage; a particular contiguous block of real storage will have a fixed set of access restrictions at any one time that applies to all processes that may wish to access the block. However, this is too inflexible if programs or data may be shared; it is often desirable for different processes to have different capabilities with respect to the same information.

Examples

1. In many MS's, a user can interrogate the status of the system from a console to obtain such information as the load on the system (number of jobs or processes on various queues) and the status of his job; continual updating of status is also occurring in parallel with this. The data areas defining the status are then generally $R \vee W$ for the updating process and R only for the systems process that displays this data to users.†

2. A proprietary compiler may be X-only to a paying user, R and X to a salesman or new systems programmer for the company marketing the compiler, and $R \vee X \vee W$ to its designers. It is possible in an MS for the first two of these user classes to be simultaneously accessing the same copy. (Why not all three simultaneously?)

If protection information is directly attached to the physical storage area being protected, it would be necessary to change this explicitly when processes are switched; the situation is complicated considerably in a multiprocessor operation, since several processes that reference the *same* storage area may be simultaneously running. A cleaner method is to approach protection from the point of view of *name space*; that is, each part (segment, normally) of name space for a process will have its own access restrictions. Protection, however, is not a static entity even within a single VM. In general, it is preferable if the access restrictions can vary dynamically as a function of the process state.

Example

Consider a multiphase "compile-and-go" subsystem that translates and executes some higher-level source language; let there be n phases in the translation and execution sequence, with execution occurring in the last phase. We treat the entire operation as a single process. While executing in phase $i, i = 1, \ldots, n$, the name space instruction part corresponding to phase i may be X-only while that for phase $j, j \neq i, j \neq n$, may not be accessed; the output data area in which the target language code is constructed may be

---

†Here, we explicitly recognize that programs are often changed and are rarely bug-free; the display process should never, of course, write in the status data areas, but protection against the high probability of errors must be designed into the system.

W-only while the symbol tables vary between R and $R \lor W$ depending on the phase. The output area changes to X-only for phase n. Thus each phase of execution defines a different set of access restrictions for the VM of the process.

A form of dynamic access control is obtained by assigning to each segment in a user's VM not only its own protection restrictions but also the type of access that segment may make on other segments. In increasing order of generality, protection information may then be attached to physical storage, statically to VM, and dynamically to VM. Next we describe the implementation of storage protection on several second- and third-generation computers.

1. *IBM 7090 with dynamic relocation hardware*

An all-or-nothing type of protection was implemented; upper- and lower-bound registers, say UR and LR respectively, were used to contain the upper and lower valid address limits. The body for $NLmap$ of Sec. 5.2.1.1 is then changed to

$$adr := ea + RR ;$$
$$\textbf{if } adr > UR \lor adr < LR \textbf{ then } Interrupt$$
$$\textbf{else } NLmap := adr ;$$

2. *ATLAS Paging System*

Each core block has a one-bit lock. Any attempt to access a "locked" block results in an interrupt. The lock may be used to prevent access to a block that is involved in an IO operation as well as locking out any blocks that are not part of the real memory space of the current process. An interrupt also occurs if a nonresident page is addressed.

3. *Pure Paging on the XDS 940*

The block number associated with each VM page has a one-bit read-only lock, say rol. If the lock is on ($rol = 1$), the block is read-only; otherwise, any type of access is allowed. Name spaces with less than the maximum eight pages have their mapping tables filled in with block numbers of 0. Block 0 is reserved for the system.

4. *Segmentation on the B5500*

Each segment table entry s also contains the length l_s of the segment and a presence bit a_s indicating whether the segment is resident in main storage. For an effective address $[s, w]$, if $w > l_s$ or $a_s = 0$, systems action is required, and an interrupt is generated by the $NLmap$ hardware. (The hardware check of segment length can be used very effectively to provide efficient run-time detection on subscripting errors in higher-level languages.)

5. *The nonpaged and paged IBM 360's*

Storage protection on a standard IBM 360 model (no dynamic relocation) is achieved through a four-bit protection key that is associated with each 2K-byte block of main core. This is an all-or-nothing type of protection. Each process has such a key as part of its state vector. On all storage accesses, the key in the state vector must match the block key; otherwise an interrupt occurs.

The 360/67, which has segmentation and paging, has an additional fetch protect bit, say f, augmenting the storage key. On a key match, any manner of access is valid as before; on a key mismatch, $f = 0$ permits read-only operations, and $f = 1$ is an invalid access resulting in an interrupt. The segment table register and each segment table entry contains a length indicator that specifies the current size of the segment table and page tables, respectively. Finally, a one-bit presence flag appears in each segment and page table entry; this flag indicates whether the page table or page is resident in main storage. We designate the entries of the mapping register and tables as follows:

STB, STL: Contents of the STR—segment table base address and length, respectively.
PTB[S], PTL[S], PTA[S]: Page table base, length, and presence flag for the page table corresponding to segment indexed by S.
BB[P], BA[P]: Block address and presence flag corresponding to page indexed by P.

Then, the *NLmap* for an effective address $[s, w] = (s, p, l)$ is†

> **if** $s > STL$ **then** *Interrupt*("Invalid Segment Number") ;
> $S := STB + s$;
> **if** $PTA[S] = 1$ **then** *Interrupt*("Page Table for Segment Not in Core") ;
> **if** $p > PTL[S]$ **then** *Interrupt*("Invalid Page Number") ;
> $P := PTB[S] + p$;
> **if** $BA[P] = 1$ **then** *Interrupt*("Page Not in Core") ;
> $NLmap := BB[P] + l$;

Thus all-or-nothing protection is provided on a VM basis, with read-only restrictions attached to real space via the f flag and storage key system.

6. *MULTICS on the GE 645*

The GE 645 employs length indicators and presence flags in a similar way to the IBM 360/67 for a first level of static VM protection. The segment and page table entries also contain fields for all combinations of the more detailed R, X, and W access restrictions, and specify the permissible control mode—master, slave, or both—of the process using the segment or page. Hardware traps occur when these restrictions are violated.

A form of dynamic protection on VM is also provided with software and hardware by using a *ring* scheme (Graham, 1968). The purpose is to permit a

†We shall ignore the associative registers here.

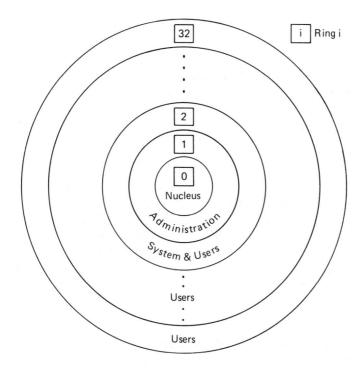

Fig. 5-8   Ring protection in MULTICS.

process's capability to vary as it moves through the programs and data of its VM. Processes in MULTICS execute within a hierarchical protection system that may be represented by a series of concentric rings; segments appearing in inner rings are most highly protected, whereas those in outer rings are more accessible in general. Figure 5-8 shows the initial ring assignments in MULTICS; ring assignments are fixed for a given segment and appear as part of the file directory entry for each segment. The operating system occupies the first three rings with the most critical parts, the nucleus, occupying ring 0; most of the system is in ring 1, and the remainder, the less sensitive segments, reside in ring 2. Rings 3 to 32 may be employed by user processes. Let S_i be the set of segments residing in ring i at any one time. The basic idea underlying this scheme is that a process executing in any segment $S \in S_i$ may "freely" access a segment $T \in S_j$ in its VM, $j \geq i$, *subject to* the X, R, W protection mode of T. An attempt to access an inward ring, i.e., $j < i$, results in an interrupt, and control is transferred to a systems routine to verify the validity of the reference. Actually, both inward ($j < i$) and outward ($j > i$) calls generate interrupts. In both cases, if control is successfully transferred out of the current ring, the "executing" ring number must be changed to that of the new ring, and arguments must be checked. For example, a call to a procedure T in an outer ring j might include, as arguments, addresses of variables in ring i, the calling ring; $T \in S_j$ will not be able to access these inner ring variables. The solution chosen is to copy the arguments into a data area accessible to T.

7. *Scientific Control Corporation SCC6700* (Watson, 1970):

Automatic dynamic VM protection is implemented by means of access path matrices. Each element a_{ij} of a matrix specifies the access permitted by segment i to segment j. a_{ij} may take values from the set $\{\neg(R \vee W \vee X),$ $R \wedge \neg(W \vee X), \neg(R \vee W) \wedge X, R \vee W \vee X\}$. Every process has a matrix giving the access path protection of its segments. When a process is running, a small block of its matrix is stored in registers to allow fast hardware validity checking.

This computer also uses the storage protection mechanisms as a means for *control* (instruction) protection in a manner originally suggested by Lampson (1968). The basic idea is to control the use of privileged instructions by placing them selectively in execute-only storage rather than having the conventional master and slave mode CPU operation. A process then uses these out-of-line instructions via "execute"† instructions. The system has complete and flexible control over the classes of privileged instructions that a particular process may use. Changes of mode from slave to master and some calls to systems routines are avoided.

How is all the protection information associated with systems and user processes made known to the system and maintained? Clearly, the owners of the various segments must specify this information when creating or editing program and data files. The file system is usually responsible for verifying and initializing access protection when segments are first loaded into storage, and for maintaining the protection data; the interaction between the file system and main storage protection is discussed in Chapter 9 (Sec. 9.4.3).

EXERCISES

1. Can you think of any other modes of protection in addition to combinations of R, W, and X?

2. Is write-only protection useful? Try to find some applications.

5.4 ALLOCATION STRATEGIES

5.4.1 Storage Allocation in Nonpaged Systems

This section is concerned with the problems of allocating and freeing *variable* size blocks of main storage in systems without paging hardware.

---

†An execute instruction, say of the form *EX OPADR* will execute the instruction located at its operand address (*OPADR*) and then continue at the next instruction following the *EX*, very much like indirect addressing of instructions.

These operations might be performed by the two commands:

1. *Request*($MAINSTORE, (SIZE, BASEADDR)$),   and

2. *Release*($MAINSTORE, (SIZE, BASEADDR)$),

where $SIZE$ is the number of contiguous storage units involved in the operation and $BASEADDR$, the first (low-order) address of the block, is an output parameter of *Request* and an input parameter to *Release*. An allocated block normally contains a logical program or data segment of some process.

Given a request for a storage block of size k, we can generally proceed as follows. If there is a hole H of size h such that $h \geq k$, then allocate k units of H to the requesting process. (The criterion for selecting one of several competing satisfactory holes was called the placement strategy in Sec. 5.1.3.) If a hole of sufficient size is not available, one can choose from a number of alternative strategies: The requesting process can be placed in blocked status until sufficient free storage becomes available; one or more used blocks may be deallocated to create a hole of adequate size (a replacement policy); or used storage may be compacted†—i.e., moved to a single contiguous area—in an attempt to create a large enough hole. We first examine two popular placement strategies.

First Fit and Best Fit Placement

Let main storage be divided into two sets of variable-size blocks, a set of empty or unused holes $\{H_i \mid i = 1, \ldots, n\}$ and a set of allocated or full blocks $\{F_i \mid i = 1, \ldots, m\}$. Given a request for a block of size k, a *first-fit* placement strategy searches for *any* hole H_i, e.g., the first one found, such that $h_i \geq k$, where h_i is the size of hole H_i. A *best fit* strategy selects that hole H_i with the closest fit; i.e., $h_i \geq k$, and for all H_j such that $h_j \geq k$, $h_j - k \geq h_i - k$ for $i \neq j$. For both strategies, when $h_i - k$ is small and nonzero, it is preferable to allocate all of H_i rather than just k units; otherwise, the newly created hole of size $h_i - k$ may be too small to be of any future value and may result in wasted time and space during all subsequent storage management activities. First fit is fast but, intuitively, it wastes larger holes by prematurely allocating parts of them. Best fit retains larger holes for future use but is a slower procedure; it also has a tendency to create many small and useless holes. It is easy to devise nonpathological examples in which either of the two methods is superior to the other.

Examples

For simplicity, we just consider a sequence of storage *Requests* and allocations, and assume that storage blocks are not *Released*.

---

†If compacting is employed, information in storage cannot be location-dependent; for example, absolute storage addresses may not be present.

1. A *Request* sequence where best fit performs better:

Storage Request	Size of Holes in Available Space	
	First Fit	Best Fit
(1) Initial "state"	2000, 1500	2000, 1500
(2) 1200	800, 1500	2000, 300
(3) 1600	blocked	400, 300

2. A *Request* sequence where first fit is better:

Storage Request	Size of Holes in Available Space	
	First Fit	Best Fit
(1) Initial "state"	2000, 1500	2000, 1500
(2) 1200	800, 1500	2000, 300
(3) 1400	800, 100	600, 300
(4) 700	100, 100	blocked

Experiments with both these methods over a wide range of simulated data were performed by Knuth (1968). In most cases, the best fit system terminated earlier ("blocked" in the above simplified examples) because of insufficient storage. The simulations indicate that one cannot always trust intuition. Note also that longest time until termination is not necessarily the best criterion to use; for example, different results might be obtained if processes were placed in blocked status on unsatisfied requests. Extensive experiments should be made using realistic statistical distributions of request size, request arrival times, and the "lifetimes" of allocations, before committing an MS to any particular policy.

The first fit method of searching available space can be speeded up with a simple trick (Knuth, 1968). Assume that the hole data (size and address) are kept in a list. A straightforward search might always start at the top of the list and continue sequentially until a fit is found. Unfortunately, this tends to cluster the smaller holes near the top of the list, since allocations are performed there first if possible; as time proceeds, it would then take longer and longer on the average before obtaining a fit. An efficient scheme that would keep the hole size more uniformly distributed over the list is to start the search at some variable point Q within the list. One possibility for Q is the next item following a selected hole on a successful search.

Available Space Administration

We first investigate data structures for maintaining information on available space or holes. The goal is to exhibit a structure in which first and best fit

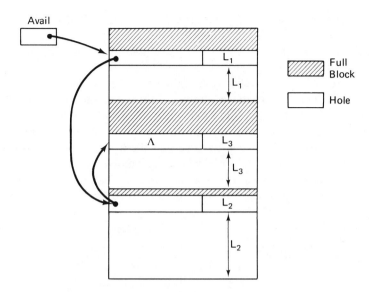

Fig. 5-9   Available space administration using a singly linked list.

searches may be done conveniently and new holes can be added as storage is released. Instead of keeping a separate storage area for the data structure, we shall use the hole space directly in the first methods discussed.

Consider the straightforward use of a simple singly linked list (Fig. 5-9). The first entries of each hole block contain the length of the block and a pointer to the next hole. A header pointer, say *AVAIL*, points to the first block of the list; Λ indicates the last element. Note that even if we start with the pointer chain sorted by storage address, for example in ascending sequence, the ordering will quickly disappear as holes are added at arbitrary points in the list (unless, of course, we go to the trouble of inserting any new hole pointer at its proper sorted place). The following difficulty arises. A block that is released can be surrounded by a free or full block on either side (Fig. 5-10). It is desirable to coalesce or merge adjacent free blocks on a release, but, in order to do this, the allocation of the blocks surrounding the released block

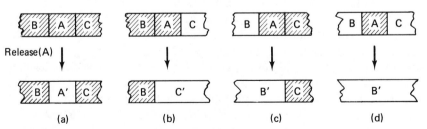

Fig. 5-10   Hole coalescing on a release.

must be obtained easily. In the data structure of Fig. 5-9, it would be very awkward to determine whether a hole or a full block is adjacent to any given block. (How would this be done?) If the available space list is maintained in sorted form, the coalescing can be accomplished easily, but the list would first have to be sequentially searched to find the surrounding holes, if any.

These problems are avoided by "tagging" the upper and lower boundaries of each full and empty block and by chaining holes with a doubly linked list. We store a single-bit tag (assumed to be a Boolean variable for this discussion) and the block size as both the first two and the last two elements of each block; a **true** tag denotes a hole, and a **false** tag indicates a full block. In addition, a forward and backward pointer is stored at the head of each hole as part of the hole chain (Fig. 5-11). The pointer changes on a block release for

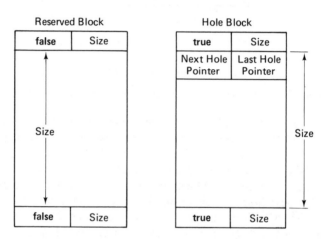

Fig. 5-11   Boundary tag data structure.

case (d) of Fig. 5-10 are illustrated in Fig. 5-12. New holes are inserted at the head of the list, since this is the most conveniently accessed place, especially for case (a) of Fig. 5-10. (The list tail would do equally as well.) This "boundary tag" scheme was devised by Knuth (1968).

Linked lists are not always the best way to keep track of available space. If storage is allocated in contiguous sequences of *fixed-size* blocks, then a separate table containing a "bit" map may be more efficient. For example, suppose that storage is broken into 32K-word blocks for allocation purposes and there are 256K words (8 × 32) of main memory. Then the allocation state of storage can be represented by a bit string: $B = b_0 b_1 \ldots b_7$, where $b_i = 0$ or 1, depending on whether block i is free or used respectively. A storage release operation can be done with a logical "and" of B and an appropriate bit mask. For example, the release of blocks 4, 5, and 6 is accom-

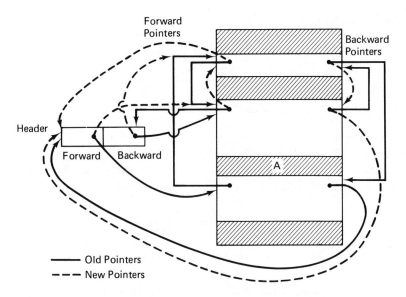

Forward Pointers

Backward Pointers

Header

Forward   Backward

A

——— Old Pointers
– – – New Pointers

Fig. 5-12 Effect of executing *Release(A)*.

plished by the statement:

$$B := B \wedge \text{"11110001"} ;$$

A first-fit search for k contiguous blocks, $1 \leq k \leq 8$, involves a number of shifts and logical operations as follows:

> *Mask* := "$0^k 1^{8-k}$" ; *Blockstart* := -1 ;
> (0^k denotes a string of k zeros.)
> **for** i := 0 **step** 1 **until** 8 $- k$ **do**
> **if** *Mask* $\wedge$ $B = B$ **then begin** *Blockstart* := i; **go to** *L* **end**
> **else** *Mask* := "10000000" $\vee$ *Rightlogicalshift(Mask, 1)* ;
> $L : \ldots$

Some Analysis of Storage Fragmentation and Utilization

It is possible to obtain some measures of the fragmentation and utilization of main storage under the above strategies for placement and release. We assume that requests and releases are equiprobable and that the system has reached an equilibrium state where the average change per unit time in the number of holes is zero. Let n and m be the average number of holes and full blocks, respectively, at equilibrium. Consider Fig. 5-10 once again. The A blocks of (a), (b), (c), and (d) of the figure represent all possibilities for full blocks. Let a, b, c, and d be the average number of full blocks of each type in storage during equilibrium. Ignoring boundary conditions at both ends of memory, we have

(1)
$$m = a + b + c + d$$
$$n = \frac{2d + b + c}{2}.$$

(2)   Since $b = c$, $n = d + b$.

Let q be the probability of finding an exact fit hole on a request and $p = 1 - q$. In Fig. 5-10, the number of holes increases by 1 in (a), decreases by 1 in (d), and remains constant in (b) and (c) as a result of the release. The probability that n increases by 1 at any change in storage allocation is

(3) $Prob(release) \times \dfrac{a}{m}.$

The probability that n decreases by 1 is

(4) $Prob(release) \times \dfrac{d}{m} + Prob(request) \times (1 - p),$

where $Prob(release)$ and $Prob(request)$ are the relative probabilities of storage requests and releases.

The equilibrium condition implies that (3) = (4). Since $Prob(request) = Prob(release)$,

$$\frac{a}{m} = \frac{d}{m} + (1 - p)$$

i.e.,

(5) $a = d + (1 - p)m.$

Substituting (2) and (5) in (1), we have

$$m = d + (1 - p)m + b + c + d = (1 - p)m + 2b + 2d$$
$$= (1 - p)m + 2n,$$

which gives the final result

$$n = \tfrac{1}{2} pm.$$

This measure of storage fragmentation was originally derived by Knuth (1968), who called it the *fifty percent* rule, since n tends to 50 percent of m as p approaches 1.

Denning (1970) has obtained the following result on storage utilization: Let the average hole size be $h = kb$, where b is the average full block size and

$k > 0$; and let p, the probability used in the 50 percent rule, be 1. Then, the fraction f of storage occupied by holes in an equilibrium state is

$$f = \frac{k}{k+2}$$

This can be easily derived by using the 50 percent rule with $p = 1$. Let M be the storage size. Then

$$h = kb = \frac{M - mb}{m/2}.$$

This leads to

$$M = mb\left(\frac{k}{2} + 1\right).$$

Therefore,

$$f = \frac{\frac{m}{2}kb}{M} = \frac{\frac{m}{2}kb}{mb\left(\frac{k}{2}+1\right)} = \frac{\frac{k}{2}}{\frac{k}{2}+1} = \frac{k}{k+2}.$$

Simulations by Knuth (1968) indicate that an average request size $b \leq M/10$ is necessary to obtain a hole fraction of $f \simeq 0.1$;† in this case, hole size is approximately $0.22b$. When b is large, say about $M/3$, f rises to 0.5, and k is then 2. The obvious conclusions are that M must be large relative to b in a dynamic environment, or else much storage will remain unused, and that some fraction f of storage will always be wasted (holes).

When a request cannot be satisfied, storage compacting may be considered as a means to produce a large enough hole. However, it is frequently the case that storage utilization is high at this point, and the results are not worth the effort. An alternative policy is to swap out enough full blocks to create the required size hole. The replacement strategies discussed for paging systems in the next section are also applicable to the swapping case.

EXERCISE

Write procedures for storage *Request* and *Release*, using a first fit placement policy and the boundary tag data structure for available space. The procedure headings are

(1) **integer procedure** *Request(size)* ;
    comment Return address of block if request can be satisfied. Otherwise return 0. *size* is the number of words requested ;

†A simulation experiment terminated on "memory overflow," i.e., on a request that could not be satisfied.

(2)   **procedure** *Release(adr)* ;
      comment Add the full block starting at address *adr* to available space ;

Let $M[a]$ be the contents of storage location a. A *full* block starting at address a will have the boundary headers:

$$M[a] = \textbf{false} \;;\; M[a + 1] = s \;;\; M[a + s + 1] = \textbf{false} \;;\; M[a + s + 2] = s \;;$$

A *hole* block starting at address a will have the header information:

$$M[a] = \textbf{true} \;;\; M[a + 1] = s \;;$$
$$M[a + 2] = address\ of\ next\ hole \;;\; M[a + 3] = address\ of\ last\ hole \;;$$
$$M[a + s + 1] = \textbf{true} \;;\; M[a + s + 2] = s \;;$$

The hole list has the header:

$$M[fh] = pointer\ to\ first\ hole\ in\ list \;;$$
$$M[lh] = pointer\ to\ last\ hole\ in\ list.$$

5.4.2 Allocation in Paged Systems

5.4.2.1   Static and Dynamic Allocation

Paging hardware can be useful in systems that allocate storage *statically* for each user, as well as in dynamically allocated ones. In the former case, paging permits the assignment of noncontiguous fixed-size storage blocks to a single name space; no placement decisions, such as first fit or best fit, are necessary, since a given page can reside in any block. Available space administration is also simplified considerably; an unordered list of free blocks is a sufficient data base for memory requests and releases. Note that static allocation implies either that user name space is less than or equal in size to real main storage, or that user-specified virtual memory overlays are used.

The arguments for dynamic allocation, for example, demand paging, are the conservation of main storage, the reduction of IO time and storage interference between IO and central processors, and the increase in the number of active processes maintained in main memory. The RCA Spectra 70/46 provides a concrete example of the second point (Oppenheimer and Weizer, 1968): IO transmission time for one page (4K bytes) between auxiliary storage (drum) and core is approximately 12.5 ms. The memory interference rate is 1.44 μsec/2 bytes; i.e., for every two bytes transmitted over a channel, main core is unavailable to the CPU for 1.44 μsec. Thus, about 3 ms are stolen from the CPU by an IO channel for each page read or written. Looking at these figures in another way, there is a degradation of CPU activity by 24 percent (3/12.5) during a page IO; if the page is not referenced, this is a total waste.

When virtual memories are implemented, the sum of the name space sizes for active processes is generally much larger than the available main storage, and storage is frequently entirely allocated. Consequently, most storage requests cannot be satisfied immediately. One often has the option of either *replacing* some page(s) in storage to make the requested block space available—a resource preemption policy—or delaying the requesting process until space becomes available by "natural" means. Replacement is commonly used, since much of the allocated storage will not be referenced again in the near future, if at all, and paging allows, in principle, efficient replacements. The selection of the particular page to replace has been the subject of much recent research. The results can also be applied to replacement decisions in pure segmented systems and in systems with high-speed buffer memories (Sec. 5.6). We also observe that, under demand paging, the fetch and placement strategies are determined *a priori*, leaving the replacement scheme as the only "variable" with which to optimize the behavior of a system with respect to its storage management policies.† In the remainder of this section, a useful model for studying allocation policies with paged systems and replacement is presented.

We consider a complete execution time trace Z of a particular program with a specific set of input data. Z is given in the form

$$r_0 \, r_1 \, \cdots \, r_k \, \cdots \, r_T,$$

where r_k is the instruction or data *page* referenced by Z at its kth storage access and r_T represents the last such reference; this type of trace has been called a *program reference string*. The subscripts in the reference string can be treated as time instants. Assume that the program and data corresponding to Z are allocated a main storage area of size m blocks, where $1 \leq m \leq n$ and n is the number of *distinct* pages in Z. An allocation policy P defines for each instant of time k the set of pages p_k that are loaded at time k and the set of pages q_k that are removed from storage or *replaced* at time k during the processing of Z. A common measure of goodness for a policy P is the total number of pages $n_p(Z)$ loaded into storage when Z is processed; i.e.,

$$n_p(Z) = \sum_{k=0}^{T} |p_k|.$$

Example

Let $Z = wzxyyxwxxxz$ and $m = 2$. The number of distinct pages $n = 4$, since Z references the pages $\{w, x, y, z\}$.

---

†We are assuming that the page size and the amount of main storage allocated to a program are fixed.

(a) Consider a policy P which always assures that storage contains one of $\{w, x\}$, $\{x, y\}$, or $\{y, z\}$. Then, the storage map could change as follows as Z is referenced:

Z Time k	w 0	z 1	x 2	y 3	y 4	x 5	w 6	x 7	x 8	x 9	z 10
p_k	$\{w, x\}$	$\{y, z\}$	$\{x\}$	—	—	—	$\{w\}$	—	—	—	$\{y, z\}$
q_k	—	$\{w, x\}$	$\{z\}$	—	—	—	$\{y\}$	—	—	—	$\{w, x\}$
Block 1	w	y	y	y	y	y	w	w	w	w	y
Block 2	x	z	x	x	x	x	x	x	x	x	z

$$n_p(Z) = 8.$$

(b) Let P be a demand paging policy in which a page is not loaded until referenced. If a page must be replaced to provide room for a "demanded" page, the removed page will be selected on a first-in, first-out basis. The storage map history then becomes

Z Time k	w 0	z 1	x 2	y 3	y 4	x 5	w 6	x 7	x 8	x 9	z 10
p_k	$\{w\}$	$\{z\}$	$\{x\}$	$\{y\}$	—	—	$\{w\}$	$\{x\}$	—	—	$\{z\}$
q_k	—	—	$\{w\}$	$\{z\}$	—	—	$\{x\}$	$\{y\}$	—	—	$\{w\}$
Block 1	w	w	x	x	x	x	w	w	w	w	z
Block 2	—	z	z	y	y	y	y	x	x	x	x

$$n_p(Z) = 7.$$

Mattson, et al. (1970) have shown that for *any* policy P and initial allocation of pages of Z, there exists a *demand* paging policy P_d such that

$$n_{p_d}(Z) \le n_p(Z);$$

i.e., an appropriately selected demand paging policy will yield the minimal $n_p(Z)$. However, one must be very careful in interpreting the results of such analyses, since the model and its assumptions may not be valid for some systems and the criterion for optimality, $n_p(Z)$, may not be appropriate. In particular, the demand paging result does *not* "prove" that this is the best policy to use; it does say, however, that it brings in the fewest pages. Suppose, for example, that the "cost" $h(k)$ of loading k pages at a time was equal to $C_1 + C_2 k$, where C_1 and C_2 are constants. This is not an unrealistic cost for transmitting from auxiliary storage to executable storage; C_1 includes housekeeping and waiting costs and $C_2 k$ assumes that the transmission cost is directly proportional to the number of pages. Then the loading costs for the policy of (a) in the above example is $5C_1 + 8C_2$ and that for (b) is $7C_1 + 7C_2$; the best possible demand paging policy for (b) (see next section) will yield $n_p(Z) = 6$ with corresponding cost of $6C_1 + 6C_2$. For *all* $C_1 > 2C_2$, $5C_1 + 8C_2 < 6C_1 + 6C_2$, and demand paging would "cost" more.

In implementing large virtual memories on a paged machine with multi-programming, real executable memory can be treated as a general "pool" from which storage requests and releases are made; alternatively, each active program can be given its own work space within which dynamic memory management takes place. Replacements in the latter case are made only from a process's own workspace, whereas, in the pooling situation, page faults from one process can cause replacements of pages of entirely unrelated programs. The above model assumes a fixed-size workspace (*m* blocks) associated with an executing process. Both approaches have been employed with varying degrees of success—and failure (Denning, 1970; Oppenheimer and Weizer, 1968).

5.4.2.2 Replacement Schemes

For later comparisons and to provide insight into practical methods, we first describe an optimal but unrealizable replacement scheme. The model and criterion of goodness of the last section are assumed. That is, program reference strings are known *a priori*, and it is required to minimize $n_p(Z)$ for each string Z. Since there exists a demand paging policy with minimal $n_p(Z)$, only this type of policy is considered. Then, minimization of $n_p(Z)$, the number of replacements, and the number of page faults are all equivalent. It can be proven that the following replacement strategy is optimal (Belady, 1966; Mattson, et al., 1970; Aho, et al., 1971):

Select for replacement that page which will not be referenced for the longest time in the future.

That is, if a page fault requiring a replacement occurs at time k, select that page r such that

(1) $\qquad r \neq r_i \qquad$ for $k < i \leq T \qquad$ (*r* not referenced again)

or if such an r does not exist,

(2) $\qquad r = r_t \qquad$ for $k < t \leq T$,
$\qquad\qquad r \neq r_{t'} \qquad$ for $k < t' < t$, $\qquad$ and $t - k$ is a maximum.

Example

The optimal replacement policy yields $n_p(Z) = 6$ for the example of the last section.

Program reference strings are virtually never known in advance, of course.

Practical replacement schemes attempt to predict future references by assuming that past reference history will be repeated in the immediate future.

The first scheme that one might consider is a *random* selection strategy; select at random the page to be replaced, using a random number generator. This may be useful if the above assumption is not valid (at least statistically so) or as a means of comparison with other methods. Probably the simplest replacement algorithms are ones based on the *"first-in first-out"* (FIFO) principle. If storage is being allocated in a work space of size m blocks, an ordered list of pages $P[0], P[1], \ldots, P[m-1]$, and a pointer k are maintained such that $P[k]$ identifies the most recently loaded page and $P[k +_m i]$ points to the ith page loaded chronologically ($i = 1, 2, \ldots, m-1$). Then, on a page fault—an attempted access to a page that is not present in main storage—page $P[k +_m 1]$ is selected for replacement and k is incremented by 1 (mod m); the number of the loaded page is subsequently entered in $P[k]$ (the new k). This method assumes that the pages residing longest in storage will be least likely to be referenced in the future. The third major strategy—and the most popular one—is a *"least-recently used"* (LRU) policy. Here, the replacement page is the one that has not been referenced for the longest time in the past. The rationale is that pages that have not been used for relatively long periods will probably not be required in the immediate future. The LRU strategy requires continual monitoring of all page references in order to accumulate usage history, whereas FIFO housekeeping is necessary only at page fault time.

A replaced page must be written onto secondary storage if its contents were changed during its last occupancy of main store; otherwise, the replaced page may be simply overwritten. A *write* bit, say w, associated with each page table entry or block is typically used to check this. When a new page is loaded, the corresponding w is reset to *OFF*; w is set to *ON* only when information in the page is modified (a write operation). One common implementation of LRU also associates a *use* bit, say u, with each resident page or block. On any reference to the page, u is set to *ON*; all u's may be reset (turned *OFF*) either periodically, or when the last u is set, or at replacement time when all u's are *ON*. The set of pages in memory is then divided into four subsets for replacement purposes. They are the sets of all pages with

1. $(u, w) = (OFF, OFF)$
2. $(u, w) = (OFF, ON)$
3. $(u, w) = (ON, OFF)$
4. $(u, w) = (ON, ON)$.

The replacement block is selected at random from the lowest-numbered, non-empty subset, thus approximating LRU.

Several more sophisticated methods for maintaining records of usage history exist. One suggested scheme employs a capacitor for each block. The capacitor is charged on a reference; the subsequent exponential decay of the charge can be directly converted into a time interval. Another attractive technique uses an aging register of n bits for each block;

$$R = R_{n-1} R_{n-2} \cdots R_1 R_0$$

On a page reference, R_{n-1} is set to 1 and every τ time units R is shifted right one unit. If the page has been referenced in the last (approximately) $n\tau$ time units,

$$\bigvee_{i=0}^{n-1} R_i = 1.$$

LRU then selects from that subset of pages with a minimum value of R, treating R as a positive integer. The original ATLAS contained a more complex mechanism for usage history-keeping which included usage information on blocks in secondary storage; the replacement decision was based both on time since last reference and time during the previous period of inactivity on the drum.

Belady (1966) tested a number of replacement algorithms on a broad sample of FORTRAN and assembly language programs, and compared the results with those using the optimal but unrealizable replacement. Generally, the basic LRU schemes required about twice as many page loads as the optimal, and were superior to ATLAS, FIFO, and random replacement. The FIFO and random strategies were least satisfactory, needing approximately three times as many page loads as the optimal. Block size and memory size, the other two parameters varied in Belady's experiments, affected the performance much more critically (we elaborate on these points in the next section).

The above discussion has generally assumed that each process has been allocated a fixed-size storage area from which replacements are made. Both this policy and the other extreme, where all memory is pooled, can lead to intolerable page traffic due to the dynamically varying storage requirements of different processes and possible overloading of the system with too many active processes. The *working set* model of Denning (1968) is a memory management policy that avoids these problems in principle. The underlying philosophy is that a process must have a "reasonable" amount of storage for its program and data information before it is activated, and that the amount required is defined dynamically by its recent past behavior. Each process at a given time t has a working set of pages $W(t, \tau)$ defined as a set of pages referenced by the process during the time interval $(t - \tau, t)$; $w(t, \tau)$ is the number of pages in W (the cardinality of W). It is assumed that both W and w

are approximately constant locally over small time intervals. Storage is managed according to the rules (Denning, 1970):

A program may run if and only if its working set is in memory, and a page may not be removed if it is a member of the working set of a running program.

Thus, the replacement scheme is a variation of LRU.

The working set strategy seems very attractive, but little experience exists to date on its practical use; for example, one question that is still unresolved is how to choose the value of the parameter τ. In one reported set of simulations of scheduling and paging algorithms for the RCA Spectra 70/46 time-sharing system, a form of working set strategy gave the best performance (Oppenheimer and Weizer, 1968). Here, the availability of W was not required; it was only necessary that w storage blocks be allocated to a process before it was activated.

EXERCISES

1. Give the storage map history for the program reference string and m of the example in Sec. 5.4.2.1, using
   (a) Optimal replacement.
   (b) LRU.
2. Devise data structures and algorithms for
   (a) Maintaining the working set of a process.
   (b) Selecting a replacement page using working set principles.

5.5. EVALUATION OF PAGING

A number of experiments have been carried out to study the dynamic behavior of programs under paging (Belady, 1966; Fine, et al., 1966; Coffman and Varian, 1968; Freibergs, 1968; Baer and Sager, 1972). The general method was to execute interpretively a sample set of programs, simulating the paging mechanism; the most significant parameters that were varied were page size and the amount of executable storage. The results of these independent studies were generally consistent and can be summarized as follows:

1. Most processes require a high percentage of their pages within a very short time period after activation; for example, about 50 percent of a process's total pages on the average were referenced during a single quantum in a typical time-sharing operation.

2. A relatively small number of instructions within a page are executed before control moves to another page; for page sizes of 1024 words—the

most common size—less than 200 instructions were executed before another page was referenced in most of the samples investigated.

3. In the range 64–1024 words per page, the number of page faults increases as the page size increases, while available memory is kept fixed (demand paging).

4. As storage decreases, there is a point at which page faults rise exponentially for a fixed page size (demand paging).

Figure 5-13 illustrates these effects qualitatively.

One conclusion from the above is that page sizes should be relatively small—certainly smaller than the common 1024 words. Some factors that we shall consider explain the larger page size, while others add more evidence supporting the first conclusion.

Among the many reasons given for paging was the reduction of memory

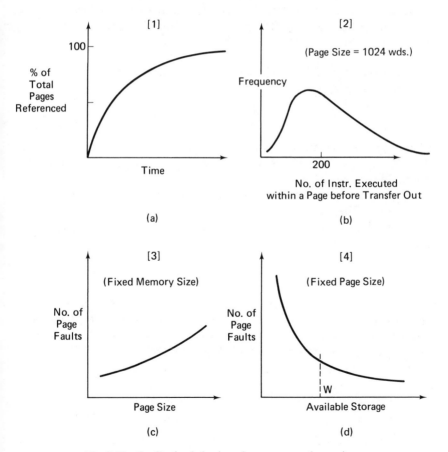

Fig. 5-13 Qualitative behavior of programs under paging.

fragmentation. Even though checkerboarding of storage is eliminated, however, two other types of memory losses occur in a paged system. The first, studied by Randell (1969), occurs because segment sizes are rarely, if ever, exact multiples of page size; the last page of a segment will then invariably have wasted storage. Randell called this loss *internal fragmentation* and performed several experiments which showed that losses could exceed those due to the more common (external) fragmentation in nonpaged systems. The second loss is in the tables required to hold the virtual to real space mapping functions, i.e., the page table storage. If it is assumed that the average segment size s_0 is much larger than the page size z, and that page tables are stored entirely in main memory, then an optimal page size can be derived (Denning, 1970; Wolman, 1965):

THEOREM

Let c_1 be the cost of losing a word of main storage to page table use and c_2 be the word cost for internal fragmentation. If $z \ll s_0$ and each segment begins on a page boundary, the optimal page size z_0 is approximately $\sqrt{2cs_0}$, where $c = c_1/c_2$.

Proof (informal): For each segment, the storage loss cost C_z for paging with page size z is

$$C_z = C_i + C_t,$$

where C_i is internal fragmentation cost and C_t is page table cost. If $z \ll s_0$, then $C_i = c_2 z/2$ approximately, since on the average, one-half of the last page of a segment is wasted.

$C_t = c_1 s_0/z$ approximately, since each segment requires roughly s_0/z page table words. Therefore, $C_z = c_2 z/2 + c_1 s_0/z$.

To find the optimum z_0, we solve $dC_z/dz = 0$, i.e., $c_2/2 - c_1 s_0/z_0^2 = 0$, leading to our result.

This result confirms our conclusion on small page sizes if we take $s_0 \leq 5000$ and $c = 1$; in that case, $z_0 \leq 100$ words. z_0 is even smaller if the typical segment sizes of 100 words (!) as measured on the B5500 (Batson, et al., 1970) are regarded as universal. However, smaller page sizes require larger page tables to address a fixed amount of virtual storage and also mean that main memory must consist of a larger number of blocks.

Larger page sizes are employed in practice because of

1. The software overhead in processing page tables.

2. The hardware cost of dividing storage into fixed-size blocks.

3. The physical characteristics of rotating auxiliary storage devices, which

perform most efficiently when transmitting larger blocks of information. (Chapter 9 contains a review of secondary storage hardware.)

Typically, a track on a drum or disc will hold several thousand words, i.e., several pages; a sizeable rotational delay is incurred on the average before the first word of a desired page appears under the read-write mechanism. A *paging drum* or disk (Denning, 1970, 1972) provides an efficient way to avoid this delay when possible. Every drum track i is divided into a number of fixed size sectors j, each corresponding to a page. A hardware sector pointer is synchronized with the rotating drum, and an IO request queue is maintained for each sector; each queue element contains a track number and read or write indicator (Fig. 5-14). When the pointer reaches a sector with nonempty queue, the read or write operation at the head of the list is automatically initiated over the drum channel. The performance of this drum is theoretically much superior to one which schedules each operation on a first-come, first-served basis. The University of Michigan Multiprogramming System (MTS, 1967) running on the IBM 360/67 is one example of a system that uses such a paging drum.

The second conclusion from the experiments on the dynamic behavior

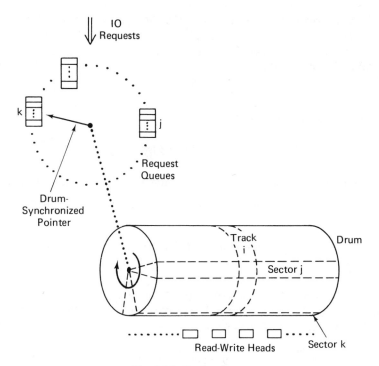

Fig. 5-14 Paging drum.

of programs is that IO activity resulting from page faults can become intolerably high and unproductive unless each active process has a sufficient amout of storage, e.g., a working set, available for program and data needs. By "intolerably high" and "unproductive," we mean that the CPU is devoting too much time to housekeeping related to paging in and out, that the CPU and channels operate sequentially instead of in parallel because all active processes are continually in need of page space, and that the same pages are continually being swapped in and out; in other words, there is a dramatic decrease in the amount of useful work accomplished. The point labelled W in Fig. 5-13(d) represents a minimum amount of storage required to avoid these effects. Most large general-purpose time-sharing systems using demand paging (e.g., MULTICS, 1965; MTS, 1967; TSS, 1967; CP-67/CMS, 1969) attempt to control the amount of paging in and out by either limiting the number of active processes that may compete for the CPU, or by using some variation of a working set policy, or, more directly, by deferring page requests if there are too many pending at the time.

Dynamic storage allocation based on demand paging has been used successfully in many time-sharing systems after an uncertain beginning and much effort. Despite the elegance of the concept, however, it is still not evident whether simpler policies, for example, using swapping and fixed- or variable-sized work spaces, may prove superior in the long run or whether dynamic allocation on a segment basis as implemented on the larger Burroughs computers may be a more useful path to follow. Too little comparative data is available to judge at this time.

5.6. STORAGE HIERARCHIES†

Computer performance is often limited by

1. The small size of main storage relative to program requirements.

2. The slow access speed of main memory relative to that of CPU registers.

3. The orders of magnitude difference between auxiliary storage access times (mechanical) and that for main storage (electronic).

Our previous discussions have implicitly assumed that main storage consisted of a set of homogeneous addressable cells with uniform access times. Within this organization, paging was introduced in order to improve storage

---

†The terminology and definitions in this section are taken from the survey paper of Denning (1970).

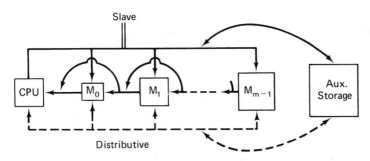

Fig. 5-15 Storage hierarchies.

utilization and processing efficiency. Another approach that is becoming widespread is based on the use of storage hierarchies.

Main storage is no longer homogeneous but is composed of an hierarchy of electronically accessed storage devices, $M_0, M_1, \ldots, M_{m-1}$, each having different speeds and sizes (Fig. 5-15). The characteristics of each level are such that

$$Accesstime(M_{i-1}^{\cdot}) < Accesstime(M_i)$$

and

$$Size(M_{i-1}) < Size(M_i), \qquad i = 1, \ldots, m-1.$$

The hardware and/or software are designed to keep the most frequently used information in M_0 with the aim of approaching the performance of a system with homogeneous memory of the same type as M_0 but size $\sum_{i=0}^{m-1} Size(M_i)$.

There are two basic schemes for connecting a CPU and auxiliary storage to the hierarchy, called the *slave* and *distributive* organizations. In the distributive method, all of main storage is directly accessible by both secondary storage (through a channel) and the CPU for fetches and stores. The slave approach, first suggested by Wilkes (1965), considers M_0 to be the (almost) only device referenced by the CPU, while auxiliary storage connections are generally restricted to the slower memories $M_{m-1}, M_{m-2}, \ldots$ When data is *stored* into any M_i by the CPU, the hardware ensures that the new copy appears in $M_{i+1}, \ldots, M_{m-1}$, by transferring the data through the hierarchy. Conversely, whenever data is *fetched* from any M_i, it is also *stored* into $M_{i-1}, \ldots, M_0$ for future use. This implies a replacement policy if any of the latter memories are full; note that such a replacement into any M_i, $i \neq m-1$, involves only overlaying the replaced storage area, since up-to-date copies exist in $M_{i+1}, \ldots, M_{m-1}$. A combination of the slave and distributive organization is also used; for example, computer processors will often have a hidden high-speed memory for instruction lookahead and small program loops, which in effect acts as a slave memory to a visible homogeneous, slave, or distributive store.

Example

One interesting and successful realization of slave memory is in the IBM 360/85 (Conti, et al., 1968; Liptay, 1968). In this system, there are two levels in the hierarchy ($m = 2$). M_0, called a *cache* or high-speed buffer, is an invisible (to the program) 16K-byte, 80-ns memory, divided into 16 sectors of 1K. Main store M_1, a standard μs core, is similarly divided into 1K sectors. A field associated with each sector s in M_0 is used to hold the address of a sector in M_1 that has been allocated to s. Information is transmitted between M_0 and M_1 in units of 64 bytes, called blocks; each sector is thus divided into 16 blocks. Corresponding to every block in the cache is a 1-bit tag t; $t = 1$ indicates that the block contains information, while $t = 0$ for undefined contents. Allocation of M_0 is done on a single sector basis, but each information transfer involves only a single block. The store and fetch operations between the CPU and main store work as follows:

1. Store data α into X (X is an M_1 storage address).
   (a) If X is in M_0, then store α in *both* M_0 and M_1.
   (b) Otherwise, store α in M_1.

2. Fetch data α from X.
   (a) If X is in M_0 (sector covering X is in M_0 and $t = 1$ for the block of X), then fetch α from M_0.
   (b) If sector of X is in M_0 but $t = 0$, then fetch α from M_1 and load the block of X into M_0 (in parallel).
   (c) If sector of X is not in the cache, then
      (i) If cache is full, use an LRU strategy to select a replacement sector and
      (ii) Fetch α from M_1 and load block of X into M_0 simultaneously.

Writes to auxiliary storage occur from M_1 only, but reads, which change memory, are treated in the same way as store operations (case number 1 above). All of the dynamic memory management is done by hardware. This organization of large sectors and small blocks appears to be a very clever engineering compromise between the smaller hardware costs of large pages, and the experimental and theoretical evidence for small page sizes. Early simulations and actual experience show that the internal computer performance is roughly from 60 to 90 percent that of an "ideal" hardware configuration with 80 ns memory of the same size as M_1. As another side benefit, channel interference is reduced considerably, since the working set is usually in M_0 and most IO operations deal with M_1 exclusively.

Problems of memory allocation between main and auxiliary storage are similar to the nonhierarchical situation. They are not as severe, however, since much larger but slower main memory systems can be used. Hierarchical storage systems are also one solution to the engineering problem of increasing the size and speed of storage beyond that presently available; with conventional technology it is not the switching times of storage components that currently limit the access speed, but the signal transmission time to each component.

Pure distributive systems are more flexible, in that software allocators have complete control over the memories. In practice, there are usually two levels in the hierarchy—a conventional fast main storage M_0 and a slower but larger core storage M_1; both operate in the μs range. Administration of M_0 and M_1 is much more complicated than the single-level memory, the critical decisions being where to load information (M_0 or M_1?) and when to move information among the three levels consisting of M_0, M_1, and auxiliary storage. In one general-purpose MS serving a university community where storage is statically allocated on a job basis (CLASP, 1971), M_0 contains batch jobs, the system nucleus, and heavily used systems routines, while M_1 holds an interactive text editor, a time-sharing language processor and associated subsystem, IO buffers, and the remainder of the operating system; the reasonable assumption here is that the batch jobs and system nucleus consume most of the CPU cycles and should be in faster store. The Carnegie-Mellon University time-sharing system on the IBM 360/67 (Vareha, et al., 1969) offers an example of a dynamically allocated system using paging. In one memory management policy, working sets for conversational tasks are maintained exclusively in a large bulk core (M_1) and executed therefrom, while heavily used operating systems components are allocated to high-speed memory (M_0) as much as possible. More complex policies, in which the access frequency of user and systems programs dynamically dictate their location in the hierarchy, have also been employed. The Carnegie-Mellon group has demonstrated the usefulness of the hierarchy as an economic method for reducing response times for interactive tasks and for reducing paging IO traffic. More analytic and experimental research on optimum allocation policies for memory hierarchies is still required.

6 PROCEDURE AND DATA SHARING IN MAIN STORAGE

A multiprogramming organization necessarily involves the sharing of a wide variety of resources among user (and system) processes. There is the sharing of hardware resources—primarily time-sharing of active CPU, channel, and IO device processors, and space sharing of central and auxiliary storage areas. Although the hardware sharing was one of the original motivations for the development of multiprogramming, it was also discovered that the principal software resources could also be time- and space-shared, and that there were real benefits for doing so.

6.1. WHY SHARE?

Sharing of computer programs and data is often accomplished by providing a user with his own private copy of the shared information. The copy could be manually incorporated into a job before submission to the computer (e.g., by insertion of a card deck) or might be automatically added by a loader referencing a library or utility file. This could still be done in a multiprogramming environment. However, several active processes often need the same code or data resident in main storage at the same time. If each process had its own copy, unnecessary systems costs would be incurred; these consist of the IO overhead in loading the excess copies and the memory to store them. A serious problem occurs when multiple copies of the same data file are updated; it is almost always necessary to have one consistent file that contains *all* updates. The problem here somewhat resembles the familiar critical section problem discussed in Chapter 3, and the same type of errors can appear unless handled carefully. For these reasons, a *single* copy in main storage is frequently shared by more than one process; the sharing occurs in a time-multiplexed fashion when several processes share a single CPU or essentially simultaneously when the processes are running on independent processors with a common memory. This chapter is concerned with the structure of programs (and data to some extent) required to perform single-copy sharing correctly and efficiently. We first look at some typical applications of data and procedure sharing.

Data Sharing

1. Several processes—possibly invoked by interactive users—simultaneously interrogating a file system: The directories or index of the files would be simultaneously in use.

2. Systems programs sharing a data base: Resource status (e.g., which elements of the resource are free or busy) is generally continually searched and updated by various systems processes. In addition, a "display" process might exist which writes the current status on some output device.

3. Critical sections are primarily used to control data sharing on a sequential basis. (See applications and examples in Chapter 3.)

Procedure Sharing

1. *Systems nucleus routines.* In an MS, all processes share the same set of nucleus routines, for example, the IO programs.

2. *Utilities and system services.* Widely used routines, such as various dumps, a tape-to-print utility, or a linking loader, may be single-copy shared.

3. *Language processors and text editors.* Popular compilers, assemblers, and interpreters are often maintained in executable storage to allow their simultaneous use by more than one job. Text editors and interactive language subsystems, such as those for APL or BASIC, are designed in many cases to handle several terminal users at the same time with a single copy of the system.

4. *Applications programs.* Some heavily used applications programs might be shared, but it is often simpler to load a copy for each requesting process; otherwise, one has to search storage to see if the sharable copy exists and keep a record of the number of processes using the program. The examples in Secs. 3.1.1 and 3.1.2 on parallel programming illustrated simple situations in which a single copy is most convenient. In those examples, several processes within a *single* job share the same code; multitasking facilities in some higher-level languages, e.g., PL/I, implicitly involve single-copy sharing.

6.2. REQUIREMENTS FOR CODE SHARING

In the early days of computing, it was often claimed that much of the power and flexibility of computers derived from the ability to modify programs during execution; instructions could be treated as data and vice versa. This claim was not so much theoretical as it was practical. The structure of the first generation of machines made instruction modification necessary in order to produce efficient and practical programs. Looping and subroutine transfer and return were the two principal areas that required programs to change themselves dynamically. For example, the following self-modifying (partial) instruction sequence will sum a set of numbers in the array A; a single-address, single-register (R) machine is assumed:

```
                      —Initialize—
LOOP    CLA    *+4        MODIFY "ADD A" TO
        ADD    = 1          GET NEXT ELEMENT
        STO    *+2          OF A.
        CLA    SUM        R := SUM ;
        ADD    A          R := R + Ai ;
                            THE MODIFIED INSTRUCTION.
        STO    SUM        SUM := R ;
                      —End of Loop Test—
        TRA    LOOP
                .
                .
                .

SUM     DS     1
A       DS     100
```

Later, the use of index registers to store and compute addresses made instruction self-modification unnecessary.

Instruction modification during execution is not considered good programming practice today for at least two reasons. Program logic often becomes very obscure and difficult to follow; the result is that programs are hard to debug and communicate. Uncontrolled program self-modification also makes it impossible to share code; a process may be interrupted after it has changed an instruction (or data item), and another process, sharing the same code and data area, may either change the same instruction (data item) or execute (use) it, incorrectly assuming that no changes have been made. For both these reasons—clarity and sharing—it is desirable to eliminate *store* operations into code areas. To do this, the data that is manipulated must be isolated in a separate area from the program.

Self-Initializing Programs

In serial sharing situations, it is possible to change code and data local to the code if the program is *self-initializing;* that is, initial values of code and data are set by the program itself and the initializing code remains inviolate. Then, a single copy is sufficient as long as each process sequentially uses the copy to completion before another process is allowed entry. The code is thus a critical section and acts as a "serially reusable" resource. A common application is in an MS that devotes a single "partition" or block of main memory to the sequential batch processing of a favorite language (e.g., compile, load, and go); the language subsystem is kept permanently in the partition in a self-initializing form. The subsystem can then include data storage for variables with its instructions, avoiding the discipline of separating the two. This approach is satisfactory when little or no multiprogramming is desired or needed in the subsystem. For example, the subsystem may be written very carefully so that IO and computing are well balanced; or the subsystem jobs are at the lowest priorities; or there is already efficient multiprogramming in the operating system.

Pure Procedures

Pure procedures are programs that do not modify their own instructions or local data; that is, internal store (write) to memory operations are prohibited. Any such program that is execute- and read-only is also called *reenterable* (IBM, 1965), since it may be "resumed" at any time with the assurance that nothing has been changed. Thus, pure procedures may be shared by more than one process, in either a time-multiplexed or multiprocessing mode.

Variable data associated with the process using a pure procedure must be stored in separate private areas. These data normally include arguments, return addresses, and temporaries. The most convenient way to access the variable information is through base registers that will point to the private storage at run time.

Example

Let ARG be the symbolic name of a location containing some variable; $[ARG]$ designates the contents of ARG. To store the contents of a register Ri into ARG, the following instruction might be employed in a nonpure procedure:

$$STO\ Ri,\ ARG \qquad [ARG] := [Ri]\ ;$$

The code is not correct in general, however, *if* the instruction is part of a procedure P shared by several processes, since each process might be simultaneously storing different values into ARG. (This could happen, for example, if the instruction were in the middle of an iteration loop.) To correct this situation, ARG is usually an agreed-upon offset or relative address within a private area of any process executing P; some (base) register, say Rb, is assumed to contain the base address of this area at run time. Then the correct referencing instruction that keeps P pure might be:

$$STO\ Ri,\ ARG(Rb) \qquad [[Rb] + ARG] := [Ri]\ ;$$

CPU registers, which are stored as part of the state vector of a process, thus provide a simple means for linking pure procedures to changeable data. Before a pure procedure is called, arrangements must be made for passing parameters, the return address, and temporary storage locations through the registers.

6.3. SHARING IN STATICALLY ALLOCATED SYSTEMS

Let storage be *statically* allocated for each job or job step as part of a linking, relocation, and loading operation. External references appearing in use tables of object modules may refer to potentially sharable items; in addition, programs requested through command and control language statements may also be sharable. We wish to examine briefly the problems and implications of general single-copy sharing by several independent processes under these circumstances. Several base registers are assumed available for accessing private or shared data, and for linking to and from shared procedures.

First consider machines *without* dynamic relocation hardware. In virtually all MS's on these computers, a sharp distinction is made between systems and users' programs, often corresponding to privileged (master) and slave hardware modes, respectively. Users invoke shared systems programs and data by executing supervisor trap instructions (*SVC*'s) but generally cannot share other users' information. To provide sharing on a more general basis, linking loaders must be modified to search main memory, as well as auxiliary storage and input files, for external references and main programs. In addition, the usual contiguity requirement for user's storage space must be abandoned. (Why?) One major problem is that of assuring adequate protection. When protection is realized through storage keys only (Sec. 5.4), the shared information and all of the memory associated with the sharing processes must have the same key, thus fully exposing the sharing processes and their data to one another. The shared areas could be protected by tagging them read and/or execute only, if this type of protection is implemented in the hardware. [Of course, this solution is not acceptable if the area in question must be updated (written), as is frequently the case, for example, in work areas for users sharing a compiler or interpreter.]

It is difficult to implement completely general sharing facilities on a virtual memory machine that dynamically relocates by *pure paging* (no segmentation). Shared data accessed by private procedures do not present any serious problems. The loader can assign a different set of sequential page numbers to the data for each private process and adjust the page tables to point to the appropriate blocks. At run time, the particular virtual space address of the data is inserted in a base register; a private procedure executing within a process accesses the data through the base register, in a manner similar to the example of the last section. Note that data areas shared in this manner cannot contain addresses either to themselves or to other areas, since these addresses would necessarily include page numbers; only pointers *relative* to the base or some other fixed point of an area can be used.

Procedures require more care, since their page numbers are *bound* (assigned) at the time of linking and loading; that is, all valid effective name space addresses (instruction and local data addresses) within such a procedure are determined at load time—the paging, recall, is invisible to the user. Therefore, the shared procedures must be accessed with the *same* page numbers by *all* processes sharing this code; page number conflicts and wasted table space can occur when a new process requires several independent, shared, and already loaded segments. (See the following exercise.) One can circumvent this problem, but the methods seem to be quite clumsy. If the total set of sharable segments are known to the system, it is frequently possible to *permanently reserve* their page numbers; the same page numbers are used for those procedures and data segments that are mutually disjoint, where two segments are mutually disjoint if they are never used together by the same process.

When a dynamic relocation mechanism works through segment tables—possibly followed by page tables—the above difficulty disappears, provided that we assume that segment numbers of running processes appear explicitly in base registers. The segment numbers become part of the invoking process rather than part of the code;† the segment tables for different users may then have their entries for the same procedure in different relative locations. The table entries point to the absolute locations of the shared procedure or, if the memory is also paged, may point to *shared* page tables. Protection, as in the pure paging case, is afforded through the address mapping hardware. References to shared data, and transfer and return of control among shared procedures is still not straightforward, since segment numbers for the same shared information will differ for each process; the linking methods described in the remainder of the chapter apply to the static case also. Restricted forms of sharing can also be accomplished in segmented systems by permanently reserving some segment numbers for shared information.

EXERCISE

Examine the problems of static sharing in a pure paged system (no segmentation) by considering the following situation: A process p_a requires programs Q_1 and Q_2, temporary storage T_1, and data D_1, of size q_1, q_2, t_1, and d_1, respectively,

---

†Segmentation on the GE 645 is done in this manner. The Burroughs B5500 and B6500 do not use base registers to hold segment numbers; the segment numbers appear explicitly in instructions.

in pages. These are combined and linked into a virtual space program of size $q_1 + q_2 + t_1 + d_1$ pages in the above order and loaded into storage. While p_a is still active, another process p_b requests loading of information Q_1', Q_2, T_1', and D_1 with page sizes q_1', q_2, t_1', and d_1, respectively, where $q_1' < q_1$ and $t_1' > t_1$. Q_2 and D_1 are to be shared between p_a and p_b. Describe a possible contents of the page tables for p_a and p_b. What problem arises if a new process p_c now enters the system and wants to share Q_1' and Q_1? Can you think of any general way to avoid page number conflicts and still allow sharing?

6.4. DYNAMIC SHARING

Dynamic sharing is considered in its most general form, where linking of procedures to shared information (other procedures or data) is deferred to the last possible moment, the time of reference; this approach could be called *"dynamic linking."* A multiple-segmented virtual name space is assumed; all name space addresses consist of a segment and word pair $[s, w]$, as in Chapter 5. Hardware relocation takes place through segment tables and a dynamic storage allocation policy may be employed in conjunction with linking. Our discussion will be based on the MULTICS system (MULTICS, 1965; Daley and Dennis, 1968) because of the elegance and generality of the techniques developed by its designers.†

Since segment numbers are assigned during execution and may differ for the same procedure or data segment depending on the referencing process, it is imperative that no segment numbers appear explicitly in segments. This applies to both internal (self) and external references. Two different processes sharing the same information segment will, in general, refer to that segment by different segment numbers, the particular number assigned being a function of the current segment number allocations for the process.

Internal references are handled easily by using a base register for the segment number of the running process; the segment number is then a part of the state vector of the process. Thus, only word numbers appear explicitly in shared code. External references must remain symbolic for two reasons. First, this is the only way to allow dynamic linking and segment number assignment for different processes simultaneously sharing. The second reason is to insure that the procedures that use shared information are immune to most changes in the latter (for example, recompilations). On the other hand, if the external references are *always* symbolic, accessing time would probably be impractically long because of the need for interpretive execution. We would like the *first* access by a given process to each external item to be performed interpretively with symbolic information; this allows retrieval of the

---

†The paging in the MULTICS system will be ignored here; the linking methods are almost independent of this aspect of memory organization.

segment by the file system, protection checking, and segment and possibly word number assignment. However, on subsequent references, it would be most desirable to bypass the interpretive software and access through hardware only via a normal [s, w] address. How to do this and, at the same time, keep the references symbolic and code pure for potential use by other processes is outlined in the next few sections. We shall use capital letters to designate symbolic references and lowercase letters for numerical (assigned) virtual space addresses. For example, [SUB, ENTRY] might be a symbolic external reference while [sub, entry] could be a corresponding segment number/word number pair after dynamic linking.

6.4.1 Form of a Procedure Segment

The MULTICS solution to the problems of dynamic sharing involves the use of two types of interfaces:

1. A *linkage section* LS is defined for each potentially sharable or sharing segment. Transfer of control and external data references occur by indirectly addressing through linkage sections. *Each* process receives a *private* copy of the linkage section when it uses a segment.

2. A private *stack* segment is allocated to each process for storing arguments, return addresses, processor states, and temporaries; the segment is organized as a stack for convenient call and return linkages and so that every procedure may be used recursively if desired.

During execution, the stack and linkage section addresses are maintained as [s, w] pairs in two base pair registers, lp (linkage pointer) and sp (stack pointer), respectively. A procedure base register pbr always contains the segment number of the code currently in execution.

Each pure procedure segment consists of three parts—a symbol table, the pure code, and the linkage section (Fig. 6-1). For simplicity, we shall take some liberties in describing the content and the pointer structure within these parts. The symbol table can be viewed as a symbol definition and use table in a relocatable object module. Figure 6-2 contains a skeleton symbol table for a hypothetical procedure segment named P. Within P, n symbols $E_1, E_2, \ldots, E_n$ are defined for possible external use (for example, entry points); that is, they may be used as [P, E_i] pairs in other segments to reference the appropriate point in P. The names $e_1, e_2, \ldots, e_n$ designate word numbers of their respective E_i in P (Fig. 6-3), while the le_i are pointers to the linkage section, used to establish run-time links to P from other segments. The procedure P itself refers symbolically to word X in data segment D and word E in procedure Q.

The pure code part of P illustrated in Fig. 6-3 contains linkage section

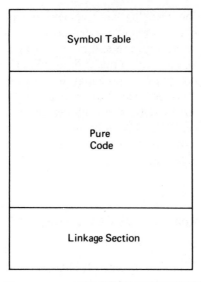

Fig. 6-1   Procedure segment.

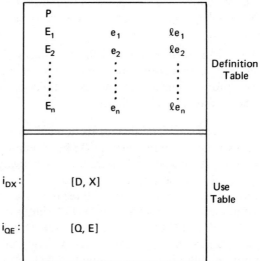

Fig. 6-2   Symbol table for a procedure P.

pointers (word numbers) l_{DX} and l_{QE} for the external references, where the ADD instruction might have been assembled from

$$ADD \quad [D, X]$$

and the TRA instruction assembled from a procedure call:

$$CALL \quad [Q, E];$$

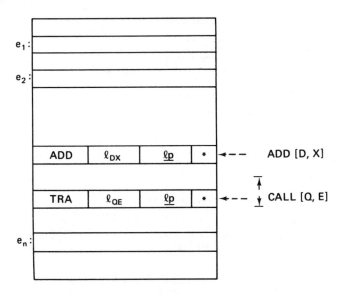

Fig. 6-3   Pure code section for procedure P.

The asterisk * indicates indirect addressing, and the lp designation means that the effective $[s, w]$ address of each instruction is computed by the hardware as

$$\left[\, segmentnumberin(lp),\ wordnumberin(lp) + \begin{Bmatrix} l_{DX} \\ l_{QE} \end{Bmatrix} \right].$$

The linkage section of P, LS_P, appears in Fig. 6-4. The references i_{DX} and i_{QE} are pointers to the symbols D, X and Q, E in the symbol table. The "*Trap Tag*" is a flag in the address field that causes a hardware trap or supervisor call when the location is accessed during indirect addressing. The code corresponding to the le_i will be described in Sec. 6.4.3.

It should be emphasized that all three parts of P will remain invariant. When a process α links to P, it is given a *private* copy of LS_P, say LS_P^α; the $[s, w]$ address of LS_P^α is inserted in lp so that all external references are accessed indirectly from P through LS_P^α.

6.4.2 Data Linkage

We now examine the method for handling the external data references. Assume that a process α is executing the segment P of Figs. 6-2, 6-3, and 6-4 and is just starting the operand fetch for $[D, X]$ in the ADD instruction; it is the first time that this particular instruction is executed by α. The pbr register contains the segment number of P in α's virtual space, and lp points to the linkage section copy, LS_P^α, associated with α [Fig. 6-5(a)]. Initially, LS_P^α is identical to LS_P.

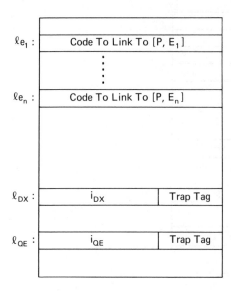

Fig. 6-4   Linkage section for P.

The operand, l_{DX}, in conjunction with lp, first produces the address a in Fig. 6-5(a). Because of the indirect addressing at a, the effective address mechanism fetches the contents of a; an internal trap results immediately from the *Trap Tag*, and control is transferred to a piece of software called the *linker*. The main functions of the latter are to establish the correct linkage to $[D, X]$, i.e., to produce $[d, x]$, and ensure that future references by α to $[D, X]$ in P are automatic.

The linker finds the symbolic name of the data, $[D, X]$, from the linkage section and P, using the pointers in an obvious way. The segment management module is then invoked; it makes D "known" to α and returns a segment number, say d, for D. This process can be quite complicated, involving calls on the file system, storage allocation for segment (and page) tables, possible storage replacements, verification of the "legality" of the access, and much table housekeeping. (Chapter 9 describes the file system functions in more detail.) The symbol table of D then allows the linker to obtain the word number x of X. The pair $[d, x]$ is inserted at a, replacing i_{DX}, and the *Trap Tag* is turned off. At this point, α is ready to continue, and the indirect addressing is completed to obtain the inserted $[d, x]$. On all subsequent executions of a, $[d, x]$ is produced without further traps [Fig. 6-5(b)]. P still remains intact for use by other processes.

Note that the MULTICS technique requires two storage accesses to retrieve this type of external data—one for the indirect addressing and the second for the actual data fetch—in addition to the memory references necessary for implementing the segmentation-paging map. It is difficult to suggest how one might always avoid the indirect addressing and still maintain

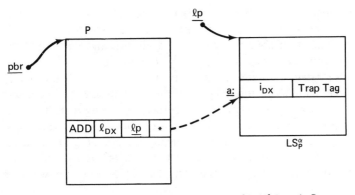

(a) First Data Reference to [D, X] by α in P

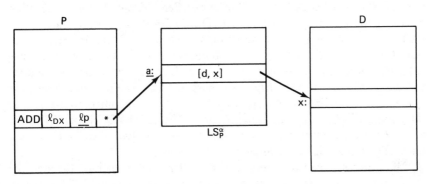

(b) Completed Linkage to [D, X]

Fig. 6-5   Data linkage by α in P to [D, X].

symbolic information in pure code. External data, in the form of arguments and return addresses, need not be symbolic, since standard calling sequences and the use of the stack assure that relative locations of this information are known. The stack pointer register provides a sufficient and efficient means for data operand retrieval in pure code.†

6.4.3 Procedure References

Transfer of control from one procedure segment to another is more complex than data linking. The system must not only establish the link but must also obtain a copy of the linkage section of the called procedure and arrange for insertion of the appropriate new [s, w] pair in lp and new segment number in the pbr. We again describe the linking mechanism through the example of Figs. 6-2, 6-3, and 6-4. A process α is executing P and is just starting the

†The MULTICS system also uses an argument register ap to point to a list of arguments.

operand fetch for $[Q, E]$; it is the first time that the TRA instruction is executed by α, and no changes have been made to LS_P^α. The instructions preceeding the call to Q must, of course, provide for argument and return address linkage and for temporary stack space, which Q might need.

The over-all strategy is to move from P through LS_P^α to LS_Q^α and finally to Q. The indirect addressing and lp again produce a trap in LS_P^α. The linker invokes a segment management module as before, providing it with a symbolic segment name Q. Q is made "known" to α by allocating a private copy, LS_Q^α, of its linkage section and assigning segment numbers for Q in α's space. The $[s, w]$ address for defined symbol E in LS_Q^α, say $[lq, le]$, is inserted in LS_P^α at the trap location, and the flag is turned off; the address in LS_P^α now points inside LS_Q^α (Fig. 6-6).

The trick now is to provide the proper code in LS_Q^α to effect the total transfer; this is the code left blank in our earlier Fig. 6-4. The first operation sets the lp to the $[s, w]$ pair of LS_Q^α. This is accomplished by letting the original TRA instruction complete its execution so that control actually transfers to word le in LS_Q^α. At this point, the pbr contains the segment number of the new linkage section;† the segment number part of lp can be set to the pbr contents and the word number part of lp to the base of LS_Q^α.‡ The purpose of the next instruction, the indirect branch ($TRA\ y$ *), is to transfer control to the desired entry point of Q, $[q, e]$, and set the pbr to q. The address $[q, e]$ corresponding to $[Q, E]$ is inserted by the linker after Q has been identified in α's virtual space. The linking is now complete.

The process Q can now return to its caller P by branching through the stack segments of α to the return address. Further execution of the $CALL$ $[Q, E]$ by α in P will automatically proceed through the linkage sections without any traps, as illustrated in Fig. 6-6.

In addition to the work in initially performing a link, two extra instructions and two indirect address fetches are the "price" of the generality of sharing of procedures. Note that the techniques described in these last sections can also be employed in statically allocated systems, with a static linking loader performing the functions of the dynamic linker; the equivalent of a *Trap Tag* is not required.

---

†Indirect transfers to new segments automatically set the *pbr* to the new segment number.

‡A linkage section is often treated as a complete segment making the base word number equal to zero; however, linkage sections for a single process may also be combined into larger segments.

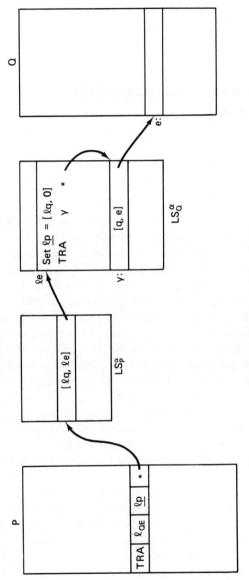

Fig. 6-6 Procedure linkage by α from P to Q.

7 PROCESS AND RESOURCE CONTROL

The highest levels of user processes in an MS are established in response to requests and definitions expressed in the job control or command language of the system. We will assume that a highest-level "supervisory" process p_J is created for each user job J. In many systems, this is actually the case; where it is not, it is still convenient conceptually to assume the existence of such p_J's, even though their functions may be performed centrally by systems processes. The process p_J has the responsibility for monitoring and controlling the progress of J through the system as well as for maintaining a global accounting and resource data structure for the job. The latter may include static information such as job identification, maximum time and IO requirements, priority, "class" (e.g., interactive, batch, IO-bound, CPU-bound), and resource needs (e.g., main storage, files, peripherals); and dynamic data related to resource usage and current processes within the job. In general, p_J will create a number of offspring processes, each corresponding to some requested unit of work, such as a job step; these processes may in turn create additional ones, either in sequence or in parallel. Thus, as a job progresses, a corresponding tree hierarchy of processes grows and shrinks. The processes are not totally independent, but interact with each other and parts of the operating system such as resource managers, schedulers, and file system components. These ideas are illustrated in Fig. 7-1, where an OS process p_S has created job processes $p_{J1}, \ldots, p_{Jn}$.

In this chapter, we specify in some detail a set of data structures and primitive operations for processes and resources, discuss the treatment of interrupts and IO processes, and examine several organizations and techniques for allocating ready processes to processors, i.e., scheduling or dispatching methods. Our purpose is to consolidate and amplify material of earlier chapters on process and resource primitives, and other parts of the system's

166

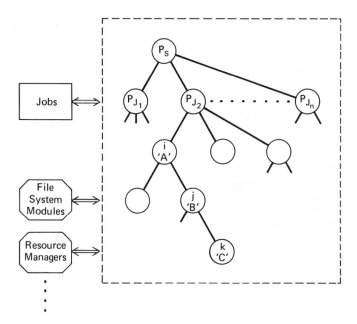

Fig. 7-1   Process hierarchy for user jobs.

nucleus; to present one possible model organization for a nucleus;† and to use the model as a framework for discussing a variety of processing techniques.

7.1.   DATA STRUCTURES FOR PROCESSES AND RESOURCES

Every resource class and process normally has a corresponding data structure containing its basic "state," identification, and accounting information. These data structures are sometimes referred to as systems *control blocks* or *descriptors*. The descriptors collectively represent the state of an operating system and, as such, are maintained, and frequently accessed by systems routines.

7.1.1   Process Descriptors

A process descriptor is constructed at process creation and represents the process during its existence. These data structures are modified and used extensively by basic process and resource operations, interrupt routines, and schedulers; and referenced during performance monitoring and analysis.

† Shaw, et al. (1973) describes an implementation of the nucleus model presented in this chapter.

Table 7-1 lists a possible set of descriptor data for a process in a general-purpose MS. The subscripted variable defining or following a component in the table will be used to denote the component and its contents; a given element may itself be a complex structure as discussed below.

Table 7-1   Process Data Structure

Process i

1. Name *Id*[*i*]

2. Virtual/Real Machine
   2.1 Processor State and Capability   *CPUstate*[*i*]
   2.2 *Processor*[*i*]
   2.3 Main Storage Map   *MainStore*[*i*]
   2.4 Other Allocated Resources   *Resources*[*i*]
   2.5 Created Resource List   *CreatedResources*[*i*]

3. Status Information
   3.1 *Status*[*i*]
   3.2 Data Associated with Status   *Sdata*[*i*]

4. Immediate Relatives
   4.1 *Parent*[*i*]
   4.2 *Progeny*[*i*]

5. Accounting and Scheduling Data   *Priority*[*i*], . . .

Identification

Each process has a unique internal identification, say an integer i, provided by the system at process creation time, and an external name $Id[i]$. The purpose of the latter is to allow convenient explicit interprocess references. To eliminate conflicts arising from the use of the same external name for more than one process, we impose the convention that the "children" of any process in the tree hierarchy have unique names and define a complete reference from process i to j as the ordered concatenation of Id's of processes on the "path" connecting i to j (including $Id[j]$); for example, in Fig. 7-1, process i can reference process k by the name $B.C$, where $Id[j] = B$ and $Id[k] = C$. (More details on this type of referencing are given in Chapter 9, where a similar scheme is used for naming files in file directories.)

Virtual/Real Machine Definition

The second component, the virtual/real machine specification, defines the process state vector in the sense of our earlier introductory discussions in Secs. 3.2 and 4.3. The state and capabilities of the virtual or real processor executing i, the address space, and any other resources allocated to i are described here. Virtual to real machine mappings, if required, are also included within each part of this component.

The element *CPUstate[i]* contains the process's capability and protection data, as well as the current instruction counter and register contents in the case where *i* is ready or blocked but not running. *CPUstate* could be equivalent to the information in the typical third- (or fourth-)-generation machine stateword—i.e., the data saved by hardware when an interrupt occurs. Capability is then expressed in terms of the set of instructions that may be legally executed, e.g., master or slave mode, and perhaps a memory protect key for its address space; a form of self-protection is specified by the types of traps (internal interrupts) that are enabled, disabled, or inhibited during execution of the process. Capability and protection may be further elaborated by software or hardware, for example, by adding "ring" protection or access path matrices (see Sec. 5.3), or by listing the resources that the process has authority to request and release. If a process *i* is running, *Processor[i]* identifies, by number, the (central) processor executing *i*.

The main storage map describes the real address space of the process and the name-location map, if used. *MainStore[i]* could contain upper and lower storage bounds, or a segment table pointer, or a page table pointer. The main storage resources allocated to the process, including those on a shared basis, are found in this component. The next component *Resources[i]* is a pointer to a list of all other serially reusable resources allocated to *i*. These might be such reusable resources as peripherals, auxiliary storage space, and critical sections; the list would contain the details of the allocation, for example, the sector addresses of disk space. Each element on the resource list and unit of *MainStore[i]* has a flag indicating whether the resource is *shared* or *owned*. The created resource list is a list of all resource classes created by the process.

Status Data

The status of a process *i* is described by an indicator *Status[i]* and a data item *Sdata[i]* pointing to a list associated with the resource responsible for the status. As introduced in previous chapters, *Status[i]* may be one of the following:

running: *i* is running on a processor (the one designated by *Processor[i]*).

ready: *i* is ready to run, waiting for a processor.

blocked: *i* cannot logically proceed until it receives a particular resource or message.

These can handle many situations but there are some applications for which a finer division of status types is desirable. Consider the following two examples:

1. A user is interactively debugging or running a program. Often, he will

wish to suspend execution to examine the state of his computation, possibly make some changes, and either continue or terminate execution.

2. An internal process might wish to suspend the activity of one or more other processes to examine their state or perhaps modify them. The purpose of the suspension may be, for example, to detect or prevent some kinds of deadlocks or to detect and destroy a "runaway" process.

In both cases one could "block" the process to achieve the suspension. However, a process could be already blocked when suspension is desired. Unless we wish to allow a process to be blocked on more than one "resource," or to be blocked by other than itself, a new "suspended" status is required.†

A process will be either *active* or *suspended*. If active, it may be running, ready, or blocked, denoted by a *Status[i]* value of *running*, *ready$a$*, or *blocked$a$*, respectively. When suspended, *Status[i]* is *ready$s$* or *blocked$s$*.

Sdata[i] points to a resource and has the meaning:

Status[i]	Sdata[i]
1. *running* *ready*$\left(\begin{smallmatrix} s \\ a \end{smallmatrix}\right)$	Pointer to a ready list used by process scheduler for allocation of the processor resource.
2. *blocked*$\left(\begin{smallmatrix} s \\ a \end{smallmatrix}\right)$	Pointer to a waiting list associated with the resource causing the block.

Details of the ready and waiting lists are provided in the next section on resource descriptors.

Other Information

At the beginning of this chapter, the method of spawning hierarchies of processes was briefly discussed. Each process i has a creator, *Parent[i]*, which created the process, and which owns and controls any of its offsprings.‡ Similarly, every process i may create other processes; *Progeny[i]* consists of a list of internal names of direct offsprings of i. The priority of a process, *Priority[i]*, is a static or dynamic entity indicating the relative importance of i; we shall use the convention that *Priority[i]* $>$ *Priority[j]* implies that process i has a higher priority than j. The priority is not necessarily an external priority assigned to a job; the latter can be viewed as a "long-term" priority used for determining when a job is to be loaded and activated, while *Priority[i]*

---

†We shall assume that blocks are always self-blocks, which is the case for all primitives except *Block(i)* discussed in Chapter 3.

‡There will be one ultimate creator, created when the system is first loaded.

is basically a "short-term" and possibly dynamic priority employed by the process scheduler when selecting a process to run. *Priority[i]* could be a complex function of an external priority, the resource demands of the process, and the current environment, i.e., other processes in the system. The last part in the process data structure is used for scheduling, charging, allocation, and performance-measuring purposes. Typical elements include CPU time used by the process, time remaining (according to some estimate), resources used, resources claimed, and the number of IO requests since creation.

7.1.2 Resource Descriptors

This section presents a data structure skeleton that can describe the state of any of a large number of entities called resources; the class is much larger than one would expect. The data structures and basic resource operations of the next section, developed by Weiderman (1971), consolidate and generalize many heretofore isolated but widely used notions.

The term "resource" is commonly applied to a reusable, relatively stable, and often scarce commodity which is successively requested, used, and released by processes during their activity. The term is most frequently used to describe hardware components. It is evident, however, that many types of software—data and programs—satisfy this common definition also. The above resources are called *serially reusable* since they are usually (but not always) shared by processes on a serial basis, i.e., by one process at a time. Each resource class requires at least three descriptive components:

1. An *inventory* listing the number and identification of available units of the resource.

2. A *waiting list* of blocked processes with unsatisfied requests for the resources.

3. An *allocator* responsible for deciding which requests should be honored and when.

There is yet another set of entities that shares the same descriptive needs as serially reusable resources. These appear in synchronization and communication situations where messages, signals, and data are transmitted among processes. For each class of messages at a given point in time, there is an "inventory" of messages that have been produced but have not been received (consumed), a waiting list (perhaps empty) of processes that have requested some information, and some allocation mechanism that matches messages to receivers. We shall call these resources *consumable*, after Holt (1971), since they are used primarily in producer-consumer applications, individually have a short life time in a system, and are not "returned" to the system after use. Units of serially reusable resources may be released or returned to the resource inventory *only* if they were previously acquired, whereas elements of consumable resources can be released independently of any previous acquisitions.

Consumable and serially reusable resources have one vital property in common: A process can become logically blocked due to an unsatisfied request for such a resource. This leads us to a general definition:

A *logical resource*, hereafter called *resource*, is anything that can cause a process to enter a logically blocked status.

A (logical) resource class will be called a *resource semaphore* for historical reasons; its descriptor has the entries indicated in Table 7-2. *Sdata* in the process descriptor will point to a resource semaphore if the process is blocked. Resource semaphores, and their descriptors, are established *dynamically* during execution when a process creates a new resource class.

Table 7-2   Resource Data Structure

Resource Semaphore i

1. Identification $Id[i]$, $SR[i]$, $Creator[i]$
2. Availability Inventory $Avail[i]$
3. Waiting Process List $Waitrs[i]$
4. Allocator Entry Point $Allocator[i]$
5. Other Information

As in the process descriptor case, each semaphore will have both an internal and external name defined by the system and creator at resource creation (definition) time. A Boolean indicator $SR[i]$ denotes whether the resource is serially reusable ($SR[i]$ = **true**) or consumable; only allocated resources of serially reusable type are described in *Resources[i]* in the process descriptor. In addition, a field $Creator[i]$ contains the internal name of the process that created the resource semaphore.

Inventory Pointer

The reference $Avail[i]$ points to the head of an availability list or inventory for resource semaphore i. The list itself could be a single bit indicating the presence or absence of a certain type of interrupt signal, or a table for main storage blocks, or a linked list for buffer pools; or some more complex and structured data such as auxiliary storage device addresses that contain availability directories for the particular unit. The head of the list also contains pointers (entry points) to at least two routines, one for insertion of new elements (released resources) and the other for removal of allocated resources; the possibilities are similar to those described next.

Waiting Process List

All processes blocked on the resource semaphore are found in this list. Each process entry will contain its unique internal identifier, an address where the details of the allocation are to be inserted, and the details of the resource request. The latter might include such things as the size of the request, its type—for example, a request for an IO-bound job from a job resource list, or a request for a 7-track or a 9-track tape—and the identification of the process(es) that may give the resource (e.g., send a message) to the requester.

The waiting list can take many forms. In the simplest case, it has a capacity of one element. This occurs in basic signalling applications in which a process is only blocked and waiting for a signal from one other process. It would probably be most efficient to combine all resources of this type into a larger class, since the allocation mechanism would be the same for each one.

A universal organization for the waiting list is that of a generalized queue structure; the header of this structure is addressed by *Waitrs[i]*. We would like to specify uniformly the insertion and removal of queue elements, regardless of the organization details of the queue. To do this, the structure of Table 7-3 is proposed for the queue header. Then the calls

1. *Insert(q, e)* ;

2. *e := Remove(q)* ;

could be used, respectively, to

1. Insert *e* onto *q*, (i.e., call the routine addressed by *Insert[q]* with argument *e*).

2. Remove an element from queue *q* and place its pointer or index in *e*.

It is also convenient to have another removal routine (or entry point to *Remove*) which removes a named element from the queue list; we shall use the call

$$e := Remove(q, i) ;$$

Table 7-3   Generalized Queue Header

Queue q

1. Insert Routine Entry Point   *Insert[q]*
2. Remove Routine Entry Point   *Remove[q]*
3. First Element   *First[q]*
4. Last Element   *Last[q]*
5. Additional Data

to take the element named i from q. Other queue access routines, such as those for searching and scanning the queue, can either be written by using the *Insert* and *Remove* routines or could appear as entry points in the last element of the queue header. The last component of the queue header may also be employed for holding queue statistics and indicators for use by performance measurement and allocation procedures, and for identifying the structure of the queue.

A FIFO queue might appear as illustrated in Fig. 7-2. The process identified p_i can just be a pointer to the process descriptor. d_i represents the details of the request and a_i is a base location where the allocation is to be placed when the request is satisfied. Note that this FIFO structure is similar to the buffer pool organization described in Chapter 2. The structure of Fig. 7-2 could be simplified by using a simple contiguous table treated as an implicit circular list. The advantage of the explicitly linked list is that lengthy arguments do not have to be moved; only pointers to the various elements need appear in the entries.

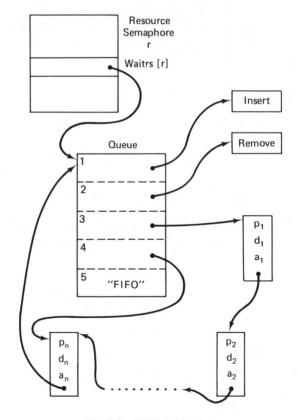

Fig. 7-2 FIFO waiting list.

Often it is useful to order the waiting list queue elements in some manner; the ordering may be based, for example, on request size or some priority of the requesting process. A forward-linked list similar to the FIFO queue could be employed and the order maintained so that the highest priority items remain at the top. This complicates insertion somewhat but might be the most efficient method if the lists are not expected to be too long. A general priority data structure is useful if the waiting lists are potentially long. Let priorities be numbered 1 to n. Then the queue can be organized as follows (Lampson, 1968): $First[q]$ and $Last[q]$ point to the first and last elements of a priority table. ($Last[q]$ is not always necessary.) Each element i of the table heads a doubly linked FIFO waiting list of processes at priority i, and has a forward queue pointer $fqp[i]$ and a backward pointer $bqp[i]$ that address the processes of priority i, if any, on the list. Figure 7-3 contains an example of such a data structure; processes 6, 8, and 5 are waiting with priority 1, no priority 2 processes are waiting, and process 2 is waiting with priority 3. Forward and

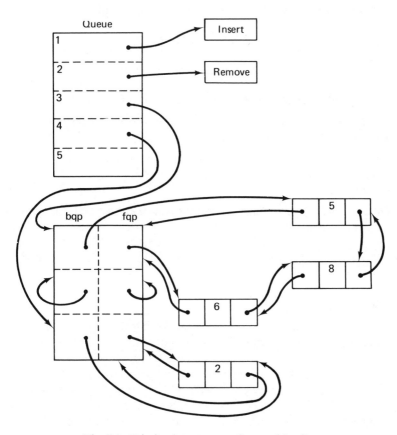

Fig. 7-3 Priority data structure for a waiting list.

backward pointers are convenient for changing the list when process priorities are dynamically changed or when processes are removed from the list. This data structure is also a natural one for a process ready list and will be used for this purpose in Sec. 7.4.2.

The Allocator

The allocator of a resource semaphore is a routine that attempts to match available resources to requests of blocked processes. If resources are allocated, it stores the allocation in the designated field of the request parameters. We shall allow the allocator to satisfy requests from one or more processes on a single call. This is certainly desirable when resources are added to the availability list, since more than one process may be unblocked as a result of such an action. Less obviously, it may be desirable to defer allocations until some future time, even though resources are available at the time of request. This might be done to prevent deadlock, or in anticipation of future requests, or for efficiency purposes. We shall assume a general call:

$$Allocator(r, k, L) \; ;$$

where k and L are output parameters with the meaning:

1. k: the number of processes allocated resources (unblocked), $k > 0$;

2. $L[i]$, $i = 1, \ldots, k$: a list of the processes to which resources are allocated (defined only when $k > 0$); and

3. r is the internal name of the resource semaphore.

Additional Information

The last field in the resource descriptor can be employed for several purposes. Since system behavior depends to a large extent on resource demands and utilization, it is convenient to maintain some measurement data in this field. The current allocation of the elements of the resource semaphore can also be kept here.

The Processor Resource

There is one resource that must be treated separately, and that is the central processor(s). The reason is that we do not consider a process to be logically blocked if it is waiting *only* for the availability of a processor. In a system with potentially more than one central processor, a data structure is required for this resource by the scheduler. For simplicity, we shall assume that *all central processors are equivalent* in the sense that a ready process may be allocated to any one. In practice, this may not be so since they may vary in speed, the amount and type of internal storage available, and their ability to communicate with other processors, storage devices, and peripherals. Our processor descriptor consists of two components:

1. *np*: the number of processors ($np > 1$)

2. *Process*[*i*], $i = 1, \ldots, np$: identification of the process executing on processor *i*.

Process scheduling is simplified if we assume that each processor is always active, running some process. To ensure this continual activity, a looping "idle" process is created for each processor; the idle process runs if there are no other *readya* processes in the system.

The process and resource descriptors are sufficient to handle a wide variety of multiprogramming applications. However, few commercial systems have such a general structure for these descriptors. Usually each resource class has its own data structure, which is bound (defined) at systems generation. The process descriptor generally contains fields for each hardware resource that may be allocated and bit strings for indicating the cause of a wait. One pays a price in efficiency for our more general structures—the storage to hold the additional pointers and the extra computing required by the basic process and resource operations. The benefits of such a systematic organization derive primarily from its clarity and uniformity. Changes can be made easily to adapt to new conditions, a system is easier to understand and therefore to analyze and evaluate, and there exists the possibility of implementing primitive operations on these structures in hardware, e.g., via microprogramming.

7.2. BASIC OPERATIONS ON PROCESSES AND RESOURCES

A set of primitive nucleus operations is specified in the following sections. The state of our hypothetical MS, the process and resource descriptors, is maintained through these primitives. We shall take the point of view that each primitive represents an instruction that is executed within the invoking process rather than treating each primitive as a separate process. The primitives are considered indivisible and are protected by a common "busy wait" type lock; for clarity, we omit the locks in the following descriptions. Error and capability checking are also omitted. These issues are discussed after the operations are presented and in Sec. 7.2.3.

7.2.1 Process Control

Five operations on processes are defined:

1. *Create:* Establish a new process.

2. *Destroy*: Remove one or more processes.

3. *Suspend*: Change process status to "suspended."

4. *Activate*: Change status to "active."

5. *ChangePriority*: Set a new priority for the process.

Interprocess communication is handled by the general resource operations outlined in Sec. 7.2.2.

To create a new offspring n, a parent process will call the *Create* primitive with the arguments: external name n, initial CPU state S_0, priority k_0, initial main storage M_0, initial inventory of other resources R_0, and perhaps accounting information and limits. The initial status will be *readys—ready* because the new process n should be in position to proceed logically and *suspended* because it may be desirable to create a process well before its activation. The system process ready list, *RL*, will be a priority organized structure of the form illustrated in Fig. 7-3. The *Create* primitive is

procedure *Create*(n, S_0, M_0, R_0, k_0, *accounting*) ;
begin
   $i := GetNewInternalProcessName$;
   $Id[i] := n$; $CPUstate[i] := S_0$;
   $MainStore[i] := M_0$; $Resources[i] := R_0$; $Priority[i] := k_0$;
   $Status[i] :=$ 'readys'; $Sdata[i] := RL$;
   $Parent[i] := *$; $Progeny[i] := \Lambda$;
   $Insert(Progeny[*], i)$; .
   Set Accounting Data ;
   $Insert(RL, i)$
end *Create*

The first instruction retrieves an internal name i for n and makes i known to the system; allocation for the name i also assumes the allocation of process descriptor space. The asterisk* designates the internal name of the invoking process and can be obtained either from a register or through software. The last statement of *Create* inserts the new process on the ready list. The initial resources, including main storage, are defined as *shared* resources for the new process and must be a subset of those of the parent process; the parent may share any of its resources with other progeny processes in a similar manner. The created process, in turn, can share its resources with its children and can also obtain further resources which it will then *own*.

A process will be permitted to suspend only its descendents. The operation of suspension could be treated in two different ways. A call, *Suspend* (n, a), where n is a process name and a points to a return storage area, could suspend only n, or it could suspend n and all of its descendants; both these options may be desirable. The last possibility is somewhat tricky, since some descendants may have been previously suspended by ancestors (which are descendants of n). The RC4000 system (Brinch Hansen, 1969) suspends in this manner but, as a consequence, requires more complex process status types (see exercise). Our solution is to permit suspension of only one process at a time, but to return enough information to the suspender so that some or all of the further descendants may also be suspended if desired. The information to accomplish this is readily available since, in order to allow a suspender to examine the state of the suspendee, a *copy* of its descriptor is returned in the storage area pointed to by the parameter a by the suspend operation. (One could, alternately, grant read-only access to the process descriptor and return a pointer to the descriptor, but this may not be feasible.)

```
procedure Suspend(n, a) ;
begin
    i := GetInternalName(n); s := Status[i] ;
    if s = 'running' then Stop(i) ;
    a := CopyDescriptor(i) ;
    Status[i] : = if s = 'blockeda' V s = 1 'blockeds' then 'blockeds'
                  else 'readys';
    if s = 'running' then Scheduler
end Suspend
```

The purpose of $Stop(i)$ is to interrupt $Processor[i]$, store the appropriate part of the processor state in $CPUstate[i]$ and set $Process[Processor[i]]$ to Ω (undefined), thereby making the processor available; the process scheduler is then invoked at the end of the operation to allocate the processor to some other *readya* process. The suspended process remains linked within the list it occupied prior to suspension.

Process activation is straightforward, involving a status change to active and a possible call on the scheduler. The latter permits the option of preemption scheduling if the activated process becomes *readya*. A process may activate any of its known descendants, in particular, its progeny. Thus, the normal sequence for introducing a new process into the system is a *Create* followed by an *Activate*.

```
procedure Activate(n) ;
begin
    i := GetInternalName(n) ;
    Status[i] : = if Status[i] = 'readys' then 'readya'
                  else if Status[i] ≠ 'running' then 'blockeda' ;
    if Status[i] = 'readya' then Scheduler
end Activate
```

For destroying a process, the same alternatives are available as in the *Suspend* operation—one can either remove a single process (a descendant) or remove that process and all of its descendants.† If the first policy were selected, the process hierarchy could easily fragment and disappear, potentially leaving isolated processes in the system with no control over their behavior. We therefore require that *Destroy* remove a process and *all* of its descendants. There remains a question of what to do with the resources of the destroyed processes. The simplest policy here—and the one we choose— is to destroy all resource semaphores created by each destroyee and to return all *owned* serially reusable resources that were created by the destroyer or its ancestors to their respective inventories. If the destroyer wishes detailed descriptor information on the destroyees, it could precede the *Destroy* by one or more *Suspend* operations.

Destroy is invoked by the call *Destroy(n)*, where *n* is the name of the "root" process of the tree to be removed. For each process *i* in the tree, the routine removes *i* from its *Sdata* list, returns all owned resources to their availability lists, destroys all semaphores created by *i*, and, finally, eliminates the process descriptor. The process scheduler is called if one of the destroyed processes was running.

```
procedure Destroy(n) ;
begin
    sched := false ;
    i := GetInternalName(n) ;
    Kill(i) ;
    if sched then Scheduler
end Destroy ;

procedure Kill(i) ;
begin
    if Status[i] = 'running' then
    begin Stop(i); sched := true end ;
    Remove(Sdata[i], i) ;
    for all s ∈ Progeny[i] do Kill(s) ;
    for all r ∈ {MainStore[i] ∪ Resources[i]} do
        if owned(r) then Insert(Avail[semaphore(r)], data (r)) ;
    for all R ∈ CreatedResources[i] do RemoveResourceDescriptor(R) ;
    RemoveProcessDescriptor(i)
end Kill
```

The final primitive, *ChangePriority(n, k)*, changes the priority of process *n* to *k*. In general, this will also require that *n* be moved to a different place in whatever list it resides to reflect the new priority. If processor preemption

---

†We shall not permit a process to destroy itself directly; it can commit suicide by sending an appropriate message to a parent process.

is desirable, the scheduler is called on a priority change. The code for *Change-Priority* is left as an exercise.

In all of the primitives, it is important that error checking be included. For example, the last four operations require a test to assure that the process name *n* is in fact a descendant of the caller; this check could be incorporated in *GetInternalName*. There is also a problem related to duplication of external names; the direct progeny of each process must have distinct external names, and path names must be given as arguments to the primitives if the possibility of ambiguity exists. The critical section implementation problems and issues discussed in Sec. 3.5 are applicable to the primitives here. We have proposed a "busy wait" implementation of a common lock for all primitives rather than including possible process blocking; blocking can occur *only* as a result of requests for resource semaphores (see next section). It is therefore imperative that these critical sections, i.e., the operations, be efficiently implemented.

EXERCISES

1. Suppose that the *Suspend* and *Activate* operations are similar to *Destroy* in that they also apply to all descendants of the named process. Also assume that *Suspend* and *Activate* may name only a direct progeny as their argument process. Modify *Activate* and *Suspend* so that a process *n* invoking *Activate* only activates those descendant processes that were *previously* suspended by *n*, and *Suspend* suspends only those processes that are active. (*Hint:* Devise additional suspended status types to indicate the source of suspension.)

2. Write an Algol-like program for *ChangePriority(n, k)*. Assume that the appropriate processor is preempted if the priority of a ready process is higher than a running one as a result of this operation.

7.2.2 Resource Primitives

As emphasized earlier, all process communication and resource allocation will occur through the resource semaphore operations. Four primitives operating on resources are defined:

1. *CreateRS*: Create a new resource semaphore.
2. *DestroyRS*: Destroy the resource semaphore.
3. *Request*: Request some elements of a resource semaphore.
4. *Release*: Release some elements of a resource semaphore.

Following a description of these operations, we present several examples of their use and consider their implementation efficiency.

A process requesting resources issues the command *Request(RS, data,*

ans), where *RS* is the name of the resource class—the resource semaphore—
ans points to a memory area for storing the results of a satisfied request—
i.e., the description of the particular allocation—and *data* specifies the details
of the request. Processes can be blocked only by their own actions (self-
blocks) and *only* through this operation. Blocking occurs if the allocator for
the resource semaphore can not or will not satisfy the request immediately.
The strategy within *Request* is to insert the process on the waiting list, *Waitrs*,
associated with *RS* and then call the allocator; this insures that the allocator
need only examine its inventory and waiting list in either a *Request* or a
Release, without distinguishing between the two kinds of calls if it wishes.
The allocator returns a list of 0 or more processes (Sec. 7.1.2). All processes
on this list, with the exception of the one calling *Request*, are set to *readya* or
readys and inserted on the ready list, *RL*, by *Request*. If the request of the
calling process * is not satisfied, * is set to *blockeda* status and the processor
is made available. The process scheduler is always called at the end of the
Request to determine any new processor allocations; this is perhaps too general for some situations where the request can be immediately satisfied, but
the implementation price is not too high, and the system has the additional
flexibility of making new scheduling decisions at that time.

```
procedure Request(RS, data, ans) ;
begin
    r := GetInternalNameRS(RS) ;
    Insert(Waitrs[r], (*, ans, data)) ;
    Allocator(r, k, L) ;
    self := true ;
    for j := 1 step 1 until k do
    if L[j] ≠ * then
    begin
        i := L[j] ; Insert(RL, i) ; Sdata[i] := RL ;
        Status[i] := if Status[i] = 'blockeda' then 'readya' else 'readys'
    end
    else self := false ;
    if self then begin Status[*] := 'blockeda' ;
                       Sdata[*] := Waitrs[r] ;
                       Process[Processor[*]] := Ω
                 end;
    Scheduler
end Request
```

When the allocator assigns resources to a waiting process, it stores the allocation information in *ans*; if the resource is serially reusable, the allocation is
also stored in the resource list of the process descriptor. The first is needed so

that the requesting process can identify the resource, while the latter record is necessary for resource sharing, process removal, and record-keeping.

If a process no longer requires a previously obtained serially reusable resource or if it wishes to add units of a consumable resource to the inventory, it does so by means of the *Release* primitive. The call is *Release*(*RS*, *data*), where *RS* is the resource semaphore and *data* defines the specifics of the freed resource; *data* would contain the same type of information as the *ans* parameter of *Request*. *Release* adds the *data* to the resource inventory and calls the allocator, which tries to satisfy outstanding requests of blocked processes. If allocations are made, the relevant processes are awakened and the scheduler is called.

```
procedure Release(RS, data) ;
begin
    r := GetInternalNameRS(RS) ;
    Insert(Avail[r], data) ;
    Allocator(r, k, L) ;
    for j := 1 step 1 until k do
    begin
        i := L[j] ; Insert(RL, i) ; Sdata[i] := RL ;
        Status[i] := if Status[i] = 'blockeds' then 'readys' else 'readya'
    end;
    if k ≠ 0 then Scheduler
end Release
```

Process status can thus be changed as a result of the *Request*/*Release* operations or any of the process primitives. Figure 7-4 summarizes the possible status changes and the operations causing these changes.

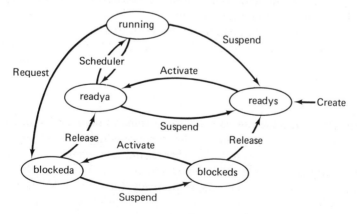

Fig. 7-4   Process status changes.

CreateRS and *DestroyRS* are concerned with dynamically establishing and removing, respectively, resource descriptors from the system. (We implicitly assume that a storage area exists for all process and resource descriptors.) Most of the hardware resources are "created" at systems generation and at systems load time, while the other resources are created dynamically by systems and users' processes. *CreateRS* requires the initialization and definition of both the inventory and waiting lists, the specification of insertion and removal routines for these lists, and the definition of the allocator for the resource. The calling sequence is

$$CreateRS(RS, sr, avail, waitrs, allocator, otherinfo);$$

where

> *RS* is the external name of the resource semaphore,
> *sr* indicates whether *n* is serially reusable,
> *avail* and *waitrs* are pointers to the inventory and waiting queue headers (Table 7-3), respectively, with appropriate initializations assumed within the queues,
> *allocator* is the allocation routine entry point, and
> *otherinfo* points to an arbitrary list of additional desired fields in the descriptor.

The internal details will not be specified. We only note that an entry is also made in the resource part of the creator's process descriptor which identifies the process as the creator of the resource.

As in the process case, a resource can be destroyed only by its creator or by an ancestor of the creator. The destroy primitive has the call *DestroyRS* *(RS)*, where *RS* is the external name of the resource semaphore. *DestroyRS* removes the resource descriptor from the system and wakes up (changes from blocked to ready status and inserts on the *RL* list), with an appropriate message, all processes waiting on the resource.

Request and *Release* can handle all the resource and synchronization situations that we have encountered. The most variable part of their internal structure lies in the allocator routine. The following examples illustrate some common applications:

1. *Dijkstra Semaphores*

Request and *Release* can be made isomorphic to the *P* and *V* operations, respectively. For a semaphore *S*, the corresponding calls are defined as *Request*(S, Ω, Ω) and *Release*(S, Ω), where Ω indicates undefined parameters. The inventory is the value of *S*; *Insert* and *Remove* for the availability list merely increments and decrements, respectively, the value of *S*. The allocator determines if an allocation is possible by comparing the length of the waiting list with *S*. *P* and *V* can be generalized to request and release any positive number of units; i.e., *Request*(*S*, *n*, Ω); and *Release*(*S*, *n*), $n \geq 1$; in this case, the allocator is more complicated (see Exercise).

2. *Message Passing*

Let us assume that a message producer sends messages to particular named processes and message consumers (receivers) can request messages from known processes. Then a message *m* may be transmitted to a process *p* by the call

$$Release(M, (p, m)) \; ;$$

where *M* is the message resource semaphore. A receiver requests a message from a process *p* by issuing

$$Request(M, p, m) \; ;$$

where *m* is a data area that will contain the message.

The allocator matches messages to receivers. Other possibilities, for example, where the receiver does not specify the sending process, can also be easily implemented.

3. *Main Storage Allocation*

For allocation and freeing of contiguous variable-length blocks of main storage, the calls might be

$$Request(MAINSTORE, NUMBEROFWORDS, BASEADDRESS) \; ;$$

and

$$Release(MAINSTORE, (BASEADDRESS, NUMBEROFWORDS)) \; ;$$

The allocator and data structure may be one of those discussed in Chapter 5.

4. *Input and Output Buffers*

Let *IFB*, *OFB*, and *EM* be resource semaphores associated with input-full, output-full, and empty buffers, respectively, in a buffer pool. The operations for *IFB*'s, say, may be

$$Request(IFB, \Omega, current) \; ;$$

and

$$Release(IFB, current) \; ;$$

where *current* is a buffer index in the pool, used as an output parameter of *Request* and input parameter of *Release*.

With such a general set of primitives, it is appropriate to examine the questions of efficiency and implementation. To maintain our convention that a process can logically block only as a result of the *Request* primitive, the operations are protected by a common busy wait lock—the same lock is used for all primitives that reference the system descriptors. The critical sections must not only be short, but there must also be a centralized control and responsibility for the allocators and list manipulation routines to assure their correctness and efficiency. This can be accomplished by maintaining a systems library of tested routines and data structures that may be referenced by users when resources are created. Weiderman (1971) has compared assembly and higher-level language implementations of similar *Request* and *Release* operations and common allocators and data structures, with Brinch Hansen's message-passing operations and the IBM OS/360 primitives (Sec. 3.6); execution times were within the same order of magnitude. Again, in this section, details of error checking and analysis have been omitted. The process tree structure and access conventions simplify this problem considerably. However, more extensive error tests would generally be required to validate and enforce restrictions on resource requests; for example, it would be desirable in many instances to limit the amount of a resource (for example, storage) that a particular process can request, or even forbid certain processes access to some resources. (We pursue these issues in the next section.)

Our final remarks relate to noncritical and delayed requests. A process might wish more units of a resource immediately *if* it were available, but otherwise it could, and may want to, continue processing; similarly, a process may wish to enter a request that need not be satisfied immediately. The first case can be handled by specifying a pair $(0, n)$ in the data field of the request; the allocator is then designed to allocate 0 units (always possible) if n units are not available. The simplest implementation of the second type of request is to send a message to another process which requests the resource in the normal fashion and releases an answer back to the original process when the resource has been allocated.

EXERCISE

(a) Implement P and V with *Request* and *Release* operations, respectively; in particular, define the data structures of the appropriate lists, the *Insert* and *Remove* routines, and the allocator.

(b) Repeat (a) for the generalized P and V described at the end of the first example of this section.

7.2.3 Capabilities

In order to prevent a process from adversely affecting itself, other processes, and the systems resources, some protection mechanisms are required. These can be formulated as process *capabilities*—the actions that a process can and cannot do to itself and other entities in the system. (See also Sec. 5.3 for a discussion of real and virtual memory protection.)

The nucleus described in the preceding sections includes a rudimentary capability scheme, governed by the process tree structure. A process can *only* *Suspend*, *Activate*, *ChangePriority*, and *Destroy* its progeny or their descendants. Similarly, a process can only give a subset of its resources to its progeny, and can only destroy, using *DestroyRS*, those resource semaphores that it or its descendants have created. We did not state any restrictions on the use of *Request* and *Release*, but it would appear consistent with our other conventions to permit a process to invoke these primitives *only* on resource semaphores created by it or its ancestors. Unfortunately, this strategy would give the greatest *Request/Release* capabilities to the lowest-level processes in the tree hierarchy, while the other capabilities were greatest at the higher levels.

A more consistent and powerful capability scheme is obtained by explicitly specifying which resources may be *Requested* and *Released* by each process. We can easily insert this control within our nucleus by adding a new field, *Capability[i]*, to the descriptor for each process i. *Capability[i]* lists those resource semaphores that a process i may *Request* or *Release*, and is set according to the following rules:

1. The creator of a resource semaphore automatically receives *Request/Release* capability for it.

2. When creating a progeny, a process may share any subset of its capability with the new process.

This protection method can be completely implemented in software. More elaborate capabilities, such as those described at the end of Sec. 5.3, require special hardware for a practical realization.

When a capability violation occurs, some action must be taken. One could simply destroy the erring process (and all of its descendants), but this seems too drastic. A more satisfactory approach is to transfer control to an error routine or process supplied by either the current process or the operating system; the error then has the same effect as an internal interrupt or trap. (Interrupt handling is discussed in the next section.) A second reasonable possibility is to return an error indicator directly to the process; the erring process can then take whatever action it wishes. This last strategy was selected for one implementation of the nucleus (Shaw, et al., 1973), primarily because of its simplicity.

7.3. INTERRUPTS AND INPUT-OUTPUT PROCESSES

The previous sections treated process and resource control for internal CPU processes. The present aim is to examine processes associated with input-output operations and to see how hardware interrupts, notably those originating from IO and timers, can be smoothly interfaced with the process and resource structures.

Our strategy is to define for each IO device D—i.e., for each peripheral auxiliary storage unit—an IO process p_D which controls the operation of that device. Process p_D receives IO requests, invokes the appropriate allocators or schedulers for channels and controllers, initiates IO operations, handles general transmission errors, decodes interrupts, and sends completion messages back to the requesting process. The lowest-level IO "instruction" consists of a message-reply sequence directed at the selected p_D and can take the general form

$$Release(Dio, ioprogr) ;$$
$$Request(Dioend, \Omega, completionmessage) ;$$

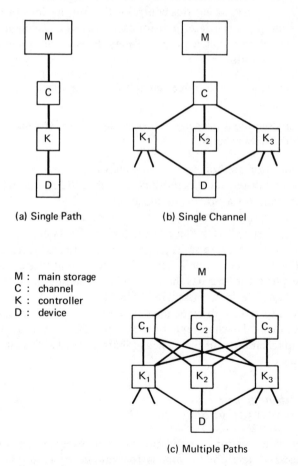

(a) Single Path   (b) Single Channel

M : main storage
C : channel
K : controller
D : device

(c) Multiple Paths

Fig. 7-5   Path(s) from memory to an IO device D

Dio is a resource semaphore corresponding to messages directed to p_D while the *Dioend* semaphore is associated with replies from p_D. The parameter *ioprogr* specifies the nature of the request—read, write, control, or some sequence of the latter. *ioprogr* could directly contain channel command or controller orders, possibly with parameterized channel or controller addresses if these may be variable; or it could be at a higher level containing, for example, only storage device addresses and the number of units to be transmitted. In general, for each device and system, a different set of *ioprogr* conventions would be established. The final results of the IO request would be returned in *completionmessage*; this would typically contain the number of units of information actually transmitted and whether any errors occurred during the operation.

More than one physical "path" between a device and storage unit may be possible, depending on the hardware connections (Fig. 7-5).† In the general case depicted in Fig. 7-5(c), a channel and controller must be assigned to establish such a path. The process p_D will, of course, vary for each device, but a typical organization might be

p_D: **begin**
      L : *Request(Dio, Ω, (p, ioprogr))* ;
          Request(PATH, D, path) ;
          Generate IO instructions from path and ioprogr ;
          Initiate IO ;
          Request(IOint, path, message) ;
          Decode interrupt ; *Possible further IO operations* :
          Produce completion message ;
          Release(PATH, path) ;
          Release(Dioend, (p, completionmessage)) ;
          go to *L*
      end

p designates the process which issued the IO request through *Dio*. The resource allocator for *PATH* allocates a channel and controller to p_D, thus defining the physical transmission path for the operation. The "further IO operations" may be necessary because the original request generates several IO sequences—for example, a disk seek followed by a read—or because of certain IO errors where the system attempts to correctly execute the IO instructions several more times before signalling the machine operator. *IOint* is associated with IO interrupts. The above algorithm assumes that only one interrupt occurs as the result of each IO initiation. This is true in some cases, but there are other common possibilities. In general, an interrupt signal may

---

†Some multiprocessing systems also have channel controllers to permit processors to connect to different channels.

result from the completion of *each* of the channel, controller, and device activities. The three signals could be produced, for example, by a rewind magnetic tape operation; two signals, one for channel completion and the other for controller/device end, are often produced for card and printer peripherals. Rather than requesting and releasing a PATH, individual *Requests* and *Releases* for each path component, i.e., channel and controller, might be issued.

All interrupt handlers are treated uniformly in this model. Their main function is to translate hardware signals into software messages. Abstractly, we view each interrupt handler IH_i as a cyclic process that waits for an interrupt, determines the internal process p_S responsible for servicing this interrupt, and *Releases* an appropriate message to p_S. To implement this idea, the handler first saves the state of the interrupted process *, changes *'s status from *running* to *readya*, and sets the processor descriptor element *Process* [*Processor*[*]], to Ω:

IH_i: *SaveStatein(CPUstate*[*])*; *Status*[*] := 'readya' ;
         Process [*Processor*[*]] := Ω ;
         Determine service process p_S ;
         Release(InterruptClass, (p_S, interruptdetails)) ;

When the *Scheduler* is called within the *Release* in IH_i, it may either reactivate the interrupted process or give the CPU to a process that changed from *blockeda* to *readya* as a result of the *Release*. Interrupts are inhibited during IH_i, since system descriptors are being modified.

For IO interrupts, the interrupt class might be the resource semaphore, *IOint*, and p_S would correspond to the device process p_D responsible for initiating the IO. Internal interrupts due to program errors such as arithmetic overflow or storage addressing violations would send messages to the appropriate error process, which could ignore the error, terminate the process, or perhaps correct the error after dispatching an error message. Timer interrupts may result, for example, in terminating a process—if it has exceeded its total allotted time—putting a process at the end of a ready list—if its time quantum has expired in a time-sharing system—or waking up some process—if the process has requested a wakeup signal at some specific time.

Example

Suppose that at a timer interrupt the running process p must relinquish the CPU to the highest-priority ready process q such that $Priority[q] \geq Priority[p]$, if such a q exists. The *Release* in the timer interrupt handler could then simply be

$Release(TIMEOUT, (p_T, *))$;

The timer process p_T associated with this interrupt could have the form

p_T: **begin**
    L: *Request*(*TIMEOUT*, Ω, p) ;
        ChangePriority(p, *Priority*[p]) ;
        go to L
    end

It is assumed that p_T has a higher priority than p in order that p_T quickly receive a CPU. The *ChangePriority* operation effectively places p at the end of the list of ready processes at *Priority*[p]. p_T could achieve the same effect without using *ChangePriority* by *Suspend*-ing the running process and *Activate*-ing the highest-priority ready one. p_T is essentially a time-driven process scheduler in this example. Other instances of the use of timers and their relationship with the scheduling mechanisms are examined in the next section.

7.4. ORGANIZATION OF PROCESS SCHEDULERS

The *process scheduler* or *dispatcher* is that part of an operating system responsible for allocating processing units to ready processes. This section is concerned primarily with the *organization* of schedulers as opposed to particular dispatching *strategies*. It is often desirable, for example, to employ different strategies for processes associated with batch jobs than for those generated by interactive users, for system processes than for user ones, or for processes dealing directly with IO than for purely internal activities. With a general priority mechanism and the careful use of timers, a uniform organization can be designed to handle a broad spectrum of such strategies.

As described earlier, there are a number of places where a scheduler must be invoked in a general multiprocessor MS. Basically, whenever a process blocks, is awakened (i.e., made ready), or has its priority changed (in a preemptive system), a new processor allocation is possible; any change in the number of processors would also result in a dispatcher call. One particularly important source of block and wakeup signals that permits close control over scheduling is an *interval timer*, which will trigger an interrupt after an arbitrary user-defined time interval.

It is imperative to establish and enforce limits on the continuous running time of each process—in order to prevent some processes from monopolizing the system, to guarantee reasonable response to users, to react to time-dependent events, and to recover from some types of program errors. For this purpose, the dispatcher can set a timer just prior to transferring control to a selected process; alternatively, a process p_T, signalled as a result of the timer interrupt, can assume responsibility for setting the timer. In both cases, a critical question is: To what value t should the timer be set? The use of p_T is feasible if t is constant over all ready processes, for example, in a simple time-sharing system with a single quantum. However, a more flexible policy is to assign different quanta to different classes of processes on a dynamic basis, reflecting, for example, their importance, their immediate past behavior, and the current load on the system. This can be accomplished by associating a time interval Δt_p with each process p on the ready list (Saltzer, 1966); when the scheduler selects a process p from the ready list, it can then reset the timer to Δt_p. The scheduler itself may remain simple and need not be concerned with evaluating and changing these time intervals. A system process that is awakened at specified time intervals can perform the latter tasks. Some form of *fixed time list* (Lampson, 1968), similar in principle to those used in simulation programs, is convenient for the administration of such time-dependent activities.

There are other applications in which a process will block itself with a request to be awakened at some specific time in the future. One example is in the systems measurement area when it is desired to "sample" the load characteristics of an MS periodically. Another occurs in time-sharing when some type of communication—perhaps a trivial one—to an on-line user is guaranteed within a given time. Applications programs are often run on a periodic basis on many large commercial systems; for example, a program (process) might be run (awakened) once a day to produce an inventory or sales summary. These kinds of time-dependent tasks can be handled by maintaining a list of processes blocked on the *time* "resource" and ordered by wakeup time. Within our nucleus framework, a resource named *TIME* may be defined. A process can request a wakeup signal at some future time by a call

$$Request(TIME, t, \Omega) \ ;$$

where t is a time interval or, perhaps, an absolute time. A high priority time process can be awakened periodically† to execute the operation

$$Release(TIME, currenttime) \ ;$$

The allocator for the *TIME* resource will control the fixed time list—i.e., the list of blocked processes waiting on *TIME*—and wake up any waiting processes with *wakeuptime* $\leq$ *currenttime*.

The above discussion illustrates the close relationship between scheduling and the time resource. This is certainly also the case for other critical resources, especially main storage. Some demand paging systems, for example,

---

†It may be convenient to do this whenever a timer interrupt occurs, whenever a new job is loaded, or, generally, whenever some event that is known to occur regularly with a reasonable frequency is triggered.

set limits on the number of processes eligible for execution, or the number of pages currently being queued for IO, or the availability of working set storage space (Alexander, 1970). Supervisory processes that oversee the current allocation and demands normally perform this task.

7.4.1 Master and Shared Schedulers

A process scheduler can be shared by processes in the system in the same manner that the nucleus developed in this chapter is shared—i.e., the scheduler is invoked by a subroutine call as an indirect result of a nucleus operation. The nucleus and scheduler are then potentially contained in the address space of all processes and execute within any process. A second method is to centralize the scheduler (and possibly the nucleus). Conceptually, this type of scheduler is considered a separate process running on its own processor; it can continuously poll the system for work, or it may be driven by wakeup signals. The master and shared alternatives are illustrated in Fig. 7-6.

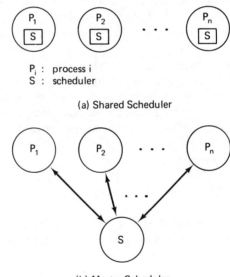

P_i : process i
S : scheduler

(a) Shared Scheduler

Fig. 7-6 (b) Master Scheduler

The master organization has been used successfully in multiprocessor systems where one processor is permanently dedicated to scheduling, nucleus, and other supervisory activities, such as spooling and loading. The operating system is then cleanly separated from user jobs, at least in principle. This scheme is employed in the CDC 6400/6600 SCOPE operating system (CDC, 1971) and, to some extent, in the IBM 360 "attached support" ASP systems. Even if a single processor is not dedicated to parts of the operating system, the master approach is still possible in uni- and multiprocessor configurations.

A logical difficulty, however, arises in these situations—namely, who dispatches the scheduler process? One solution is to transfer control to the scheduler whenever a process blocks or is awakened; the scheduler then exists above, or at a higher level, than the remaining processes.

Lampson (1968) suggested another possibility for the master case which seems particularly attractive within current technology. A small fast processor is dedicated to a microprogrammed scheduler, which continuously polls a number of input lines for signals from other processors and from external IO sources. Each signal normally represents a wakeup message, accompanied by the name and priority of the process to be awakened. The functions of the scheduler are to change the status of the process to ready (if not presently ready or running), insert it in a ready list, and transmit a processor "switch" signal if there exists a running process of lower priority.

The shared approach was selected in our nucleus model for the following reasons. Because the nucleus components are automatically included in every process, they are independent of the number of available processors and need not be permanently associated with any particular one. The view that the nucleus really defines a set of machine operations necessary to transform a standard computer into an operating systems machine naturally leads to such a shared organization. A final point, advocated by the MULTICS designers who employ this method, is that different processes may in principle have different types of operating systems controlling them; for example, a variety of schedulers may coexist simultaneously, each one attached to a different set of processes. When the nucleus code is pure and single-copy shared, the difference between the shared organization and the master one with non-dedicated processors is more a difference of points of view and less one of implementation strategy.

7.4.2 Priority Scheduling

A general and relatively complex priority scheduler is presented first. Following this, we discuss a number of simplifications that may be made in common practical situations.

Assume that the scheduler, a module or subroutine named *Scheduler*, is called only within the nucleus primitives of this chapter, i.e., within *Suspend*, *Activate*, *Destroy*, *ChangePriority*, *Request*, and *Release*. The ready list *RL* is structured on a priority basis as in Fig. 7-3 and contains all processes p such that $Status[p] \in \{running, readya, readys\}$. A *preemption* dispatching policy is used. That is, the scheduler ensures that, at all times, the priority of any *running* process is greater or equal to that of any *readya* process. Figure 7-7 illustrates a global view of the *Scheduler* and its relation to the system data structures and other primitives.

The tasks of the *Scheduler* can be succinctly defined. At any time, let S_r

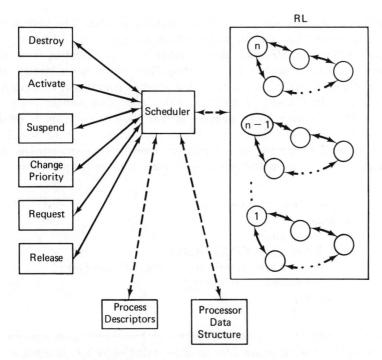

Fig. 7-7 Global view of scheduler with respect to systems data structures and nucleus primitives.

be the set of running processes and S_{ar} be the set of *readya* and *running* processes in the system. Define S_a as the set of processes that *should* be running at a given time. S_a is the largest subset of S_{ar} with the properties

$$|S_a| = np \text{ (number of processors)},†$$

and for all $p \in S_a$ and $q \in (S_{ar} - S_a)$, $p \neq q$,

1. *Priority*[p] $\geq$ *Priority*[q].
2. If *Priority*[p] $=$ *Priority*[q] then p precedes q in the *RL*.

The *Scheduler* guarantees that $S_a = S_r$ by allocating all members of $S_a - S_a \cap S_r$ to processors—to preempted processors of all members of $S_r - S_r \cap S_a$ and to inactive processors when $|S_r| < np$.

An implementation, however, requires some care. One source of difficulty lies with the process, designated *, within which the *Scheduler* is called. If * is being blocked—as a result of issuing a *Request*—or if * is preempted from

---

†Recall from Sec. 7.1.2 that there exists an "idle" process for each processor; the priority of an idle process is less than that of any "worker" process.

its processor, it is necessary to defer the transfer of control to some other process until *all* other allocations have been accomplished; otherwise, the *Scheduler* will not be able to complete the latter, since it is executing in the processor of *. When a processor *c*, including *Processor*[*] is reallocated, the state of *c* must be saved in the process descriptor component *CPUstate*[ ]. This can be a little tricky in the * case; the instruction counter stored in *CPUstate*[*] must point to an instruction that allows * to properly return from the *Scheduler* (and therefore exit from the nucleus, since the *Scheduler* is only invoked at the end of a primitive) upon its later resumption. We accomplish a switch from process *p* to *q* on processor *c* by the procedure

> **procedure** *Switch*(*p*, *q*, *c*) ;
> **begin**
>   *Interrupt*(*c*) ;
>   *StoreState*(*c*, *CPUstate*[*p*]) ;
>   **if** *p* = * **then** *StoreInstrCntr*(*RA*, *CPUstate*[*p*]) ;
>   *LoadState*(*c*, *CPUstate*[*q*])
> **end** *Switch*

Interrupt(*c*) interrupts processor *c* if *Processor*[*] $\neq$ *c*; otherwise, it is treated as a "no-op." *RA* is the return address of the caller of *Switch*. In addition to transferring control to the new process, *LoadState* may also set an interval timer. The details of *Switch* will, of course, be highly dependent on the particular computer characteristics.

In order to simplify the description of the *RL* manipulations in *Scheduler*, the forward pointer of each process entry *p* will also be designated by *fqp*[*p*]. The priority numbers *n*, *n* − 1, . . . , 1 are assumed distinct from the process numbers to avoid conflicts. The general *Scheduler* is given below. The global flow is

1. Get the highest priority *readya* process *p*.

2. If there are inactive processors, allocate *p* to one and go to step 1.

3. Try to preempt a running process. If successful, go to step 1.

Special processing for * is performed at the end of the algorithm.

> **procedure** *Scheduler* ;
> **begin**
>   *p* := Π := *n*; *cpu* := 1 ;
>   **comment** Find highest priority 'readya' process ;
>   *Nextreadya* :
>   *b* := **true** ;

```
while b ∧ Π ≠ 0 do
begin
  p := fqp[p] ;
  if p = Π then Π := Π − 1
  else b := Status[p] ≠ 'readya'
end ;
if Π = 0 then go to Wrapup* ;
comment Look for an inactive processor for p ;
while cpu ≤ np do
if Process[cpu] ≠ Ω then cpu := cpu + 1
else
begin
  Process[cpu] := p ; Processor[p] := cpu ;
  Status[p] := 'running' ;
  if cpu ≠ Processor[*] then Loadstate(cpu, CPUstate[p])
  else p* := p ;
  cpu := cpu + 1 ;
  go to Nextreadya
end ;
comment All processors are allocated. Try for a preemption.
        Is there a running process with priority < Priority[p] ;
Πmin := Π;
for c := 1 step 1 until np do
begin
  q := Process[c] ;
  if Priority[q] < Πmin then
  begin Πmin := Priority[q] ; cp := c end
end ;
if Π ≠ Πmin then
begin
comment Perform a preemption on processor cp ;
  q := Process[cp] ; Status[q] := 'readya' ;
  Processor[p] := cp ; Process[cp] := p ; Status[p] := 'running' ;
  if q = * then p* := p else Switch(q, p, cp) ;
  go to Nextreadya
end ;
comment Final fixup of calling process * ;
Wrapup* :
  if Status[*] ≠ 'running' then Switch(*, p*, Processor[*])
end Scheduler
```

The scheduler, while manageable, can nevertheless be considerably simplified if some of the underlying assumptions are relaxed. Consider first the

elimination of preemption. The scheduler then need not be called on a *ChangePriority* operation and about half of the code (and time) is eliminated. The very common situation in which only a single central processor is available ($np = 1$) leads to a much less complex scheduling algorithm. In this case, *Suspend* would never invoke the *Scheduler* and, at most, one process switch could occur. Another possibility is to limit allocators so that at most *one* process is ever taken off a blocked list (awakened) at any time. Various combinations of the above are also widely used.

EXERCISES

1. Give a complete *Scheduler* for each case when the following restrictions are imposed on the system:
   (a) Processes are never directly preempted from their processors.
   (b) $np = 1$ (uniprocessing system).
   (c) A *Release* operation wakes up at most one process.
   (d) Restrictions (a), (b) and (c) combined.

2. Consider a system with a separate processor dedicated entirely to the scheduling of other processors. Let the *Scheduler* poll the other processors for work on a cyclic basis. Assume that the *Scheduler* is invoked indirectly through our nucleus primitives. However, instead of a subroutine call, a special processor register, say R_i for the ith processor, is first set by the primitive and then, in a separate operation, a busy loop on R_i is executed until it is reset by the *Scheduler*. Give an algorithm for a general priority *Scheduler* with preemption in this type of computer system.

7.5. SCHEDULING METHODS

A number of common scheduling strategies are presented within the framework of our nucleus. After a discussion of the preemption issue and two basic scheduling methods, criteria for statically and dynamically determining priorities are considered.

Preemption, Nonpreemption, and Selective Preemption

The last section defined a uniform preemption scheduler based on process priorities. Preemption in this manner is one way of assuring that "important" processes—for example, those responsible for acquiring and disposing of real-time signals—quickly receive a processor when they are active and ready. (A less general approach, applicable to interrupt-driven high-priority processes, is to implicitly initiate the preemption through hardware interrupts by directly transferring control to the higher priority process associated with the interrupt.) Often, however, a more economical nonpreemptive policy may be adequate. Preemption costs include process switching times and the additional logic in the scheduler; preemption can also lead to other inefficiencies, such as swapping data or programs to auxiliary storage. Between these two extremes lies another set of possibilities, which we label *selective preemption*.

One such "selective" policy would assign a bit pair, say (u_p, v_p), to each process p with the interpretation:

$$u_p = \begin{cases} 1 & \text{if } p \text{ may preempt another process} \\ 0 & \text{otherwise.} \end{cases}$$

$$v_p = \begin{cases} 1 & \text{if } p \text{ may be preempted by some other process} \\ 0 & \text{otherwise.} \end{cases}$$

Thus u_p defines the preemptive capability of a process and v_p is really a running priority. (u_p, v_p) would be another component of the process state vector, used in an obvious way by the scheduler. Proceeding in the direction of even more generality, the priority of a process p may be changed to a pair (Π_p, ρ_p) where Π_p represents the ready status priority of p and ρ_p is the priority of p when it is running. Some control is then possible over the preemption power of one process relative to another. Finally, a universal, and probably impractical, scheme requires a preemption matrix with entries (i, j) indicating whether or not process i can preempt process j. Many of the above affects, however, can be obtained through the judicious use of the *Suspend* and *ChangePriority* operations by high priority "controlling" processes, in conjunction with the preemption mechanisms presented earlier.

FIFO and Round-Robin Scheduling

A FIFO strategy would dispatch processes according to their arrival time on the ready list *RL*—the earlier the arrival, the higher the scheduling priority. This can be easily implemented in our nucleus by restricting all processes to the same priority. The *Insert* routine for *RL* merely places the argument process at the end of the single-priority queue. While the entire process set in an MS is rarely treated on a FIFO basis, it is certainly the most common—and, in the absence of other information, rational—policy for administrating a ready list queue within *each* priority.

An important variation of the FIFO method is a *round-robin* discipline wherein processes are dispatched according to the FIFO rule but a fixed limit, *quantum*, or *time-slice t* is imposed on the amount of *continuous* processor time that may be used by any process. If a given process has run for *t* continuous time units, it is preempted from its processor and placed at the end of the *RL*; the processor is allocated to the next (first) process on the *RL*, again for at most *t* time units. The time interval *t* may be constant over long periods of time, or it may vary with the process load. If the time *T* for one complete round robin of all active processes is kept constant, then *t* can be computed dynamically every T seconds by using $t = T/n$, where n is the number of active processes on RL. The example at the end of Sec. 7.3 implements a round-robin policy if all processes, except p_T, have the same priority. Methods based on the round-robin scheme are used by most time-sharing systems for handling "interactive" processes—i.e., processes that directly or indirectly communicate with interactive terminals.

The normal scheduling disciplines in medium- and large-scale MS involve the use of many different priorities (also called priority levels). How and when these priorities are selected are important policy decisions.

Static Priorities

In the static case, the process priority remains fixed at the value assigned at process creation time. A wide variety of criteria and methods have been employed to determine priority values. One popular technique, used in batch multiprogrammed systems, is to *externally* generate the priority value. User jobs are submitted at a given priority level, and the processes subsequently spawned by each job are each given the job priority. A cost, based on a resource charging algorithm, is usually associated with each level; the user selects that priority for his job which will give him adequate service (response) at a price he can afford. For example, a job at priority Π could be charge $\$f_1(\Pi)$/sec for processor time, $\$f_2(\Pi)$/word/sec for main storage, $\$f_3(\Pi)$/card for input, and $\$f_4(\Pi)$/line for output. Systems processes are assigned fixed priorities by the designers and/or installation management.

More satisfactory results are obtained if the static priority is based on the characteristics of user jobs and processes, including perhaps an external priority; these characteristics are declared by the user. Two example and priority policies are

1. *Running Time*

An appealing philosophy adopted by many installations is that the shorter the job, the better its service should be. We give two arguments leading to this philosophy. The first is that users will not be satisfied unless they receive fast service for short jobs; otherwise, if possible, they will take their business elsewhere.† The second reason derives from a theoretical consideration. If each job is processed sequentially to completion (no multiprogramming), average job completion time is minimized by dispatching jobs in a shortest-job-first order (see exercise). Thus, one suspects that in a more complicated multiprogramming environment including interacting processes, average

---

†Supermarkets have long recognized this elementary fact by providing special checkout counters for customers with few items.

turnaround time will be minimized by giving the shortest jobs the highest priorities.

2. *Type of a Process*

A job or process is classified in terms of its relative IO and CPU requirements and the urgency of fast response—for example, a batch or interactive job, a background or foreground process in a real-time system, or a CPU-bound or IO-bound job. Often, the highest (CPU) priorities are assigned to processes with heavy IO needs; at the same time, the IO requested by CPU-bound processes is given a high priority. This policy provides good response to interactive and real-time users and also maintains a high degree of overlap between IO and central processing.

Dynamic Priorities

Both response and machine efficiency can be controlled more precisely when the priority of a process can be changed during its existence; this feature has been especially valuable in time-sharing systems. The criteria for selecting new priorities have been similar to those used in the static case, but more often based on measurements of process behavior rather than *a priori* declarations. Most of the dynamic schemes are designed to move interactive and IO-bound processes to the top of the priority queues and to let CPU-bound processes drift to the lower priorities. Within each level, entries are serviced on a FIFO or round-robin basis. The degree of IO activity can be measured directly by counting the number of times a process *Requests* an IO operation over a given period of time. Alternatively, the priority will directly reflect the IO frequency if a process's priority level is automatically increased after an IO *Request* (provided, of course, that the priority is not already sufficiently high).

The almost classic example of the above type of dynamic method is the multilevel technique used originally in the CTSS time-sharing system (Corbato, et al., 1962). At each priority level Π, there is a corresponding time T_Π, which is the maximum amount of processor time any process may receive at that level; if a process exceeds T_Π, its priority is decreased to $\Pi - 1$. A satisfactory scheme—basically the one used in CTSS—is to let $T_\Pi = 2^{n-\Pi} \times t_n$, where t_n is the maximum time on the highest-priority queue; t_n is a multiple of the basic quantum or time slice. Many present systems employ a similar algorithm. Typically, a process is moved to the highest level when it is awakened because of an IO completion.

Many other variations exist. A given set of processes may be restricted to a range of priorities. A process might also be automatically assigned a higher priority if it has been waiting on the *RL* without receiving service for an excessive amount of time. More detailed treatments of scheduling methods may be found in Coffman and Kleinrock (1968) and Alexander (1970).

EXERCISE

Given a set of independent sequential processes $\{p_1, \ldots, p_n\}$ with corresponding running times $\{t_1, \ldots, t_n\}$, prove that the *average* process completion time is minimized by running them sequentially in a shortest process first order; i.e., for all $i, j, i \neq j$, p_i is run before p_j if $t_i < t_j$. Assume that only one processor is available and that the processes do not interact.

8 THE DEADLOCK PROBLEM

The notion of deadlock was informally introduced in the buffer pooling example of Sec. 2.4.4; the unrestricted competition for empty buffers lead to the undesirable state wherein all processes capable of releasing empty buffers were blocked on this same resource. When some processes are blocked on resource requests that can *never* be satisfied unless *drastic* systems action is taken, the processes are said to be *deadlocked*. This condition normally occurs because the producers of the requested resources are themselves blocked on the same resources. The "drastic" systems action referred to above may consist of involuntary preemption of resources or liquidation of processes.

Why are deadlock studies important? The problem was certainly considered in the design of many present systems, but it has received significant attention in only a few. Deadlock has not been of major concern because in most MS, parallel programming and process interaction facilities are restricted to systems processes only—and even then often on a limited basis—and because resources are allocated statically to user processes at creation time. However, dynamic resource sharing, parallel programming, and communicating processes are expected to be operating characteristics of many medium- and large-scale systems of the future at all levels of systems and user programs. The deadlock possibilities will increase accordingly. The problem can also be critical in a number of real-time applications, such as computer control of vehicles or monitoring and control of life-supporting systems, e.g., during human surgery. There are other reasons why we should examine deadlock in some detail. The work in this area represents one of the few successful examples of a theoretical and realistic treatment of some aspect of operating systems, and gives some idea about the possible form of a theory of operating systems. Finally, deadlock studies attempt to partially answer one of the most fundamental questions in computer science: Can a process progress to completion?

This chapter contains a relatively formal treatment of the deadlock problem, *based primarily on the research and model of R. C. Holt (1971b, 1972)*.† Following some examples and definitions, deadlock detection, prevention, and recovery are discussed with respect to both conventional (serially reusable) and message-like (consumable) resources.

8.1. EXAMPLES OF DEADLOCK IN COMPUTER SYSTEMS

Examples of different types of deadlocks that can arise with serially reusable (SR) and consumable (CR) resources are presented. The purpose is to illustrate the variety of situations in which deadlock is possible and to motivate the following formal model.

1. *File Sharing*

Suppose processes p_1 and p_2 both update the file D and require a scratch tape during the updating. Let T be the only tape drive available for scratch purposes. Assume further that p_2 needs a scratch tape immediately prior to the updating for some other reason, for example, to reorganize the input data for the update. Let D and T be SR resources representing permission to update the file and permission to use the tape drive, respectively. Then p_1 and p_2 may have the following forms:

p_1:	p_2:
Request(D) ;‡	*Request(T)* ;
r_1: *Request(T)* ;	r_2: *Request(D)* ;
Release(T) ;	*Release(D)* ;
Release(D) ;	*Release(T)* ;

†Some earlier studies are surveyed in the paper of Coffman, et al. (1971). Dijkstra (1965a, 1968b) was one of the first and most influential contributors in the deadlock area.

‡A process is blocked on a *Request* until the resource is allocated; *Release* returns the resource to the system.

It is possible for p_1 and p_2 to reach r_1 and r_2, respectively, at the same "time"; for example, p_2 first gets T, then p_1 gets D, then p_1 is at r_1, and finally p_2 reaches r_2, in a purely sequential manner. The two processes will become deadlocked immediately after this point. Process p_1 will block on T holding D while p_2 blocks on D holding T; p_1 can not proceed unless p_2 proceeds, and vice versa, and the processes are locked in a "deadly embrace." Figure 8-1(a)

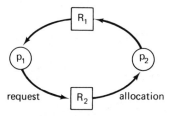

(a) Simple Example of Deadlock

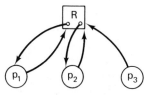

Fig. 8-1 Deadlock with SR resources.   (b) Single Resource Sharing

graphically portrays the deadlock condition. Boxes denote resources, and circles represent processes. An arrow (directed edge) from a resource to a process indicates an allocation, while an arrow from a process to a resource is a request. Substitute D for R_1 and T for R_2. (Note that this example would be even more realistic if T were another data file; p_1 and p_2 are then requesting the same data files but in the opposite order.)

2. *Single Resource Sharing*

A single SR resource R, such as main or auxiliary storage, contains m allocation units and is shared by n processes $p_1, \ldots, p_n$, $2 \leq m \leq n$. Let each process use elements of R in the sequence

$$Request(R);\ Request(R);\ Release(R);\ Release(R);$$

where each *Request* and *Release* is for one unit of R. Then a deadlock can easily result when *all* units are allocated; all processes holding units of R could be forever blocked on their second *Request*, while some processes could be similarly blocked on their first *Request*. Such a system state is illustrated in Fig. 8-1(b) for the case $n = 3$ and $m = 2$. This type of deadlock is relatively common. For example, it may arise in a spooling subsystem in which several input and output processes compete for auxiliary storage space; if the space becomes completely allocated to (a) input files of jobs waiting to be loaded and (b) output records of partially executed jobs, the system deadlocks.

3. *Static Resource Allocation for Jobs and Job Steps*

Consider a batch MS that allocates storage statically (at process creation time) for processes corresponding to jobs and job steps. Suppose a two-step job J_1 requires a data file D for the entire job, a magnetic tape T_1 for its first step, and a tape T_2 for the last step; T_1 might be a 7-track tape, while T_2 could be a 9-track tape. Let there also exist a one-step job J_2 that uses both D and T_2 for its execution. D, T_1, and T_2 are considered SR resources. The job controller processes p_1 and p_2 associated with J_1 and J_2 may appear as follows:

p_1:   *Request*(T_1) ; p_2:   *Request*(T_2) ;
           Request(D) ; r_2:   *Request*(D) ;
           Execute Step 1;   *Execute Step* 1;
           Release(T_1) ;   *Release*(T_2) ;
r_1:   *Request*(T_2) ;   *Release*(D) ;
           Execute Step 2;
           Release(T_2) ;   .
           Release(D) ;   .
                                                      .
                   .
                   .
                   .

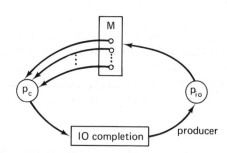

(a) SR and CR Resource Sharing

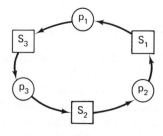

(b) Message Passing

Fig. 8-2   Deadlock with CR resources.

If p_1 and p_2 reach r_1 and r_2 at the same "time," we have the deadlock situation of Fig. 8-1(a) again. (Substitute D for R_1 and T_2 for R_2.) Thus, allocating resources in an arbitrary order, say in the order they are specified on job control cards, can be very dangerous. The original allocation philosophy of the IBM OS/360 system was similarly unrestricted until these dangers were recognized (Havender, 1968).

4. SR and CR Resources

A compute process p_c communicates with an IO process p_{io}. Assume that the run time of p_c is inversely proportional to the amount of storage space that it can acquire dynamically; for example, p_c may be a complex list processing task. Consequently, p_c requests all available storage blocks from the system, say by the operation "$Request(M, all)$;". The IO process, however, occasionally requires a storage block for buffering purposes, which it acquires through a "$Request(M)$;". The two processes p_c and p_{io} might be synchronized as follows:

p_c: $Request(M, all)$; p_{io}: $Request(IOrequest)$;

      $Release(IOrequest)$;   .

r_c: $Request(IOcompletion)$; r_{io}: $Request(M)$;

      .   .

      .   .

      .   .

      $Release(M, all)$; $Perform\ IO$;
                                 $Release(IOcompletion)$;

                                  .

                                  .

The two processes will *always* deadlock at the *Request*s at r_c and r_{io}. The compute process p_c can not acquire an "IO completion" signal until p_{io} receives its buffer, but the system has no memory to allocate to p_{io} until p_c receives its "IO completion" and subsequently releases M. The deadlock state is shown in Fig. 8-2(a); for CR resources (*IOcompletion* and *IOrequest*), an arrow is directed from the resource to the producer. (The producer "*owns*" an unlimited number of units of the resource.)

5. Message Passing

Let process p_1 produce messages S_1, p_2 produce messages S_2, and p_3 produce messages S_3; S_1, S_2, and S_3 are CR resources. Suppose that p_1 receives messages from p_3, p_2 from p_1, and p_3 from p_2. If the message communication for each process occurs in the order:

$$p_i: \ldots Release(S_i) \ ; \ Request(S_j) \ ; \ldots$$

where for $i = 1, 2, 3, j = 3, 1, 2$, respectively, then no difficulties arise. However, reversing the two operations causes deadlock [Fig. 8-2(b)]:

$$p_1: \ldots Request(S_3) \; ; \; Release(S_1) \; ; \ldots$$
$$p_2: \ldots Request(S_1) \; ; \; Release(S_2) \; ; \ldots$$
$$p_3: \ldots Request(S_2) \; ; \; Release(S_3) \; ; \ldots$$

6. An Extreme Example in PL/I

Holt (1971b) gave the following program to illustrate how easily a user can deadlock a process:

```
REVENGE: PROCEDURE OPTIONS(MAIN, TASK) ;
         WAIT(EVENT) ;
         END REVENGE ;
```

The "$WAIT(EVENT)$" is equivalent to "$Request(EVENT)$" in our notation. The $EVENT$ never occurs and $REVENGE$ blocks forever, theoretically.

7. Effective Deadlock (Holt, 1971a)

Suppose that a system allots 200K of main storage to user jobs and that a job will require either 100K or 200K for its duration. Assume that two 100K jobs are loaded initially and that the job queue *always* contains some 100K jobs. Then, if a new job is selected for loading immediately after a job completion and storage availability is used as the selection criterion, a 200K job will *never* be run. It is possible to prevent this without "drastic" action by delaying the allocation to 100K jobs if a 200K one has been waiting for a sufficiently long time. This kind of situation in which a scheduler or allocator can prevent a process from going to completion even though it is logically possible to do so has been called "effective deadlock" by Holt. Effective deadlock could also occur, for example, in a system that gives highest priority to short jobs and keeps long (heavy compute) jobs waiting until all short jobs are completed. This type of deadlock will be ignored in the rest of the chapter.

As illustrated by the examples, deadlock involves the interaction of potentially many processes and resources; therefore, it must be treated as a global systems problem. The deadlock problem can be divided into three principal parts:

1. *Detection.* Given a system of processes sharing resources and communicating with one another, how can it be determined if some subset of them is deadlocked? One clue obtained from the first five examples above is the existence of a cycle (a directed path from a node to itself) in the process-resource graphs.

2. *Recovery.* What are the "best" ways to recover from deadlock?

"Drastic" systems action is necessary, but we want to disrupt the operation as little as possible.

3. *Prevention.* How can deadlock be avoided in the first place? The input spooler of Sec. 3.4.3 contained a simple technique for preventing deadlock on one particular resource. Changing the order of *Requests* and *Releases* in Examples 1 and 5 makes deadlock impossible. We are interested in some general prevention techniques. Examples 1 to 6 consist of simple sequential code with *no* conditional branching; consequently, there is a fixed sequence of resource operations for each process which can be determined easily by inspection. However, in the general (and still practical) case, the best that one could do would be to enumerate all the "paths" through the code; one of these paths might lead to deadlock, in combination with other processes, but it is impossible to know *a priori* for an arbitrary process whether a particular path will in fact ever be taken. [This is the famous halting problem in disguise (e.g., see Minsky, 1967).]

It is interesting to note that one can find examples of deadlock in other systems in addition to computing systems, such as transportation systems and ecological systems. The same three problems are present—prevention, detection, and recovery—regardless of the domain.

EXERCISE

List some examples of deadlock in other types of systems in addition to computing systems.

8.2. A SYSTEMS MODEL

For the model of this chapter, the state of an operating system will represent the allocation status of the various resources in the system (free or allocated). The system state is changed by processes when they request, acquire, and release resources; these will be the *only* possible actions by processes. If a process is not *blocked* in a given system state, it may change that state to a new one. However, because it is generally impossible (undecidable) to know *a priori* which path an arbitrary process may take through its code, the new state may be any one of a finite number of possibilities; processes are therefore modeled as nondeterministic entities. The above notions lead to the following formal definitions:

1. A *system* is a pair $\langle \sigma, \pi \rangle$ where σ is a set of *systems states* $\{S, T, U, V, \ldots\}$ and π is a set of *processes* $\{p_1, p_2, \ldots\}$.

2. A *process* p_i is a partial function from systems states into nonempty

subsets of systems states; this is denoted

$$p_i : \sigma \longrightarrow \{\sigma\}$$

If p_i is defined for state S, then the range of p_i is designated as $p_i(S)$. If $T \in p_i(S)$, then we say that p_i can change the state from S to T by an *operation* and use the notation $S \xrightarrow{\ i\ } T$. Finally, the notation $S \xrightarrow{\ *\ } W$ means that

(a) $S = W$, or

(b) $S \xrightarrow{\ i\ } W$ for some p_i or

(c) $S \xrightarrow{\ i\ } T$ for some p_i and T, and $T \xrightarrow{\ *\ } W$.

In other words, the system can be changed by 0 or more operations by 0 or more different processes from state S to state W.

Example

Define a system $\langle \sigma, \pi \rangle$ with $\sigma = \{S, T, U, V\}, \pi = \{p_1, p_2\}, p_1(S) = \{T, U\}, p_1(T) = \Omega, p_1(U) = \{V\}, p_2(S) = \{U\}, p_2(T) = \{S, V\}, p_2(U) = \Omega, p_1(V) = \{U\}$, and $p_2(V) = \Omega$, where Ω indicates undefined. Figure 8-3(a) represents this system.

Some sequences of state changes are

$$S \xrightarrow{\ 1\ } U, T \xrightarrow{\ 2\ } V, S \xrightarrow{\ *\ } V \ (\text{e.g.}, S \xrightarrow{\ 1\ } T \xrightarrow{\ 2\ } V \text{ or } S \xrightarrow{\ 2\ } U \xrightarrow{\ 1\ } V).$$

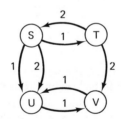

(a) System with Deadlock States

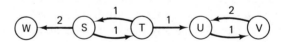

(b) System with Deadlock and Safe States

Fig. 8-3 Examples of systems.

A process is blocked in a given state if it cannot change state; i.e., the process can neither request, acquire, or release resources in that state.

3. A process p_i is *blocked* in state S if there exists no T such that $S \xrightarrow{i} T$.

A process is deadlocked in a given state S if it is blocked in S and if no matter what operations (state changes) occur in the future, the process remains blocked.

4. A process p_i is *deadlocked* in state S if for all T such that $S \xrightarrow{*} T$, p_i is blocked in T.

In Fig. 8-3(a), p_2 is deadlocked in both U and V, while p_1 is blocked but not deadlocked in T; thus, for the latter case, $T \xrightarrow{2} V$ and $T \xrightarrow{2} S$, and p_1 is not blocked in either V or S.

5. S is called a *deadlock state* if there exists a process p_i deadlocked in S. Deadlock is prevented, by definition, by restricting a system so that each possible state is not a deadlock state.

6. A state S is a *safe state* if for all T such that $S \xrightarrow{*} T$, T is not a deadlock state.

The system of Fig. 8-3(b), where $\sigma = \{S, T, U, V, W\}$ and $\Pi = \{p_1, p_2\}$, has both deadlock and safe states. U and V are safe; S, T, and W are not safe (why?); and W is a deadlock state.

Example

Consider the first example of the last section ("File Sharing") and assume that p_1 and p_2 are cyclic processes. If we sequentially scan through the code of p_1 and p_2, the following *process* states can be easily derived:

States for p_1	States for p_2
0. Holds no resources	0. Holds no resources
1. Requested D, holds no resources	1. Requested T, holds no resources
2. Holds D	2. Holds T
3. Requested T, holds D	3. Requested D, holds T
4. Holds T, holds D	4. Holds D, holds T
5. Holds D (after release of T)	5. Holds T (after release of D)

Let the *system* state where p_1 is in process state i and p_2 is in state j be S_{ij}. Then, the system can be represented by the diagram of Fig. 8-4. State changes (operations) by process 1 are graphed horizontally, while those by process 2 appear vertically. Processes p_1 and p_2 are deadlocked in $S_{3,3}$; p_1 is blocked but not deadlocked in $S_{1,4}$, $S_{3,2}$, and $S_{3,5}$; p_2 is blocked but not deadlocked in $S_{2,3}$, $S_{4,1}$, and $S_{5,3}$.

With this model of a system, we next examine the components of a sys-

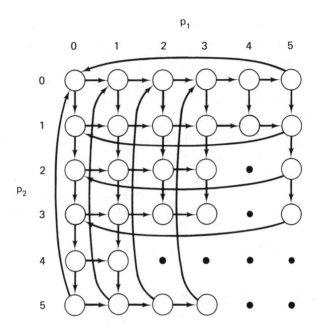

Fig. 8-4   System state changes in file sharing example.

tems state, the operations for changing state, and the deadlock problem, when the resources are SR only.

EXERCISES

1. Using the definitions of this section, prove that "S is not a deadlock state" does *not* imply that "S is a safe state." Safeness and deadlock are not complementary.

2. (Holt, 1971a) Let two processes p_1 and p_2 share a resource R containing two identical units. Each process can be in one of the following states:

   0. Holds no resources.

   1. Requested 1 unit of R, holds no resources.

   2. Holds 1 unit of R.

   3. Holds 1 unit of R, requested 1 unit.

   4. Holds 2 units.

   Each process can change from state 0 to 1 by a request, from 1 to 2 by an acquisition of a unit of R, from 2 to 3 by a request, from 3 to 4 by an acquisition, from 4 to 2 by releasing one unit, and from 2 to 0 by releasing one unit; these are the only state changes possible. Let the system state be S_{ij}, where i is the state of p_1 and j is that of p_2. Derive a state diagram for this system similar to Fig. 8-4. In what state(s), if any, is the system deadlocked and/or blocked?

8.3. DEADLOCK WITH SERIALLY REUSABLE RESOURCES

A *serially reusable* resource (SR) is a finite set of identical units with the properties:

1. The number of units is constant.

2. Each unit is either available, or allocated to one and only one process (no sharing).

3. A process may release a unit (make it available) only if it has previously acquired that unit.

The definition abstracts those essential features of conventional resources necessary for our deadlock studies; in particular, it is not necessary to identify each unit of such a resource explicitly. Examples of SR resources are hardware components such as main storage, auxiliary storage, peripherals, and perhaps processors, and software such as data files, tables, and "permission to enter a critical section."

8.3.1 Reusable Resource Graphs

The state of an operating system is represented by a process-resource graph, called a *reusable resource* graph in the SR case. A *directed graph* is defined as a pair $\langle N, E \rangle$ where N is a set of *nodes* and E is a set of ordered pairs (a, b), $a, b \in N$, called *edges*. A reusable resource graph is a directed graph with the following interpretation and restrictions:

1. N is divided into two mutually exclusive subsets, a set of process nodes $\pi = \{p_1, p_2, \ldots, p_n\}$ and a set of resource nodes $\rho = \{R_1, R_2, \ldots, R_m\}$. Each resource node $R_i \in \rho$ denotes an SR resource.

2. The graph is "bipartite" with respect to π and ρ. Each edge $e \in E$ is directed between a node of π and a node of ρ. If $e = (p_i, R_j)$, then e is a *request* edge and is interpreted as a request by p_i for 1 unit of R_j. If $e = (R_j, p_i)$, then e is an *assignment* edge and indicates an allocation of 1 unit of R_j to p_i.

3. For each resource $R_i \in \rho$, there is a nonnegative integer t_i denoting the number of units of R_i.

4. Let $|(a, b)|$ be the number of edges directed from node a to node b. Then the system must always work within the limits:
(a) No more than t_i assignments (allocations) may be made for R_i, i.e., $\sum_j |(R_i, p_j)| \leq t_i$, for all i.
(b) The sum of the requests and allocations of any process for a particular

resource cannot exceed the available units, i.e., $|(R_i, p_j)| + |(p_j, R_i)| \leq t_i$ for all i and j.

Examples

1. Figure 8-1(a) of the last section is a reusable resource graph.

$$\rho = \{R_1, R_2\}; \qquad \pi = \{p_1, p_2\}; \qquad N = \rho \cup \pi; \qquad t_1 = t_2 = 1;$$
$$E = \{(p_1, R_2), (R_2, p_2), (p_2, R_1), (R_1, p_1)\}.$$

2. Example 2 of the last section is represented by the graph of Fig. 8-1(b).

$$\rho = \{R\}; \qquad t = 2; \qquad \Pi = \{p_1, p_2, p_3\};$$
$$E = \{(p_i, R) | i = 1, 2, 3\} \cup \{(R, p_1), (R, p_2)\}.$$

The systems state is changed to a new state only as a result of requests, releases, or acquisitions of resources by a single process.

1. *Request.* If a system is in state S and process p_i has *no* requests outstanding (no request edges), then p_i may *request* any number of resources, including any number of units of a particular resource, subject to the limitations of restriction 4 above. The system then enters state T, say $(S \xrightarrow{i} T)$. T differs from S only in the additional request edges from p_i to the requested resources.

2. *Acquisition.* A system can change from state S to state T by an *acquisition* operation by p_i $(S \xrightarrow{i} T)$ if and only if p_i has outstanding requests and *all* such requests can be satisfied; i.e., for *all* resources R_j such that $(p_i, R_j) \in E$, we have

$$|(p_i, R_j)| + \sum_k |(R_j, p_k)| \leq t_j.$$

The graph of T is identical to S, except that all request edges (p_i, R_j) of p_i are reversed to (R_j, p_i) to reflect the allocations.

3. *Release.* p_i can cause a state change from S to T by a *release* operation if and only if p_i has *no* requests and some allocations; i.e., if there exist no edges (p_i, R_j) for any j and there exist some edges (R_j, p_i) for some j in the reusable resource graph of state S. p_i may release *any* nonempty subset of its resources in this operation. The resulting state graph is identical to that of state S, except that some acquisition edges of p_i have been deleted; each unit of R_j released has its corresponding edge (R_j, p_i) deleted.

Figure 8-5 illustrates these operations for a system with one resource (3 units) and two processes.

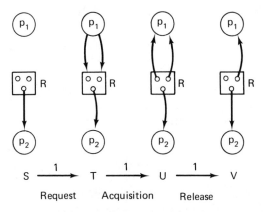

Fig. 8-5   Process operations.

Note that processes are nondeterministic; subject to the above restrictions, *any* operation by *any* process is possible at *any* time. Unless execution time traces are available or processes are restricted in their operations and resources; this nondeterministic feature is necessary, because there is no way of knowing precisely which resource a process will request or release at any time. Also in a multiprogramming environment, there is no general way of knowing *a priori* which process is allocated a given resource at any time, and which process is running on the CPU and therefore able to effect a state change. After treating the general case, we examine the effects of restricting some of the process operations and resources.

8.3.2   Deadlock Detection

To detect a deadlock state, it is necessary to determine whether each process *can* ever progress again. (It *may* be *possible* for a process to perform an operation in some present or future state, but this does *not* assure us that the process *will* in fact ever move again; a resource allocator or process scheduler might prevent it from doing so, either deliberately or inadvertently. This effective deadlock was discussed in Example 7 of Sec. 8.1.) Because we are looking at the possibility of process progress rather than the certainty of it, it is sufficient to examine only the most "favorable" state changes. The strategy for detecting deadlock will be to simulate the most favorable execution of each unblocked process in a nonmultiprogrammed (sequential) mode as follows:

An unblocked process acquires any resources it needs, releases *all* of its resources, and remains dormant thereafter; the released resources may wake up some previously blocked processes. We continue in this fashion until there are no remaining unblocked processes. If there are some blocked processes at the termination of this execution sequence, the original state S is then a deadlock state, and the remaining processes are deadlocked in S; otherwise, S is not a deadlock state.

We now formally develop and prove these notions.

A process p_i is blocked if it is unable to perform any of the three operations defined in the last section. This can only arise if p_i has outstanding requests that exceed the available resources; i.e., there must exist at least one resource R_j such that

$$|(p_i, R_j)| + \sum_k |(R_j, p_k)| > t_j.$$

The most favorable operations for an unblocked process p_i can be represented by a *reduction* of the reusable resource graph:

1. A reusable resource graph is *reduced* by a process p_i, which is neither blocked nor an isolated node, by removing all edges to and from p_i. This is equivalent to p_i's acquiring any resources for which it has pending requests and then releasing all of its resources; p_i then becomes an isolated node.

2. A reusable resource graph is *irreducible* if the graph cannot be reduced by any process.

3. A reusable resource graph is *completely reducible* if there exists a sequence of reductions that deletes *all* edges of the graph.

Figure 8-6 illustrates a sequence of reductions; the graph in state S is completely reducible, since $S \xrightarrow{*} U$ and U contains no edges. Note that p_2 is blocked in S on R_1 but becomes unblocked after the reduction by p_1.

For SR resources, the order of reductions is immaterial; all sequences lead to the same irreducible graph. This is proven in the following lemma:

LEMMA 1

All reduction sequences of a given reusable resource graph lead to the *same* irreducible graph.

Proof: Assume that the lemma is false. Therefore, there must exist some state S that is reduced to an irreducible state T_1 by reduction sequence seq_1 and to an irreducible state T_2 by seq_2, such that $T_1 \neq T_2$ (i.e., all processes in T_1 and T_2 are either blocked or isolated). We shall now derive a contradiction whose only resolution is that $T_1 = T_2$. Suppose seq_1 consists of the ordered list of processes $(q_1, q_2, \ldots, q_k)$. Now seq_1 must contain a process q that is not contained in seq_2; if not, $T_1 = T_2$, because a reduction only deletes edges already present in state S and if seq_1 and seq_2 contain the same process set (in a different order), exactly the same set of edges must be deleted. An

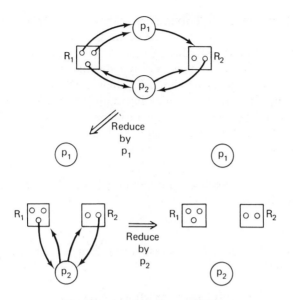

Fig. 8-6 A sequence of reductions.

inductive proof will now show that $q \neq q_i, i = 1, 2, \ldots, k$, resulting in our contradiction:

1. $q \neq q_1$, since S can be reduced by q_1 and seq_2 must therefore also contain q_1. (Why?)

2. Let $q \neq q_i, i = 1, 2, \ldots, j$. But, since a reduction by q_{j+1} is possible after reduction by $q_i, i = 1, \ldots, j$, the same must be true for seq_2 regardless of the ordering or intervening processes; the same set of edges is deleted by the q_i. Thus $q \neq q_{j+1}$.

Therefore, $q \neq q_i$ for $i = 1, 2, \ldots, k$ and q cannot exist, contradicting the assumption that $T_1 \neq T_2$. Therefore, $T_1 = T_2$.

A simple necessary and sufficient condition for deadlock exists and will be proven with the aid of Lemma 1.

Deadlock Theorem

THEOREM 1

S is a deadlock state if and only if the reusable resource graph of S is *not* completely reducible.

Proof: (a) Suppose that S is a deadlock state and process p_i is deadlocked in S. Then, for all T such that $S \xrightarrow{*} T$, p_i is blocked in T. Since the graph reductions are identical to a series of process operations, then the final irreducible state of a reduction sequence must leave p_i blocked. Therefore, the graph is not completely reducible.

(b)   Suppose that S is not completely reducible. Then there exists a process p_i that remains blocked on all possible reduction sequences by Lemma 1. Since any reduction sequence terminating in an irreducible state assures that all SR resources that can ever possibly be made available are in fact released (why?), p_i is blocked forever and therefore deadlocked.

COROLLARY 1.1

A process p_i is not deadlocked if and only if a series of reductions leaves a state in which p_i is not blocked.

COROLLARY 1.2

If S is a deadlock state (on SR resources), then at least two processes are deadlocked in S.

The proofs of the corollaries are left as exercises.

The Deadlock Theorem directly yields algorithms for detection. One simply attempts to reduce the graph in an efficient manner; if the graph is not completely reducible, the original state was a deadlock state. Lemma 1 permits the reductions to be ordered in any convenient way. A reusable resource graph can be represented by either matrices or lists; in both cases, storage is conserved by compressing several acquisition edges or request edges between a particular resource and a given process into a single edge and an associated *weight* giving the number of units:

1. *Matrix Representation*
The graph is represented by two $n \times m$ matrices:
(a) An *allocation* matrix A, where entry A_{ij}, $i = 1, \ldots, n$, $j = 1, \ldots, m$ gives the number of units of resource R_j allocated to process p_i; i.e.,

$$A_{ij} = |(R_j, p_i)|.$$

(b) A *request* matrix B, where $B_{ij} = |(p_i, R_j)|$.

2. *Linked List Structure*
The resources *allocated* to any process p_i are linked to p_i:

$$p_i \longrightarrow (R_x, a_x) \longrightarrow (R_y, a_y) \longrightarrow \cdots \longrightarrow (R_z, a_z),$$

where R_j is a resource node and a_j is the weight; i.e., $a_j = |(R_j, p_i)|$. Similarly, the resources *requested* by a process p_i are linked together. Analogous lists are used for resources. The allocations of a resource R_i form a list:

$$R_i \longrightarrow (p_u, b_u) \longrightarrow (p_v, b_v) \longrightarrow \cdots \longrightarrow (p_w, b_w),$$

where $b_j = |(p_j, R_i)|$; a similar list contains the requests of R_i.

For both representations, it is also convenient to maintain an *available units* vector $(r_1, \ldots, r_m)$, where r_i gives the number of available (unallocated) units of R_i, i.e.,

$$r_i = t_i - \sum_k |(R_i, p_k)|,$$

A straightforward detection method is to loop through the process request lists (or matrices) in order, making reductions where possible, until no more reductions can be made. The worst-case situation occurs when the processes are ordered $p_1, \ldots, p_n$ but the only possible order of reductions is $p_n, \ldots, p_1$; and when every process is requesting all m resources. Then, the number of process inspections is $n + (n - 1) + \cdots + 1 = n(n + 1)/2$, each inspection requiring the examination of m resources; thus, the worst-case execution time is proportional to mn^2.

A more efficient algorithm can be obtained at the expense of maintaining some additional information about requests. A *wait count* w_i is defined for each process node p_i, consisting of the number of resources (not resource units) that cause the process to be blocked at any time; we also keep the request for each resource ordered by size. Then, the following reduction algorithm has maximum execution time proportional to mn:

$$L := \{p_i \mid w_i = 0\} ;$$
for all $p \in L$ **do**
begin
    for all $R_j \ni |(R_j, p)| > 0$ **do**
    begin
        $r_j := r_j + |(R_j, p)| ;$
        for all $p_i \ni 0 < |(p_i, R_j)| \le r_j$ **do**
        begin
            $w_i := w_i - 1 ;$
            if $w_i = 0$ **then** $L := L \cup \{p_i\}$
        end
    end
end ;
$$Deadlock := \neg(L = \{p_1, \ldots, p_n\}) ;$$

L is the current list of processes that can perform a graph reduction. The program selects a process p from L, reduces the graph by p by incrementing the available units r_j of all resources R_j allocated to p, updates the wait count w_i of each process p_i that can have its request satisfied for a particular resource R_j, and adds p_i to L if the wait count becomes zero.

The graph structure provides a simple necessary, but not sufficient, condition for deadlock. For any graph $G = \langle N, E \rangle$ and node $a \in N$, let $P(a)$ be the set of nodes "reachable" from a, i.e.,

$$P(a) = \{b \,|\, (a, b) \in E\} \cup \{c \,|\, (b, c) \in E \wedge b \in P(a)\}.$$

Then, G has a *cycle* if there exists some node $a \in N$ such that $a \in P(a)$.

THEOREM 2

A cycle in a reusable resource graph is a necessary condition for deadlock.

Proof: See Exercise 3.

The Deadlock Theorem and cycle Theorem 2 are the most general statements one can make about deadlock detection when no restrictions are made on the use of the SR resources. The deadlock test can be accomplished more efficiently, however, if it is done on a *continuous* basis. The following theorem provides the basis for continuous detection.

THEOREM 3

If S is not a deadlock state and $S \xrightarrow{i} T$, then T is a deadlock state if and only if the operation by p_i is a request and p_i is deadlocked in T.

Proof: The proof is left as an exercise.

The implication of Theorem 3 is that a deadlock can be caused only by a request that cannot be granted immediately. In terms of continuous deadlock detection by graph reductions, this means that one need only apply reductions after a request by some p_i and that, at any stage, one should attempt to reduce by p_i first; if p_i can be reduced, no further reductions are necessary.

Special Cases

Restrictions on the allocators, the number of resources requested simultaneously, and the resource units lead to simpler conditions for deadlock. For some of these special cases, another graph theoretic concept is useful:

A *knot* in a directed graph $\langle N, E \rangle$ is a subset of nodes $M \subseteq N$ such that for all $a \in M$, $P(a) = M$.

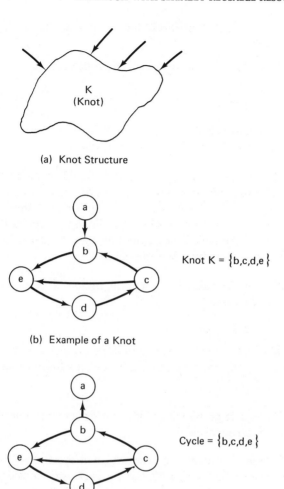

(a) Knot Structure

Knot K = $\{b,c,d,e\}$

(b) Example of a Knot

Cycle = $\{b,c,d,e\}$

(c) A Cycle but not a Knot

Fig. 8-7 Illustration of knots.

That is, every node in a knot is reachable from every other node in the knot and a knot is a maximal subset with this property. Figure 8-7 illustrates this idea. Note that a cycle is a necessary but not sufficient condition for a knot.

1. *Immediate Allocations*

If the system state is such that all satisfiable requests have been granted, a simple sufficient condition for deadlock exists. This situation occurs if resource allocators do not defer satisfiable requests but grant them immediately when possible; most allocators follow this policy. The resulting states are called "expedient":

An *expedient* state is one in which all processes having requests are blocked.

THEOREM 4

If a system state is expedient, then a knot in the corresponding reusable resource graph is a sufficient condition for deadlock.

Proof: Suppose the graph contains a knot K. Then all processes in the knot must be blocked *only* on resources in K, since no edges may be directed out of K by definition. Similarly, all allocated units of resources in K are held by processes in K for the same reason. Finally, all processes in K must be blocked because of the expediency condition and the definition of a knot. Hence, all processes in K must be deadlocked.

A knot detection algorithm is given at the end of this section in the discussion of single unit requests.

2. *Single-unit Resources*

Assume that each resource has one unit, i.e., $t_i = 1, i = 1, \ldots, m$. With this restriction, a cycle also becomes a sufficient condition for deadlock.

THEOREM 5

A reusable resource graph with single unit resources is a deadlock state if and only if it contains a cycle.

Proof: Theorem 2 proves the necessity of a cycle. For the sufficiency proof, let us assume that graph contains a cycle and consider only those processes and resources on the cycle. Since each such process node must have an entering and exiting edge, it must have an outstanding request for some resource in the cycle and must hold some resources in the cycle; similarly, every (single unit) resource in the cycle must be held by some process in the cycle. Therefore, every process in the cycle is blocked on a resource in the cycle that can be made available only by a process in the cycle. Hence, the processes in the cycle are deadlocked.

To detect deadlock in the single unit resource case, we have merely to test the reusable resource graph for cycles. Let a *sink* be any node that does not have edges directed from it. One efficient cycle detection algorithm is based on the successive deletion of edges directed into sinks; if the resulting graph contains only sinks, then no cycle was present in the original.

Let $w_i = \sum_k |(i, k)|$, the number of edges directed from node i.

Cycle Detection for graph $\langle N, E \rangle$:

$S := \{i \,|\, node\ i\ is\ a\ sink\}$;
for all $i \in S$ **do**
begin
   for all $j \ni (j, i)$ *is an edge* **do**
   begin
     $w_j := w_j - 1$;
     if $w_j = 0$ **then** $S = S \cup \{j\}$
   end
end ;
$Cycle := \neg(S = N)$;

Execution time is proportional to the number of edges in the graph which, in the worst case, is *mn*.

For continuous detection, we can take advantage of Theorem 3. Then it is necessary only to test whether the requesting process p_i is on a cycle. This can be accomplished by tracing all paths starting with p_i, looking for the reappearance of p_i.

Single-unit resources are not uncommon in present systems; for example, the *ENQ/DEQ* macros of IBM OS/360 (see Sec. 3.6) deal exclusively with resources of this type.

3. *Single-unit Requests*

Assume that a process may request only one unit at a time; that is, at most one request edge can be connected to any process node. Then, for expedient states, a knot also becomes a necessary condition for deadlock.

THEOREM 6

A reusable resource graph with single-unit requests in an expedient state is a deadlock state if and only if it contains a knot.

Proof: By Theorem 4, it is required only to prove the necessity of a knot. Assume that the graph does not contain a knot; we shall show that for any process node p_i, there exists a sequence of reductions involving p_i. Consider any process node p_i which is not an isolated node. (The latter can clearly be ignored.) Since there is no knot in the graph, p_i is either (a) a sink or (b) on a path leading to a process node that is a sink. The sink node in (b) cannot be a resource, since the state is expedient. (Why?) In case (a), a reduction by p_i is obviously possible. For case (b), let the processes on the path be $p_i, p_j, p_k, \ldots, p_x$, where p_x is the sink node. The graph may be reduced by processes $p_x, \ldots, p_k, p_j, p_i$ in that order; a simple inductive argument based on single-unit requests will establish this fact. Therefore, a reduction by an arbitrary process p_i can always be made eventually, and by Lemma 1, the graph is completely reducible.

Knot detection can be accomplished in a similar but simpler manner than cycle detection. A count variable w_i is not necessary for any node i connected to a sink because, regardless of the number of edges directed from i, node i cannot be part of a knot. The algorithm for a graph $\langle N, E \rangle$ is

$$S := \{i \,|\, node\ i\ is\ a\ sink\} \;;$$
for all $i \in S$ **do**
   for all $j \ni (j, i)$ *is an edge* **do**
      if $j \notin S$ **then** $S := S \cup \{j\}$;
$$Knot := \neg(N = S) \;;$$

If continuous detection is desired, Theorem 3 can again be used. It is necessary only to test whether or not the requesting process p_i is on a knot. We can do so by tracing all paths from p_i, looking for a sink.

EXERCISES

1. Prove Corollary 1.2 of Theorem 1.
2. Prove that the "efficient" deadlock detection algorithm using wait counts has maximum execution time proportional to mn.
3. Prove Theorem 2. (*Hint:* Use the following property of directed graphs: If a directed graph does not contain a cycle, then there exists a linear ordering of the nodes such that if there is a path from node i to node j then i appears before j in that ordering.)
4. Prove Theorem 3.
5. Prove, by counterexamples, that:
   (a) A cycle is not a sufficient condition for deadlock.
   (b) A knot is not a necessary condition for deadlock in expedient state graphs.
6. Prove that the successive deletion of edges directed into sinks will result in a graph containing only sink nodes if and only if the graph contains no cycles.
7. Describe an algorithm for continuous deadlock detection on a system with
   (a) Single-unit resources.
   (b) Single-unit requests.

8.3.3 Recovery from Deadlock

There are two general approaches for recovering from deadlock states. The first relies on process *terminations*. Deadlocked processes are successively terminated (destroyed) in some systematic order until enough resources become available to eliminate the deadlock; in the worst case, all but one of the originally deadlocked processes are liquidated. (Why?) The second approach is based on resource *preemption*. A sufficient number of resources are preempted from processes and given to deadlocked processes to break the deadlock; processes in the former set are left with outstanding requests for their preempted resources.

Perhaps the most practical and straightforward technique is a termination strategy that destroys lowest termination cost processes first. The termination "cost" of a process may be, for example:

1. The priority of the process.

2. The cost, according to the normal system accounting procedures, of restarting the process and running it to its current point.

3. A simple external cost based on the type of job associated with the process; e.g., student jobs, administrative jobs, production jobs, research jobs, and systems programming jobs may each have fixed termination costs.

The recovery algorithm would terminate the least expensive process by destroying the process and releasing its resources, and then reduce the graph as far as possible; these steps are repeated until the graph contains only isolated nodes. After recovery, the initial systems state is the original deadlock state with the terminated processes removed. This method has the virtue of simplicity but unfortunately also indiscriminately destroys those processes that have little effect on the deadlock.†

A more satisfying but less efficient termination scheme performs a minimum cost recovery. Let C_i be the cost of destroying process p_i. Then a minimum cost policy terminates a proper subset π' of the process set such that:

1. The termination of all members of π' eliminates the deadlock.

2. For all other subsets $\tilde{\pi} \subset \pi$ whose liquidation removes the deadlock condition,

$$\sum_{p_i \in \pi'} C_i \leq \sum_{p_i \in \tilde{\pi}} C_i.$$

The minimum cost for recovering from deadlock state S, $rcmin(S)$, satisfies the relation

$$rcmin(S) = \underset{\substack{\text{All } p_i \\ \text{deadlocked} \\ \text{in } S}}{minimum}(C_i + rcmin(U_i)),$$

where U_i is the state following S upon the termination of p_i. An algorithm

---

†We have ignored one important practical problem in this discussion: a process that is executing inside a critical section must, in general, be permitted to leave the critical section before it is terminated; otherwise, common data areas may be left in incorrect or "unstable" states.

for obtaining $rcmin(S)$ and the corresponding destroyed processes can be derived directly from the above relation. The algorithm systematically produces new states by process destruction until a nondeadlocked state appears. Let $d(T)$ be the set of processes destroyed to reach state T from the initial deadlock state S and let L be the list of new states produced from S, *ordered* by (partial) recovery costs. At the termination of the following algorithm, T is the initial minimum cost recovery state, $d(T)$ lists the terminated processes, and $rc(T)$ is the minimum recovery cost:

$$rc(S) := 0 \; ; L := \{ \} \; ; T := S \; ;$$
while *deadlocked*(T) **do**
begin
    for all p_i *deadlocked in T* **do**
    begin
        Terminate p_i to create state U_i from T ;
        $d(U_i) := d(T) \cup \{p_i\}$;
        $rc(U_i) := rc(T) + C_i$;
        Insertinrecoverycost(rc)order(U_i, L)
    end ;
    $T := firststatein(L)$;
    Remove(T, L)
end ;

The test for deadlock *deadlocked*(T) can be done by reducing the graph. Because the elements T in the list L are ordered by $rc(T)$ and examined in that order, the first nondeadlocked state is the minimum cost recovery state.

The "exhaustive search" nature of the minimum cost algorithm makes it impractically inefficient for complex deadlock situations. For example, if C_i is a constant, all m resources are single-unit resources, $n = m$, each resource R_i is assigned to p_i, and each p_i requests all resources except R_i, then the minimum cost deadlock recovery requires time and space proportional to at least $n!$. However, if the system is restricted to single unit requests, an efficient and more practical recovery method exists.

Assume that the system states are expedient and that requests may only be of the single unit type. Then, by Theorem 6, a minimum cost recovery need merely eliminate knots in the serially reusable resource graph in a minimal cost manner. To eliminate a knot, it is sufficient to delete all edges directed *from any* selected node in the knot, thus making the node a sink. This leads to the following algorithm:

1. Find all knots in the graph.
2. For each knot, select a resource node R_i such that for all $R_j \neq R_i$ in the knot,

$$\sum_{|(R_i, p_k)|>0} C_k \leq \sum_{|(R_j, p_k)|>0} C_k$$

3. Eliminate each knot by terminating all processes having allocations of the selected R_i; i.e., terminate all p_k such that $|(R_i, p_k)| > 0$.

One way to identify the knots in a graph (step 1 above) starts by making equivalence classes of all nodes in common cycles. All paths from a given node are systematically traced until the node repeats or the graph has been searched. In the former case, a cycle has been detected and all nodes in the cycle are replaced by a single node representing the equivalence class; edges entering or leaving any node in the cycle similarly enter or leave the equivalence class node. This process is repeated until no further cycles are found. The knots in the original graph then correspond to those equivalence classes that are sinks and contain at least two nodes. For a reusable resource graph with single unit requests, the knot identification and remainder of the algorithm have execution times proportional to $(n + m)^2$ in the worst case.

The two minimum-cost algorithms presented above could also be based on resource preemptions. A preemption cost may be associated with each unit of a resource. Instead of terminating deadlocked processes a minimum-cost set of resources is preempted to break the deadlock. When a resource is preempted by a process, the process receives an assignment of the resource, and the preempted process has its assignment changed to a request.

If deadlock detection is done on a continuous basis, then Theorem 3 offers a simple recovery technique. The deadlock can be removed by either terminating the requesting (deadlocked) process or by preempting resources and assigning them to the requesting process.

EXERCISES

1. Analyze the minimum-cost recovery algorithm, using process terminations for the case where C_i is a constant, all resources are single-unit type, $n = m$, and each process p_i holds one resource R_i and requests the remaining resources. Determine the time and space requirements.

2. Develop a minimum-cost recovery algorithm that uses resource preemption rather than process terminations.

3. Try to develop a general minimum-cost recovery algorithm based on the knot and cycle structure of the reusable resource graph.

8.3.4 Prevention Methods

Recall that a *safe* state was defined in Sec. 8.2 as one that cannot ever lead to deadlock. The general approach to deadlock prevention is to restrict the system so that all states are safe. For serially reusable resources, this can be accomplished trivially by permitting only one process at a time to hold resources; in practice, a policy of this type essentially produces a uniprogramming rather than multiprogramming operation, and can therefore be dismissed as impractical except in isolated situations.

A more practical restriction is to insist that every process request and acquire at *one* time the resources it may conceivably need; normally, this will be the first operation that a process performs. Processes with allocated resources will never be blocked because they cannot make any further requests, and will eventually release all of their resources, not necessarily at the same time. Thus a given process will either have assignments or requests, but never the two together. Deadlock is therefore impossible and every state is safe. From another point of view, it is impossible for the reusable resource graph to contain a cycle—a necessary condition for deadlock (Theorem 2 in Sec. 8.3.2). The principal disadvantages of such a policy are that resources will often be allocated long before they are actually used and that resources may be unnecessarily requested in anticipation of a possible use that does not materialize.

An *ordered resource* policy, originally devised by Havender (1968) for IBM OS/360, prevents deadlock with less drastic restrictions than the above "collective" request scheme. Reusable resources are divided into k classes, $K_1, K_2, \ldots, K_k$. A process is permitted to request resources from any class K_i *only* if it has no allocations from classes $K_i, K_{i+1}, \ldots, K_k$. (If $k = 1$, the last method and this method are identical.) It can be proved by induction on k that no state with the above restrictions can be deadlocked. The key part of the proof is that a request for the highest class K_k will always be honored eventually. This must be true, since no process with allocations from K_k can make any further requests until it releases its resources in K_k; thus all allocations from K_k are guaranteed to be released. Figure 8-8 illustrates a systems state within this policy.

Example

In IBM OS/360, job initiator processes obtain and release resources for a user job and each step within the job using an ordered resource strategy. $k =$

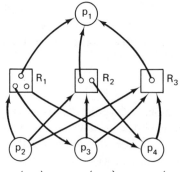

$$K_1 = \{ R_1 \} \quad K_2 = \{ R_2 \} \quad K_3 = \{ R_3 \}$$

Fig. 8-8 State using an ordered resource policy.

3 and the resource classes are:

$$K_1 = \{\text{data sets or files}\}, \quad K_2 = \{\text{main storage}\}, \quad \text{and} \quad K_3 = \{\text{IO devices}\}.$$

By assigning the most expensive or scarce resources to the highest classes, the requests of the most valuable resources can be deferred until they are actually needed. However, the same disadvantages of the first collective scheme are present here also; some resources must be allocated well in advance of their need.

Deadlock prevention is also possible in the important case where the *maximum claim* of all resources is known *a priori* for each process. The maximum claim for any process is the largest number of units of each resource that the process will need at one time. It can be represented as a claims matrix $c_{ij}, i = 1, \ldots, n, j = 1, \ldots, m$, where c_{ij} gives the maximum claim of process i for resource j. A system of this type has the following additional restriction on the serially reusable resource graph:

For each process p_i and resource R_j,

$$|(p_i, R_j)| + |(R_j, p_i)| \le c_{ij} \le t_j,$$

That is, the sum of the allocations and requests of any process cannot exceed its maximum claims.

The *claim graph* of a state S is defined as the serially reusable resource graph of S with the addition of n_{ij} request edges (p_i, R_j) for each process p_i and resource R_j, where

$$n_{ij} = c_{ij} - (|(p_i, R_j)| + |(R_j, p_i)|).$$

The claim graph obtained from S represents a *worst case* future state T such that $S \xrightarrow{*} T$ through successive requests by all processes of the maximum number of resources permitted by their claims. Figure 8-9 contains claim graphs for several states; the added edges are dotted.

Deadlock can be prevented in maximum claim systems by not allowing any *acquisition* operations unless the resulting claim graph is completely reducible. The complete reducibility of the claim graph means that the worst future state can be handled: If all processes successively request the remainder of their claim, the requests can be satisfied. This prevention policy can be restated as a theorem.

THEOREM 7

If acquisition operations that do not result in a completely reducible claim graph are eliminated, any system state that is not deadlocked is safe. Furthermore, any policy that eliminates fewer acquisitions (and makes no further

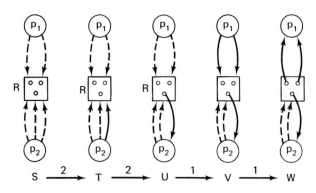

Fig. 8-9 Examples of claim graphs.

restrictions on request or release operations) produces some system states which are not safe.

Proof: See Exercise 2.

The reduction procedure that determines whether the claim graph is completely reducible should attempt to reduce by the acquiring process p_i first. If the claim graph was completely reducible before the acquisition, it is completely reducible after that operation if and only if an eventual reduction by p_i is possible. This result is analogous to the continuous detection Theorem 3 in Sec. 8.3.2. When resources are of the *single-unit* type, a more efficient method of testing the reducibility of the claim graph exists. An acquisition yields a completely reducible claim graph if and only if the acquiring process p_i is not in a cycle in the claim graph; therefore, a simple path tracing algorithm from p_i can be employed.

There does not seem to be any simple way to determine whether a state in a general unrestricted maximum claim system is safe. One could test a state for safeness by an exhaustive search procedure, but this approach, while guaranteed to terminate, is inordinately time- and space-consuming (see Exercise 4). However, a maximum claim system limited to *single-unit resources* can be easily tested for safe states by using the following results.

Consider the *undirected* claim graph obtained by treating each edge of the claim graph as an *unordered* pair. An *undirected cycle* is defined as a sequence of unordered edges $(a, b), (b, c), \ldots, (r, s), (s, a)$ in which no edge appears more than once; note that the edge (a, b) is the same as the edge (b, a) in the undirected graph. Then, safeness can be determined by testing for cycles.

THEOREM 8

A state in a maximum claim system with single-unit resources is safe if and only if the undirected claim graph contains no undirected cycles.

Proof: (a) Assume that the undirected claim graph contains no cycles. Then the claim graph (directed) clearly does not contain any cycles, which implies that no future state is deadlocked. (Why?)

(b) Let the undirected claim graph contain a cycle. The edges can now be changed to directed edges so that the undirected cycle becomes a directed cycle. Thus a reusable resource graph containing a cycle—a sufficient condition for deadlock in single-unit resource systems—can be constructed from the undirected claim graph. Either the original state can eventually be transformed to the (deadlock) state represented by the above graph, or the system deadlocks before reaching that state. In both cases, the original state is not safe.

We have really proved a stronger result, since the undirected claim graph is identical for all states:

THEOREM 9

All states in a maximum claim system with single-unit resources are safe if and only if the (unique) undirected claim graph contains no undirected cycles.

Maximum claim systems were introduced and studied by Dijkstra (1965a) and Habermann (1969). When users are required to specify their (reusable) resource needs on job control cards, maximum claim information is readily available. Deadlock prevention based on maximum claims, however, still potentially wastes resources, since a process might not ever need its maximum claim of all resources simultaneously.

A systems designer thus has two options with respect to SR resources. He can either permit deadlock and employ some detection and recovery techniques, or he may decide to prevent deadlock, sacrificing some potential resource usage. A realistic approach taken in many systems is to prevent deadlock on some classes of resources and processes for which recovery is difficult and to permit its occurrence on other classes; for example, a deadlock prevention policy may be implemented for systems processes while detection and recovery are limited to user processes.

The deadlock problem with respect to reusable resources has been studied extensively. Other approaches, which we have not examined in this chapter, were developed by Shoshani and Coffman (1969), Hebalkar (1970), and Russell (1972).

EXERCISES

1. Prove that the serially reusable resource graphs never contain cycles in the following two cases:
   (a) The system has a "collective" requests policy.

(b) The system has an ordered resource policy.

2. Prove Theorem 7. Note that the safeness or lack of safeness must result only from the acquisition restriction; requests and releases may be made in any order and quantity, subject only to the maximum claim limitations.

3. For any single-unit resource maximum claim system, prove that an acquisition operation produces a safe state if and only if the acquiring process is not in a cycle in the resulting claim graph.

4. Design an algorithm that determines whether a given state is safe in a general maximum claim system. Estimate the maximum time and space requirements for your algorithm.

8.4. CONSUMABLE RESOURCE SYSTEMS

A *consumable resource* (CR) can be distinguished from an SR in several important ways:

1. The number of available units of a CR varies as elements are acquired (consumed) and released (produced) by processes, and is potentially unbounded.

2. A (producer) process increases the number of units by releasing one or more units it has "created."

3. A (consumer) process decreases the number of units by first requesting and then acquiring one or more units. Units that are acquired are not, in general, returned to the resource but are consumed by the acquiring process.

Many signals, messages, and data generated by both hardware and software have these characteristics and may be treated as CR resources for deadlock studies. These include IO and timer interrupts; process synchronization signals; messages containing requests for various services or data, and the corresponding answers; and data such as a job "descriptor" which may be passed from one process to another as a user job progresses through an MS.

We first informally consider *unrestricted* CR systems. As in the SR case, the system changes state when any *unblocked* process p_i executes one of the three operations: *Request, Acquisition,* and *Release* of CR resources. Note that there are no theoretical limits on the number of units requested or released, provided that they remain finite. The deadlock properties of such a system are easily deduced. A state is deadlocked if and only if all processes are blocked. If there is one unblocked process in a given state, it can acquire its requested resources, if any, and then release enough units of all resources to wake up every blocked process. The second property is that *no* state is safe; all unblocked processes can always request, in succession, an amount of resources exceeding the current supply. More practical and interesting results can be derived when some additional information about the process interactions is available. CR systems can then be modeled and analyzed by using techniques similar to those developed for SR resources.

Producers Are Known

Assume that the *producer* processes for each resource are known *a priori*; that is, the set of processes that may execute *release* operations are specified. Then the state of a system containing only CR resources can be represented by a directed graph $\langle N, E \rangle$, called a *consumable resource graph*, with the following characteristics:

1. $N = \pi \cup \rho$, where π is a set of process nodes $\{p_1, \ldots, p_n\}$ and ρ is a set of CR nodes $\{R_1, \ldots, R_m\}$.

2. The graph is bipartite with respect to π and ρ; each edge is directed between a node of π and one of ρ.

3. If an edge $e = (p_i, R_j)$, then e is a *request* edge and is interpreted as a request by p_i for one unit of R_j.

4. For each $R \in \rho$, there is a nonempty set of *producer* processes $\pi_R \subseteq \pi$. The graph contains a *producer edge* (R, p), directed from R to p, for all $p \in \pi_R$. (Producer edges are permanent fixtures of the graph and are never removed.)

5. A nonnegative integer r_i, the *available units*, is associated with each $R_i \in \rho$.

Figure 8-2(b) contains a consumable resource graph; $\pi_{S_i} = \{p_i\}$ and $r_i = 0$, $i = 1, 2, 3$. Another example is given in Fig. 8-10(a).

A process p_i, with no outstanding requests, may perform a *request* for any finite number of units of any number of resources; the new state has the appropriate request edges added. If p_i has outstanding requests, it can perform an *acquisition*, provided that it is not *blocked*, i.e., provided that for all R_j such that $(p_i, R_j) \in E, |(p_i, R_j)| \leq r_j$; the available units of each acquired resource R_j are updated:

$$r_j := r_j - |(p_i, R_j)|,$$

A process p_i which has no outstanding requests and is a producer of one or more resources may execute a *release* operation in which any finite number of units are added to one or more of the resources; the corresponding available units counters (r_j's) are increased accordingly. Figure 8-10(b) illustrates these operations and the resulting states.

Graph reductions are central to our deadlock studies for CR's also. A CR graph can be *reduced* by a process p_i which is neither blocked nor an isolated

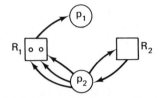

(a) A Consumable Resource Graph

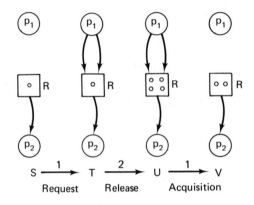

(b) Operations on CR Graphs

Fig. 8-10   Consumable resource graphs.

node. The reduction consists of the following two operations:

1. Satisfy any outstanding requests for p_i by deleting its request edges and decrementing the appropriate available units counters.

2. For each R_j such that p_i is a producer of R_j, release enough units to satisfy all outstanding requests for R_j and delete the producer edge (R_j, p_i). We avoid keeping track of available units of R_j by setting r_j to a special "number" ω with the property: for any integer i, $\omega > i$ and $\omega + i = \omega - i = \omega$.

Figure 8-11 illustrates a sequence of reductions by $\langle p_1, p_2, p_3 \rangle$; the original state S was completely reducible, since all edges are deleted in the *irreducible* state V. (See Sec. 8.3.2 for definitions.) Note that while a reduction in an SR graph never decreases the available units, the CR graph reduction may in fact leave a smaller r_j; thus in the figure $r_2 = 1$ in state S and $r_2 = 0$ in state T. The example of Fig. 8-11 also illustrates another important difference in CR systems—the *order* of reductions is significant. State S can be reduced by p_1, but if S is first reduced by p_2, it is no longer possible to reduce by p_1. Lemma 1 of Sec. 8.3.2 does not hold here.

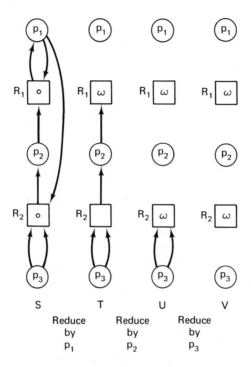

Fig. 8-11 Reductions of a CR graph.

Theorem 1 of Sec. 8.3.2, which states that S is a deadlock state if and only if the graph of S is not completely reducible, is also not true here as shown by Fig. 8-12; the illustrated state is not a deadlock state, yet the graph is not completely reducible. However, we can still employ graph reductions to determine if a particular process is deadlocked.

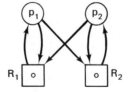

Fig. 8-12 A state which is not deadlocked and not completely reducible.

THEOREM 10

A process p_i is not deadlocked in a CR system if and only if there exists a sequence of reductions leaving a state in which p_i is not blocked.

Proof: (a) Suppose that there exists a sequence of reductions that leaves p_i not blocked. Then p_i is not deadlocked, since the reductions are equivalent to a sequence of operations.

(b) Suppose that p_i is not deadlocked in state S. Then there exists a sequence I (possibly empty) of operations by processes $p_{i_1}, p_{i_2}, \ldots, p_{i_x}$ leaving a state T in which p_i is not blocked. Consider a sequence J of reductions by processes $p_{j_1}, p_{j_2}, \ldots, p_{j_y}$, where for $k = 1, 2, \ldots, y, p_{j_k}$ is the first process in the I sequence that has not previously appeared in the J sequence and that is not an isolated node in state S; let p_{j_y} be the last process in the I sequence satisfying this property. Note that any reduction which decreases the available units will only do so by requests existing in state S. Then state S can be successively reduced by the processes in the J sequence since, before a reduction by any p_{j_k}, the available units of each resource must be at least as large as that preceding the first operation by p_{j_k} in the I sequence. Hence p_i is not blocked following the reductions, because it is not blocked following the I sequence of operations.

To detect deadlock, one must search for a *different* reduction sequence for each process, a very inefficient task in general. Whereas a deadlock can be caused only by a request operation in SR systems, both requests and acquisitions can result in deadlocks in the CR case. An example appears in Fig. 8-12, where the acquisition by p_1 of one unit of R_1 and one unit of R_2 puts p_2 in deadlock. In a manner similar to the proofs of Theorems 2 and 4, it can be shown that a knot is a sufficient condition for deadlock in expedient states and that a cycle is a necessary condition for deadlock.

Deadlock detection is considerably simplified if the system is restricted to *single-unit requests*; that is, at most *one* request edge may be directed from any process node. Then, Theorem 6 is valid here also.

THEOREM 11

A consumable resource graph with single-unit requests in an expedient state is a deadlock state if and only if the graph contains a knot.

Proof: See Exercise 3.

The knot-finding algorithm in Sec. 8.3.2 can then also be employed for deadlock detection in this important special case.

The only practical way to recover from deadlock is by termination of the deadlocked processes. Liquidation of nondeadlocked processes does not help, since their CR resources have been consumed; preemption of resources is not possible, because there is nothing to preempt. Process termination is more complex than in the SR case, since the candidate for liquidation might well be a producer of resources required by other processes; i.e., other processes might eventually need the messages produced by the deadlocked process. This problem can be solved by releasing appropriate error messages when an attempt is made to interact with the destroyed process or, in the worst case, also terminating the interacting processes, if known. For example, if a process associated with a user job or job step is deadlocked, then the entire job or job step may be aborted.

When only the producer processes are known *a priori* and any process is a potential consumer, no system state is safe, by the same argument presented at the beginning of this section for unrestricted systems. However, knowledge of consumers as well as producers permits one to test for safeness and establish a simple prevention policy.

Producers and Consumers Are Known

Assume that both producers and consumers of each resource are known *a priori*; i.e., for each resource R, there exists a nonempty set of producer processes π_R^P and a nonempty set of consumer processes π_R^C. A process p may request and acquire units of R *only* if $p \in \pi_R^C$, and it may release units of R only if $p \in \pi_R^P$. A system state is again represented by a consumable resource graph. Within each such system, there is one state, called the *claim limited* state, which has a special role. The claim limited state is defined as follows:

1. A process p has an outstanding request for one unit of a resource R_j if and only if $p \in \pi_{R_j}^C$. No other requests appear.

2. All resources have zero available units; i.e., $r_i = 0, i = 1, \ldots, m$. The corresponding graph is called the *claim limited consumable resource graph* for the system. An example appears in Fig. 8-13; $\pi_{R_1}^P = \{p_1, p_2\}$; $\pi_{R_1}^C = \{p_2\}$; $\pi_{R_2}^P = \{p_1\}$; $\pi_{R_2}^C = \{p_2\}$. The principal result is given in Theorem 12.

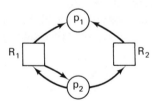

Fig. 8-13 A claim limited consumable resource graph.

THEOREM 12

All states in a consumable resource system in which producers and consumers of each resource are known are safe if and only if the claim limited consumable resource graph is completely reducible.

Proof: (a) Assume that all states are safe. Then the claim limited state is safe and is completely reducible, since the reductions correspond to a possible sequence of operations by processes.
(b) Suppose the claim limited state V is completely reducible by the sequence of processes $p_{v_1}, p_{v_2}, \ldots, p_{v_k}$. It is relatively easy to show that *any* sequence of

reductions of a claim limited consumable resource graph leads to the same unique irreducible graph. (This is analogous to Lemma 1 of Sec. 8.3.2. See Exercise 4.) Therefore, V is a safe state. We now demonstrate how any state S can be reduced by the same sequence that reduces V. The first process in the V reduction, p_{v_1}, cannot be blocked in state S. (p_{v_1} cannot be a consumer of *any* resources, because it would then be blocked in V.) Let S be reduced by p_{v_1} to state S_1. The second process p_{v_2} cannot be blocked in S_1, since p_{v_2} must be a consumer *only* of resources produced by p_{v_1}. (If p_{v_2} is an isolated node in S, we ignore it.) Otherwise, p_{v_2} would not be able to perform the second reduction from V. Continue in this manner, terminating after the reduction by p_{v_k}. The resulting state, S_k, say, must consist of isolated processes, because the V sequence includes *all* producer and consumer processes. Thus S is completely reducible. Since S is an arbitrary state, no state in the system is deadlocked. Therefore, all states are safe.

Theorem 12 provides one scheme for preventing deadlocks: the claim limited graph is tested for complete reducibility. If it is completely reducible, the system can be run without worrying about deadlock; otherwise, the systems designer attempts to modify the process interactions to achieve reducibility. The latter may not be feasible, however. For example, the claim limited graph is not completely reducible unless there exists at least one process that consumes no resources; if a system is designed so that every process must both receive and send messages, then this property is not satisfied. Deadlock can also be prevented by eliminating any cycles in the claim limited graph; the absence of cycles is an even stronger restriction than complete reducibility. Note that lack of safeness does not necessarily mean that a given system will ever, in fact, deadlock; the logic of the code of each process might be such that deadlock "paths" are never taken during execution.

EXERCISES

1. Prove that in a CR system with known producers
    (a) A cycle is a necessary condition for deadlock.
    (b) If a system state is expedient, a knot is a sufficient condition for deadlock.

2. Consider a CR system with a *single* resource R and known producers of R. Derive a simple necessary and sufficient condition for deadlock in such a system.

3. Prove Theorem 11. See the proof of Theorem 6 of Sec. 8.3.2.

4. Show that for any state S in a CR system with known producers and consumers, $S \overset{*}{\longrightarrow} V$, where V is the claim limited state.

5. Prove that *all* possible reduction sequences of a given consumable resource graph with known producers and consumers lead to the *same* irreducible graph.

8.5. GENERAL RESOURCE GRAPHS

The models of Secs. 8-3 and 8-4 can be combined to represent systems containing both serially reusable and consumable resources. We assume that *producers* are known for consumable resources. The state of an operating system is represented by a *general resource* graph $\langle N, E \rangle$, where

1. $N = \pi \cup \rho$. π is a nonempty set of process nodes $\{p_1, \ldots, p_n\}$, and ρ is a nonempty set of resource nodes $\{R_1, \ldots, R_m\}$.

2. $\rho = \rho_s \cup \rho_c$. ρ_s is a set of serially reusable resources, and ρ_c is a set of consumable resources.

3. Each edge $e \in E$ is directed between a node of π and one of ρ. If $e = (p_i, R_j)$, then e is a *request* edge and is interpreted as a request by p_i for one unit of R_j. If $e = (R_j, p_i)$, then (a) if $R_j \in \rho_s$, then e is an *assignment* edge and indicates an allocation of one unit of R_j to p_i or (b) if $R_j \in \rho_c$, then e is a *producer* edge and indicates that p_i is a producer of R_j. A producer edge is permanently directed from each resource to all its producer processes.

4. For each $R_i \in \rho_s$, there is an associated positive integer t_i denoting the *total units* of R_i; i.e., $r_i = t_i - \sum_j |(R_i, p_j)|$.

5. For all $R_i \in \rho_s$ and processes p_j, the following must always hold:
(a) $\sum_j |(R_i, p_j)| \leq t_i$.
(b) $|(R_i, p_j)| + |(p_j, R_i)| \leq t_i$.

6. For each $R_i \in \rho_c$, there is a nonnegative integer r_i giving the *available* units of R_i.

Figures 8-2(a) and 8-14 contain examples of general resource graphs; in Fig. 8-14, $\rho_s = \{R_1, R_3\}$, $\rho_c = \{R_2\}$, $t_1 = 2$, $t_3 = 3$, $r_1 = 1$, $r_2 = 2$, and $r_3 = 0$.

Request, acquisition, and release operations are defined as in Secs. 8.3.1

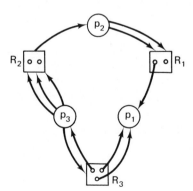

Fig. 8-14 A general resource graph.

and 8.4. Reductions are similarly defined. The following basic deadlock theorems are proven easily by using the results of the two previous sections.

THEOREM 13

A process p_i in a general resource system is not deadlocked if and only if there exists a sequence of reductions leaving a state in which p_i is not blocked.

THEOREM 14

In a general resource graph,
(a) A cycle is a necessary condition for deadlock.
(b) If the systems state is expedient, a knot is a sufficient condition for deadlock.

Theorems 6 and 11 are also valid for general resource graphs.

Deadlock can be detected by graph reductions but, because the order of reductions is significant, this method is quite inefficient. For single-unit requests, the knot detection algorithm permits fast testing for deadlock. Few additional results for the general resource case are known.

EXERCISES

1. Prove Theorems 13 and 14.
2. Prove the analogue of Theorems 6 and 11 for the general resource case.
3. Assume that maximum claims are known for SR resources and that producers and consumers are known for CR resources. Try to postulate and derive results similar to Theorem 7 of Sec. 8.3.4 and Theorem 12 of Sec. 8.4.

8.6. DYNAMIC ADDITION AND REMOVAL
OF PROCESSES AND RESOURCES

The models developed in this chapter assume a constant set of processes and resources in a system. This is usually the case for most systems processess and many serially reusable resources. However, even in present systems, processes are continually being created and destroyed, and some resources are dynamic. An example of the latter occurs in IBM OS/360 which permits users to request and release their own SR resources via the *ENQ/DEQ* macros. In this section, we briefly examine systems deadlocks in an environment allowing the dynamic creation and termination of processes and resources.

Consider first the effects of allowing processes to enter and leave a system containing a *constant* set of SR resources. The removal of a process is essentially equivalent to a reduction by that process and can only help the deadlock situation, since the number of available units of SR resources may increase. On the other hand, the introduction of a new process increases the competition for resources in general; it thus becomes easier to reach a deadlock state. In both cases, the deadlock detection algorithms presented in Sec. 8.3.2 are immediately applicable to the new set of processes. Two new operations are added to the system:

1. *Create* a process. This adds either an isolated process node or, possibly, a process node with some initial allocation to the graph.

2. *Destroy* a process. A process node and all its assignment and request edges are deleted from the graph.

The discussion on deadlock prevention with SR resources (Sec. 8.3.4) is also applicable to the dynamic situation. The addition or deletion of a process in a system following an ordered resource policy still leaves a safe system. If deadlock prevention is based on maximum claim information with the acquisition restriction of Theorem 7, the removal of processes only simplifies the testing of acquisition operations; the addition of a new process to a system in a safe state still results in a safe state, since the new process can clearly be reduced *last* in the reduction of the claim graph.

Dynamic processes working with CR resources have slightly more complex effects. If only the producers are known, then either the creation or termination of a process can cause deadlock. Deletion of a producer process may produce a deadlock, while the deletion of a process that produces no resources can in some cases prevent a future deadlock (Fig. 8-15). In the former case, some processes may be waiting forever for a message from the deleted producer if only one producer process was associated with the message resource; this can be easily handled in practice by providing a message to the requesting processes stating that the producer no longer exists. (Brinch Hansen's communications primitives are implemented in this fashion; see Sec. 3.5.) Similarly, the introduction of a new producer process can prevent a possible deadlock (or even break a deadlock), whereas the addition of a consumer may aggravate the situation (Fig. 8-16). If both producers and consumers are known, the same effects can be observed. However, the results of Sec. 8.4 remain valid and can be employed for deadlock detection and prevention in a straightforward manner.

The dynamic addition and removal of resources can also be handled within the graph models. Removal of an SR resource will, at worst, have no deadlock effect and, at best, prevent or even break a deadlock; in the latter case, a cycle or knot in the SR graph could disappear as a result of the resource liquidation. (Of course, in a practical sense, removal of an SR resource, such as a data file or buffer area, might be disastrous for a process assigned or

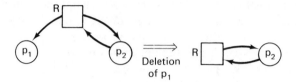

(a) Process Deletion Producing a Deadlock

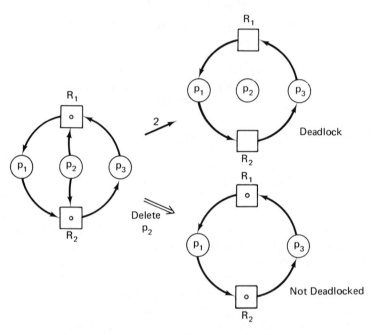

(b) Preventing Future Deadlock by Process Deletion

Fig. 8-15   Deletion of processes.

requesting the resource, making it necessary also to terminate the process.)
The definition of a new SR resource has the sole effect of complicating the
deadlock detection methods. For deadlock prevention using maximum claim
information on SR resources, the addition of a new resource makes sense only
if all processes claiming that resource are introduced *after* the new resource
has been defined. If the system is safe before the new resource is established,
it remains safe, provided that the acquisition restriction of Theorem 7 is not
violated thereafter. Removal of a CR resource is similarly beneficial only with
respect to deadlock. The deadlock effects of adding a new CR resource are
left as an exercise to the reader.

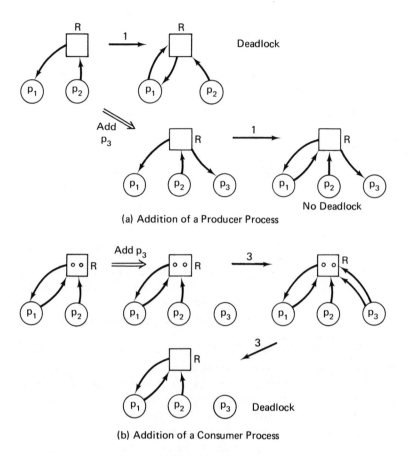

(a) Addition of a Producer Process

(b) Addition of a Consumer Process

Fig. 8-16 Effects of adding processes.

9 FILE SYSTEMS

The third and last major component of multiprogramming systems,† the file system, normally requires the most substantial design and coding efforts, and is the largest part of many MS. This chapter identifies the primary functions of file systems and describes a number of techniques and organizations for realizing these functions.

A *file* is usually defined as a collection of data records grouped together for purposes of access control, retrieval, and modification; a data *record* is just a linear list of information items. Examples of files are source and machine language programs, applications data, such as payroll or inventory files, user jobs, file directories, and systems accounting and performance data. In fact, virtually all program and data information accessed by a computer system—i.e., all computer software—is treated as file at some point during processing. Files may reside on any of a large variety of storage media including cards, disks, drums, magnetic tape, main memory, and paper; associated with each kind of storage is a processing unit that permits reading and/or writing data on that storage device, as well as control and testing operations. The same file often occupies different storage media during its lifetime. Thus a card file containing a user program could successively appear in cards, disk, and main storage as the program is spooled and loaded; or a payroll file may simultaneously reside on magnetic tape and paper.

A *file system* (*filing system, data management system*) is that software responsible for creating, destroying, organizing, reading, writing, modifying, moving, and controlling access to files; and for management of the resources used by files. Without a file system, general multiprogramming would essen-

---

†The other two components covered throughout the earlier chapters are the process and resource management subsystems, respectively.

tially be impossible. It is this component that permits the use of many language processors, on-line user libraries of programs and data, spooling operations in batch systems, and practical interactive computing. As we have mentioned earlier, all input-output in an MS is normally serviced through the file system.

9.1. VIRTUAL AND REAL FILE STORAGE

Our conventional definition of a file as a set of related data records imposes little structure on a file—only subdivision into records—and is almost independent of the medium on which a file is stored. It is useful to carry these features one step further and specify uniform formatless *virtual file memory* (MULTICS, 1967; Madnick and Alsop, 1969). At the most abstract and unstructured level, we shall consider a file to be an ordered sequence of elements with a symbolic name, where a file *element* is the smallest addressable unit in the virtual space, such as a byte or word. The eth element of a file with name F is addressed by the pair $[F, e]$. The reader will note that a file is now identical to a virtual memory *segment* as defined in Sec. 5.1.3.

The purpose of the virtual file storage concept is to provide users with one simple uniform linear space for their files. As with real computer and file memories, this space may be further structured in any convenient fashion to reflect the natural organization of the data and its processing, or, if the actual hardware storage devices are known, to take advantage of their physical characteristics.

The most basic file system operations are (a) to map access requests from virtual to real file space and (b) to transmit elements between file storage and main computer memory. The study of these and other operations requires some knowledge of the properties and behavior of *real* file storage devices. The remainder of this section briefly reviews the features of the most widely used devices. More detailed descriptions may be found in manufacturers' manuals and in several texts, for example, Gear (1969, Chapter 6). We restrict the discussion to on-line auxiliary storage that is *reusable*—storage media that may be both read and written many times. Ignored are read- and write-only stores such as cards, paper tape, and paper, and their associated processing units.

The main auxiliary storage devices that have been employed as file memories are magnetic tape, disk, drum, and core. Some properties of concern to the systems designer and user are listed below. No distinction is made between the *device* on which data is stored and the *controller* that controls device selection, reading, writing, and other operations:

1. *Capàcity.* This is the maximum amount of data that can be stored on the device.

2. *Record Size.* A physical record is the smallest set of contiguous information that may be addressed on a device. The device may allow *fixed* or *variable length* records.

3. *Access Method.* *Direct* access of any record on a device may be possible, or the device may be restricted to *sequential* access only. In the former case, a hardware record address directs the read/write mechanism directly to the record. With sequential access only, a specific record is reached by explicitly skipping forward or backward over intervening records; the normal mode of operation is to access the records sequentially in the same linear sequence in which they are stored.

4. *Removability.* Magnetic tape and some types of disks are *removable*, permitting the off-line storage of files on these devices. This feature substantially increases the amount of virtual storage provided to a user, since the machine operator can be instructed to mount active files and remove inactive ones.

5. *Data Transfer Rate.* This is the rate of speed, usually expressed in bits, bytes, or words/second, at which data can be transferred between main storage and the device. During the transfer, the IO has priority over the CPU for memory, and "steals" memory cycles from the CPU if they are both accessing the same main memory box.

6. *Latency.* After a read or write command is accepted by a device controller, it normally takes an additional time increment, the *latency* time, before the start of the accessed record is under the read or write heads and the data transfer can begin. This is either the start-up time for magnetic tape to accelerate to its rated speed from a dead stop or the rotational delay of rotating disks or drums. The CPU, if programmed carefully, can execute at its rated speed during latency time.

7. *Seek Time.* Disk devices with moving read/write heads often must precede each read or write operation by a *seek*, which physically moves the head over the track containing the desired record. In the same way as during latency, the CPU can completely overlap the seek time.

8. *Relative Cost.* As one would expect, the cost of a device increases with the speed and convenience of accessing a record.

Table 9-1 lists typical characteristics of the four main classes of auxiliary storage devices in terms of the above properties. The main liabilities of magnetic tape for on-line file storage are the sequential accessing requirement and the inability in practice (on most tapes) to make selective changes to records without rewriting the entire tape. On the other hand, tapes are inexpensive, small, and removable—features that make them useful for off-line archive storage as well as for stores for sequential files. Disks are currently the most widely used auxiliary storage devices, primarily because of their combination

Table 9-1   Typical Characteristics of Auxiliary Storage Devices

	Magnetic Tape	Disk	Drum	Core
Capacity	$\sim 10^7$ B/reel	$\sim 10^6$–10^8 B/unit	$\sim 10^7$ B	$\sim 10^7$ B
Record Size	V	F or V	F	F
Access Method	S	D	D	D
Removability	R	R or NR	NR	NR
Data Transfer Rate	$\sim 30{,}000$– $300{,}000$ B/sec	$\sim 150{,}000$– $300{,}000$ B/sec	$\sim 300{,}000$– $1{,}200{,}000$ B/sec	$\sim 10^7$ B/sec
Latency	~ 5 ms	~ 12 ms	~ 8 ms	—
Seek Time	—	~ 75 ms	—	—
Relative Cost†	1	2	3	4

Legend: B: bytes
   F: fixed length; V: variable length
   S: sequential; D: direct
   R: removable; NR: nonremovable

Note: Memory technology changes so rapidly and such a wide spectrum of devices are available within each class that the above figures and properties should be taken as very approximate.

†The larger the entry, the greater the cost.

of large capacity, direct access capability, and low price, relative to drums and bulk cores. Drums generally provide higher data transfer rates and lower latency than disks, and are often used to store the most active files and for swapping purposes in paging and other dynamic memory systems. Core is a relatively recent medium for file storage and is a direct application of conventional, but slower, main memory core technology to auxiliary storage. Its main advantages are the absence of both latency and seek times, and an effective data transfer rate comparable to main storage access times.

9.2. FILE SYSTEM COMPONENTS

Most of the principal components and tasks of a file system for a general-purpose MS can be identified by examining the "path" of a typical file access request that originates at the virtual file level. We consider the simplest possible example—a request to read the next record from a virtual card file.

A user U assumes that he is reading his data cards from a card reader. To read the next card (record), U† may issue either of the following two commands:

(1)   *ReadaCard*(A) ;
        or
      *Read*1 (*MyCardFile, A*) ;

†For simplicity, let the process associated with U be also identified as U.

Either command has the effect of reading the next 80-character record of the file *MyCardFile* into main storage locations $A[0], \ldots, A[79]$, say; *MyCard-File* is a virtual file addressed as $[MyCardFile, 0]\ [MyCardFile, 1], \ldots$ and is stored on an auxiliary storage device—perhaps as a result of a spooling operation.

MyCardFile would have a *structure* imposed upon it corresponding to the 80-character/record sequential card storage. This data structure and sequential organization can be easily produced. Let r be a pointer to the next record to be read in sequence in *MyCardFile*. Then the command (1) can be translated by the file system to

(2) $Read2(MyCardFile, A, r, 80)$;
      $r := r + 80$;

The first two reads, *Read* 1 and *Read* 2, employ the symbolic name to reference the file. The next step is to find the *internal* name of *MyCardFile*, say *mcf*, which uniquely defines the file to the system and permits the retrieval of its *descriptor; mcf* could simply be the secondary storage address of the descriptor. If the file had been previously declared or referenced by U, it most likely has been "opened" and the descriptor appears in an *active file directory* (AFD) in main storage; otherwise, a *directory* of all files in the system must be searched by *MyCardFile*. The following operations are then performed:

$(3)_1$ *open* := **false** ;
        if $LookInAFD(MyCardFile, descr)$ **then** *open* := **true**
        else $SearchSystemsDirectory(MyCardFile, mcf)$;

LookInAFD is a Boolean procedure that searches the AFD for a file; it returns **true** and the descriptor of the file in *descr* if successful. *SearchSystems-Directory* returns the file identifier in *mcf*.

After the directory search, the file must be opened—i.e., made active—if not already so, and the validity of the read request checked. Opening a file essentially involves retrieving the descriptor and inserting it in the AFD. (If *MyCardFile* were not on-line, the machine operator would locate the file in off-line storage and "mount" it.) The opening of *MyCardFile* can be expressed:

$(3)_2$ **if** $\neg open$ **then**
        begin
          $GetDescriptor(mcf, descr)$;
          $InsertInAFD(descr)$
        end ;

The descriptor for *MyCardFile* includes the following information:

Name:	*MyCardFile*
Location:	⟨*DeviceNumber, Address*⟩
Organization:	*Sequential*
Length:	*L*
Type:	*Temporary*
Owner:	*U*
Users:	{*U*}
Access:	{*Read*}

⋅

⋅

⋅

The descriptor is now used to verify that the read request by *U* is legitimate:

$(3)_3$ **if** $\neg(U \in descr(Users) \wedge Read \in descr(Access)$
      $\wedge \; r + 79 \leq descr(Length))$
   then *Error* ;

where *descr(X)* returns the contents of the field named *X* of the descriptor. The *Error* routine could either abort *U* or send *U* an appropriate message. Finally, if the read is indeed valid, the descriptor is passed to the next stage:

$(3)_4$ *Read3(descr, A, r,* 80) ;

Thus, the four file system steps of (3) are invoked by the *Read2* operation of (2).

The record specified in command $(3)_4$ is next mapped into the actual record address (and length) on auxiliary storage where the desired record is physically located. In many cases, some type of buffering scheme is employed. If it is assumed that a buffering system for *MyCardFile* has previously been established, say on opening, $(3)_4$ could invoke the following buffer operations:

$(4)_1$ *GetBuf(k); Move(Buf*[*k*], *A*) ; *ReleaseBuf(k)* ;

GetBuf(k) returns the index *k* of the next full buffer *Buf*[*k*] while *ReleaseBuf(k)* frees *Buf*[*k*] (see Sec. 2.4). The completion of $(4)_1$ would complete the original request. Synchronized with the file buffering would be a process that reads in the next sequential block of records whenever sufficient buffer space is available. The read command might take the form

     Read4(Device, RecordAddress, Buffer, No.ofElements) ;

For example, the next set of records for *MyCardFile* could be located at physical record address *pra* on device number 17; the buffering system may be designed to accept 800 characters (10 logical records) into 10 contiguous buffers of length 80. Assume that *MyCardFile* is sequentially stored on the device. The *Read*4 would then be

$(4)_2$ *Read*4(17, *pra*, *Buf*[*nextR*], 800) ;
        $pra := pra + 800$; $nextR := nextR +_n 10$;

[*nextR* is assumed to be a pointer to a circular buffer storage area containing n 80-byte buffers. (See Sec. 2.4.2.)] When this operation is completed, the space on secondary storage could be deallocated. A sequence of channel commands and device orders—an IO program—must be generated from the *Read*4 of $(4)_2$ to perform the desired operation. If the file is stored on a moving arm disk, the IO program may also contain instructions to initially move the arm to the track containing the desired record. The fully translated request is then inserted in a queue for the channel allocator. The request reaches the top of the queue, and the IO of $(4)_2$ is actually performed. On completion, an appropriate message is passed to the waiting processes. This completes the servicing of the *Read* operation of (1).

The simple read request apparently leads to a quite formidable set of operations. This is the price one pays for a general-purpose file system. However, in the example, we have tried to include most paths through the system; in practice, many shortcuts and simplifications exist. For example, once *MyCardFile* is opened and buffering is established, the external directory search is thereafter avoided and an efficient table look-up in the AFD retrieves the necessary file descriptor; the read request would then essentially translate into the buffer retrieval sequence of (4). Also, much of the translation of the original read request could be done at compile or assembly time rather than at run time.

File systems admit to a wider variety of organizations, but the functions remain similar. One possible organization distinguishes the following five modules, related as illustrated in Figure 9-1:

1. *Organization and Accessing Language.* This is the part of the file system that is interfaced to the user. Facilities for defining different logical organizations in virtual file space and language constructs for accessing files are provided in this component. The latter include commands and declarations to create, destroy, read, write, modify, and control the access to files. In many systems, these facilities are extended to the physical file level so that users may bypass large parts of the system and directly specify physical organizations and IO commands to some extent.

2. *Accessing Procedures.* This consists of routines for file directory man-

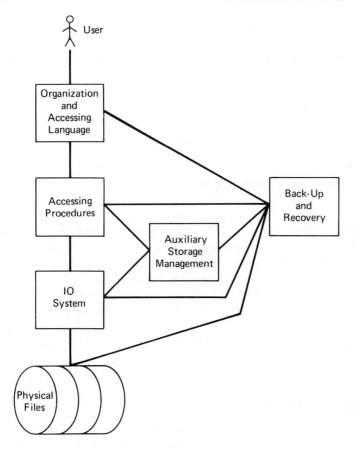

Fig. 9-1 Modules of a file system.

agement and searching, opening and closing files, mapping symbolic file names to their real addresses, controlling the access of files to legitimate users, managing internal buffers, and generating appropriate IO programs. As the long list illustrates, the accessing procedures comprise the largest part of most systems.

3. *IO System.* The IO system is responsible for maintaining queues of IO requests, scheduling and initiating the operations, servicing IO errors, and handling IO completion signals.

4. *Auxiliary Storage Management.* This module has the responsibility for keeping track of available space on secondary storage, and allocating and deallocating blocks of secondary storage on request. In a complex system, we might also include facilities for moving files of information through a hierarchy of storage devices; actual or expected activity might be one major factor in determining where a file is stored at any time.

5. *Back-up and Recovery.* It must be possible for the system to recover from hardware or software errors. For this purpose, the final component ensures that the file system (and the entire OS) can be recovered when errors occur.

The next sections describe some of the principal functions of these modules and the techniques employed within them in more detail. User "languages" for accessing and describing files are not discussed.

9.3. LOGICAL AND PHYSICAL ORGANIZATIONS

Several common file organizations are examined from two points of view—the logical organizations imposed by a user and the corresponding physical ones that may be efficiently implemented on secondary storage devices. (We shall also use the terms "virtual" and "real" for "logical" and "physical," respectively.) A virtual file is dynamically or statically partitioned into a set of *records* $R_0, R_1, \ldots$, where a record is a contiguous block of information transferred during a logical read or write operation. Similarly, a real file is divided into physical records; the record size is determined by the characteristics of the storage medium. A physical record may consist of several logical records, or, conversely, a logical record may be spread over several physical ones.

Sequential Methods

A *sequential* organization (*sequential file*) is one in which the records are ordered and accessed in sequence according to the ordering. If the ith record R_i was last read or written, the next record accessed is automatically R_{i+1}. This is the oldest type of structure and has been employed for magnetic tape files since the earliest days of computing.

Records may be of *fixed* or *variable* length within a file. These two variations are illustrated in Fig. 9-2. The fixed-length record file has records of length n units; in the variable-length case, a length header n_i directly precedes each record R_i. To impose this structure on a virtual space file (a segment), it is sufficient to maintain a pointer r to the next sequential record. Then the read and write file operations between a file $[F, 0], [F, 1], \ldots$ and a memory block with start location M can be simply expressed:

1. Fixed length:

(a) *Read*(F, M, r, n) ; $r := r + n$;

(b) *Write*(F, M, r, n) ; $r := r + n$;

The transfer occurs between $[F, r + i]$ and $M + i, i = 0, \ldots, n - 1$.

File Space Addresses

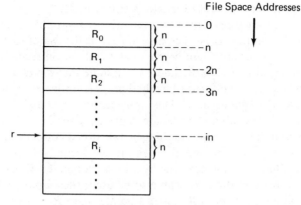

(a) Fixed Length

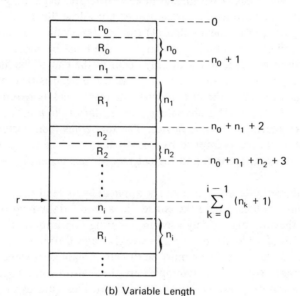

(b) Variable Length

Fig. 9-2 Sequential files.

2. Variable length:

(a) $Read(F, T, r, 1)$;
$Read(F, M, r + 1, T)$;
$r := r + T + 1;$

The main storage location T will contain the record length after the first *Read*.

(b) $Write(F, M, r, M + 1)$;
$r := r + M + 1;$

It is assumed that the record length is stored in M.

One can also *backspace* over the records; for variable-length records, however, the length field must then also appear at the *end* of each record.

The sequential structure can be physically realized on secondary storage by either *sequential* or *linked* methods; we assume that *direct access* devices are used. The most straightforward method maps logically contiguous records into physically contiguous ones. This implementation is also illustrated by Fig. 9-2; the real file reads and writes are in principle similar to 1 and 2 above. The records of a linked file are not, in general, stored contiguously in order. Instead, they may be scattered throughout the secondary storage device. Each record is linked to the next one by a forward pointer. If backspacing is also desired, a backward pointer can also be used; then a physical record R_i would contain a pointer p_i to R_{i+1} and a pointer q_i to R_{i-1}. Records may be inserted and deleted easily within the linked structure, expanding and contracting the file. The sequential method does not allow this flexibility, since the contiguity of records means that (1) the maximum file size must be declared and a sufficient block of secondary storage must be allocated *a priori* and (2) insertions and deletions can only occur at the end of the file. On the other hand, if a moving head disk is employed, the head is theoretically always positioned to access the next record, whereas a seek is required before a read in the linked case. This advantage may be illusory in practice if several active files are sharing the same device. The mappings from virtual to real space are not as simple as implied by our discussion, since we have ignored the fact that physical records and logical records are generally of different sizes.

Sequential methods are particularly applicable to read-only (input) or write-only (output) files, where the entire file is sequentially read or written, respectively; they are also widely used in updating applications that involve a complete scan of a file, for example, a weekly payroll run. There are many other situations wherein records must be directly obtained in some arbitrary order rather than sequentially. Examples are the real-time interrogation and updating of inventory, reservation, or credit card files, and dynamic paged memory management. Direct access techniques for both logical and physical space are appropriate here; in addition, they also permit sequential access, if desired.

Direct Access

Continue to assume that the records of a file are ordered $R_0, R_1, \ldots$, but that it is now required to directly access any arbitrary record R_i. Each record R_i is assumed to have a logical identification or *key* given by i; the keys could be the result of some transformation or sorting procedure on more complex alphanumeric keys. If the file is logically organized as in Fig. 9-2(a), the

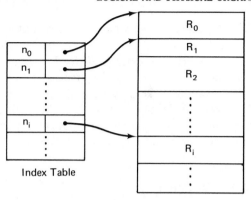

Fig. 9-3 Index table organization.

address of the first element of R_i is simply $i \times n$. The structure of Fig. 9-2(b) is not satisfactory for the direct access of variable-length records. (One could, of course, move sequentially forward through each record until the desired one is reached, but this is far too inefficient in general.) To handle this type of file, an *index table* is added, as shown in Fig. 9-3. The table is ordered so that the ith entry contains the length and address of R_i. Two operations are then required to read or write R_i; the first is a read of the appropriate index table entry, and the second is the actual access to R_i.

If records are stored sequentially and contiguously on the physical storage media, then the address of any logical record R_i in a fixed-length record file can be obtained in principle by a calculation $B + i \times n$, where B is the location of R_0 on secondary storage. (This assumes that physical and logical records are the same size.) Variable-length record files and/or files that employ a linked record organization can be handled in real space by the index table technique. The logical record number acts as an index in a linear table to retrieve a pointer to the corresponding physical records. Records need not be stored contiguously or explicitly linked, thus permitting dynamic allocation and deallocation of secondary storage space. This method also allows an efficient implementation of partially filled files. Each index table entry could have a tag bit indicating whether the corresponding record contains information or is unused; if the latter is true, then the record space need not be allocated. Files that are logically sequential in nature can also be accessed with the index table method; one just sequentially moves through the table.

The index table can be organized as a fixed length record file I in the form of a tree (Madnick and Alsop, 1969). For example, if the record length is m and there are $k \leq m$ records in the file F indexed by the table, then one record in I is sufficient. For $m < k \leq m^2$ records in F, each entry in the first record I_0 of I potentially points to another table of length m, which, in turn, contains the address of records of F. The address of the ith record of F is obtained from the entry $I_r[i \bmod m]$ where $r = i/m$. For $k = m^2$, we have $m + 1$ tables — I_0 at the first level and $I_1, \ldots, I_m$ at the second tree level. The tree structure is extended to further levels for $k > m^2$.

Other organizations may be constructed by means of more complex index table structures. One example is an *associative* file in which records are directly accessed by a key field in the record; here, the key can be "hashed" or transformed to produce an index table entry. (Of course, one must provide for the case in which two or more keys hash to the same entry.)

9.4. ACCESSING PROCEDURES

9.4.1 File Directories

All systems have a set of *directories* (*dictionaries*, *catalogs*), which identify and locate all files accessible to user and systems processes. Minimally, a directory entry contains the name and physical address of a file or its descriptor; at the other extreme, a complete file "descriptor" may be stored in each entry. Since directories are themselves data objects that are searched and modified, they are often treated as another file, albeit with a special role; then the operations of the file system can be also used for directory management. We examine methods for organizing directories and for naming files.

The most general practical directories organization is a *tree* structure, where each node of the tree is a directory (file) and each branch is a directory entry that points to either another directory or a data file. If data files are added to the tree, they will occupy all the *leaves*. The *root* of the tree is called the *master* directory. These concepts are illustrated in Fig. 9-4. (Ignore the dotted connections for the moment.) If we require that all files (data and directory) with the *same* parent node have unique symbolic branch names in the parent, then an unambiguous name for each file exists—the symbolic "path" name from the root to the file. The name is formed by concatenating the branch identifiers starting from the master directory and tracing through the tree to the desired file. (Note that we have implicitly assumed that a given file is pointed to by one and only one directory branch; otherwise, the symbolic name is no longer unique—more than one path may exist from the root to the file—but each path name still defines *one* file.)

Examples

1. In Fig. 9-4(a), data file 14 has the name *C.E.G.K.* Directory 8 has the name *C.D.*

2. A typical example of a file directory tree is given in Fig. 9-5. The master directory has six entries, pointing to the directories for the operating systems routines (*OS*); authorized (paying) users (*ACCOUNT*); basic utilities such as

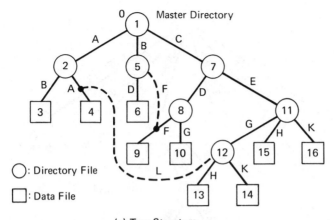

(a) Tree Structure

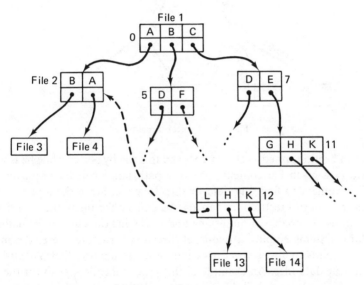

(b) Directory Contents

Fig. 9-4 Tree structured directories.

card to print and dumps (*UTILITIES*), language processors (*LANGUAGE*), public libraries of programs and data submitted by external users (*PUBLIB*), and individual user libraries (*USERLIB*). The unique identification for the run time library associated with the FORTRAN system is *LANGUAGE. FORTRAN.RUNTIME.*

The naming scheme avoids any file identification conflicts among users while permitting an almost arbitrary assignment of branch names. The branch

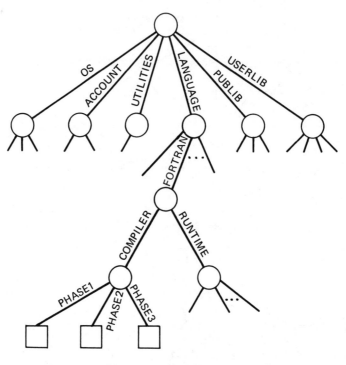

Fig. 9-5 Typical directory.

name can be interpreted as the name given to a file by a user while he is working within a given file context. The tree path name can be employed as a
search argument to find any data or directory file. Since the directories are
files, access control restrictions can also be defined for them, thus controlling
the set of users capable of modifying and retrieving directory information.

Many systems employ a two-level directory structure; here, the master
directory points to directories for various systems and user files. A third level
contains the data files. An example of this type is the file system for the University of Cambridge ATLAS computer (Wilkes, 1968, Chapter 6). This
organization is certainly simpler than a multilevel one but reduces the flexibility in naming, and collecting and controlling the use of related files. (Why?)
MS with more than two directory levels for files include IBM OS/360 (IBM,
1965), MULTICS (1967), and TENEX (Bobrow et. al, 1972). Some interesting aspects of the MULTICS methods are discussed in the next paragraph.

In MULTICS, each user (process) obtains a *working* directory; files are
then referenced *relative* to the current working directory. For example, if the
working directory of user *U* is directory 7 in Fig. 9-4(a), *U* would identify file
16 by the path name *E.K.* A convention for moving up the tree permits the
identification of both ancestral and other groups of files that are not descen-

dants of the working directory. Assume that an asterisk ('*') indicates the *parent* of a given file. Then file 6 in Fig. 9-4 is referenced by *.*B.D* with respect to file 7; similarly, if the working directory were number 12, then file 9 would be located as *.*.*D.F*. To increase the efficiency of these cross-directory references, *links* may be established between directory entries. A link is an entry in a directory that points directly to another directory *entry*, rather than a file. This is illustrated by the dotted lines in Fig. 9-4; links exist from directory 12 to the *A* entry of directory 2 and from directory 5 to the *F* entry of directory 8. Note that links are assigned names in the same manner as branches. Then, the name of file 9 with respect to working directory 5 is either *.*C.D.F*. or, using the link, just *F*; as another example, file 4 could be referenced with respect to directory 11 by either *.*.*A.A* or by *G.L*. One must be careful with links because they destroy the basic tree organization and can lead to inconsistencies; for example, if file 4 and the corresponding branch *A* of directory 2 were deleted, then the link *L* in directory 12 would point to a nonexistent entry.

Since directories can contain many entries and a potentially large number of these files may be defined, most directories are stored in secondary memory. For removable libraries and self-contained systems of files, the "local" directories are often on the same storage device as the files to which they point. It is normal for part or all of the master directory to reside in main storage, temporarily or permanently; in either case, the descriptor for the master directory is permanently maintained in main memory so that file searching can be initiated.

EXERCISE

Assume the following form for all directory files:

1. Each directory entry contains the symbolic branch name, auxiliary storage address, and length of a child file (directory or data).

2. The first two words of the file contain the auxiliary storage address and length, respectively, of the parent directory.

Suppose a working directory *D* resides in main memory at locations $W[i]$, $i = 1, \ldots, w$. Write a Boolean procedure

$$SearchDirectory(Path, n, Addr) ;$$

which searches the directory tree for a file identified by the path name $Path[i]$, $i = 1, \ldots, n$, relative to *D*. The routine should return **false** if the requested file is not found; otherwise, it returns **true** and the secondary storage address of the file in *Addr*. Each element of *Path* may be an asterisk or a symbolic branch name; for example, the path *.*.*B.C.* would be stored as $Path[1] = Path[2] = '*'$, $Path[3] =$ $'B'$, $Path[4] = 'C'$. (Assume that links are not used.)

Use the following given procedures in your program:

(1) $Read(FileAddr, M, Length)$;

Read a file of length *Length* located in auxiliary storage at address *FileAddr* into main storage words $M[1]$, $M[2]$, . . . , $M[Length]$.

(2) $Search(M, Length, Name, Addr, Len)$; (Boolean procedure)

Search the name field of a file stored in main memory $M[i]$, $i = 1, \ldots, Length$ for the symbolic name *Name*. If unsuccessful, return **false** ; otherwise, return **true**, the auxiliary storage address of *Name* in *Addr*, and its length in *Len*.

9.4.2 Descriptors for Files

A *file descriptor*, associated with each file, contains the descriptive information required by the file system in order to perform its servicing functions. In particular, it is the data in the descriptor that permits the mapping from virtual to real file space—from logical to physical records—as well as the many other file operations. A descriptor is established when a file is first created, and is updated when it is moved, contracted, expanded, or accessed.

If a given file may be addressed by only *one* directory entry in the system, then the most logical location for each descriptor is within the directory itself as part of each entry. In practice, it is often stored in a separate area on the storage device containing the corresponding files. This convention permits the use of relatively large descriptors and allows the contents of an auxiliary storage device to be directly identified within the storage itself; also, several directory entries can then conveniently point to the same file. The descriptor is normally kept resident in main storage from the time the file is made active (opened) until it is closed; during this time, it is usually augmented by processing dependent information such as buffer locations and accessing routines.

Three basic data items appear in descriptors in virtually all file systems: the file identification, where the file is stored, and access control information:

File Identification

This item normally consists of a symbolic name N and an internal identifier I. N could be a nonunique character string, such as the branch names in the directories tree discussed in the last section, or it may be a unique symbolic name, such as the path name from the master directory to the named file; one advantage of the second scheme is that the name information is then helpful both in reconstructing the directory after a systems "crash" and in testing the file system for consistency. The purpose of I is to provide a unique simple identifier for each file so that the descriptor can be easily located and the file may be conveniently referenced. This identifier might be the actual location of the descriptor; or a pair (i, d) indicating the ith file on device d; or the result of some straightforward counting method, for example, file number 325; or something more esoteric, such as the time the file was created.

Physical Address

The location and extent of a file are defined here. For files that are not stored sequentially, the address and length of each physical record must be specified—either directly by a list, or indirectly, for example, by a pointer to an index table or to the first record of a linked set of records. The mapping between logical records—contiguously addressed words of virtual file space—and the corresponding physical record addresses appear in this component either implicitly through the physical address information or explicitly, for example, by a table.

Access Control Information

The facility to control *who* can access a given set of files and *how* is one of the central and most important services provided in multiuser, resource-sharing systems. The "who" and "how" information is stored in this descriptor item. The file system must rigorously enforce these access control specifications and keep them tamperproof. The next section is devoted to this aspect of files.

A variety of other useful data appear in the descriptor. Examples are

1. *Historical and Measurement Information.* This may include date of creation, date of last change or last read, number of times the file has been opened, and other usage data.

2. *Disposition.* A file could be *temporary*, to be destroyed at "closing" time at the end of the job for which it was created, or it may be stored indefinitely as a *permanent* file.

3. *Coding of Information.* File data may be coded as uninterpreted *binary* strings meant to be directly loaded into the machine, or as *characters* (for example, in EBCDIC or USASCII code) that must be decoded and encoded or unpacked and packed during input and output, respectively.

4. *Physical Organization.* E.g., sequential, linked, indexed; fixed/variable-length records; etc. This information could be part of the *Physical Address* component of the descriptor.

9.4.3 Access Control

The access control information specifies the protection accorded to a file *within* a computer system. (The problems of securing an installation from external forces, such as theft or electromagnetic wiretapping, are not considered.) The "who" and "how" lists in the descriptor must be enforced during the main storage residency of the file as well as during all file IO operations. The latter is handled in the file system by passing all access requests through software control procedures that check their legitimacy. However, after a file has been loaded into main storage, this last method is impractical, since the entire range of CPU operations is possible. Instead, the access control data in the descriptor is employed to set the appropriate hardware storage and control protection flags (Sec. 5.2.3 describes some of these mechanisms); this type of protection is consequently limited by the characteristics of the central processor and storage control.

Files must be immune from several kinds of deliberate or accidental protection violations. These include the impersonation of one user by another, the access of files by unauthorized users, and the incorrect use of files by authorized users, including the owners. The access control data definable in most systems can be represented as *capability* lists of pairs $\langle C, A \rangle$, interpreted as: "If a user meets conditions C, then he may access the file in ways A." C essentially defines an authorized user or group of users—i.e., *who* can access the file—and A, the *access attributes*, indicates *how* the file can be used.

The access attributes generally specify permission to do one or more of the following operations: *read, write, load for execution, truncate* (delete part of the file) or *append* (add data to the file). In addition, the authority to change the contents of the capability lists must be an attribute of at least one user, the *owner*. The allowable set of conditions in C may be an explicit list of users, e.g., by name or account number, or tests based on such items as correct password submission or particular location of the user.

An even more general scheme permits file owners to define arbitrary procedures that intercept all file accesses. The owner can then devise any elaborate protection mechanism that he requires—for example, specifying the time of day at which certain classes of users may access files, or engaging in a lengthy security dialogue with the file user.

Examples

1. The MULTICS file system (MULTICS, 1967) stores access control lists in the branch entries of directories. The access attributes are *read, write, execute, append,* and *trap*. The "trap" is employed to implement the scheme described in the last paragraph. If the *trap* attribute is "on" when a file access is requested, a procedure is invoked to return the effective access attributes; otherwise, the attributes in the list are directly used. A distinction is made between directory files and data files in the interpretation of the attributes; for directory files, the *execute* attribute specifies permission to search the directory, while *read* defines permission to read only those directory items available to the user.

2. On the Cambridge multiple-access system (Wilkes, 1968), users of the set of files specified in a single directory are divided into four classes: the owner, a set of partners (defined by the owner), a set of keyholders (those who know the password given by the owner), and the remainder. Access privileges are defined for each class as global "authority" lists in the owner's directory. An element in an authority list represents an expression of the form:

$$\text{If } p_{i_1} \wedge p_{i_2} \wedge \cdots \wedge p_{i_k} \text{ are satisfied,}$$

$$\text{then accesses } a_O \, a_P \, a_K \, a_R \text{ are permitted,}$$

where the p_i are conditions such as "The name of the user is X," "User is working at a console," or "User has given a correct password," and a_O, a_P, a_K, and a_R indicate the accesses allowed as an owner, partner, keyholder, and anyone else, respectively. Each a_x is a bit string indicating some combination of the privileges: *read, load for execution, write, delete,* and *change access privileges*. Similarly, each file also has four strings b_O, b_P, b_K, and b_R, which define the access allowed by each class of user to the particular files. Thus an access request must pass through both the global restrictions of the authority lists and the local ones associated with each file. There is also a second kind of global authority list that is directed towards creation of new files, changing directories, and changing authority lists.

There is another type of security, not represented in the access control information, that must be provided. It is needed when several processes may potentially use a given file simultaneously. No problems arise if more than one user is reading the same file at the same time. However, if a user is involved in *writing* a file, it is desirable that no other read or write accesses be permitted to that file during this activity; otherwise, the results may be unpredictable. This is another variation of our familiar critical section problem and can be handled by using techniques developed in Chapter 3 (see also Courtois, et al., 1971). As one example, the Cambridge file system (Cambridge, 1967) ensures that (1) once a file has been opened for updating, no other user can access it, and (2) the access control data of a file cannot be changed during the time the file is being used in any way; concurrent reading is allowed.

EXERCISE

Consider n cyclic processes ($n > 1$), each accessing a common file F. All processes execute the two file system calls *Read* and *Write* to retrieve elements of F and write on F, respectively. The ith process p_i has the form

begin L_i: ... *Read* ; ... *Write* ; ... **go to** Li **end** ;

Any number of *Read*'s can occur simultaneously, but each *Write* is a critical section with respect to both *Read*'s and other *Write*'s. More precisely, each element a_{uv} of the following array answers the question:

> When a process p_i is in routine u, can another process
> p_j, $i \neq j$, be executing routine v?

		v	
		Read	*Write*
u	*Read*	Yes	No
	Write	No	No

Using the Dijkstra P and V operations and appropriate semaphores (Chapter 3), insert code around the *Read* and *Write* of p_i to *just* satisfy these constraints.

9.4.4 Opening and Closing Routines

After a process declares its intent to use or create a particular file, a set of file *opening* procedures are normally called to perform several initialization activities. Opening could occur at the time a job is selected for loading and execution, in response to an explicit *OPEN FILE* command, or, in the most dynamic case, as a side effect of the first request for a file operation.† Similarly, *closing* routines are invoked at the termination of a file's processing. These are typically executed at the end of a job or process, or as a result of an explicit *CLOSE FILE* command. The closing operations essentially release the resources used for the file IO and render the file inactive for the particular user.

The opening routines are responsible for obtaining the resources required for the file IO and for making the file active. This includes the following tasks:

A_1. For *old* files that are catalogued in the system:
   1. Find the file and make it available for processing: Search the directory to locate the file. If the file is off-line, on magnetic tape or removable disk, allocate a unit and physically mount the file.
   2. Use the access control information in the descriptor to check that the user has authority to access the file in the manner requested.

A_2. For *new* files that are to be created: Allocate secondary storage and/or device(s) for the file. A block of secondary storage, or a tape or disk unit might be reserved.

B. For old and new files:
   1. Obtain any main memory needed for IO buffers.

---

†An *OPEN FILE* or *CLOSE FILE* command is either explicitly given by a user, or it is *generated* by the system.

2. Load routines for accessing the file and effecting the virtual to real space mappings.

3. Possibly generate a skeletal form for the IO command sequences to be employed.

4. Insert the data of A_1 or A_2 and B, and the descriptor, into an active file directory (AFD); other names for the AFD entry are *file control block* and *data control block*. Each user may have a private AFD, or the AFD could be consolidated into one system-wide structure.

If the file is already active, due to previous opening by another user, many of the above steps can be bypassed.

The closing routines reverse the opening work. Specifically, closing involves the following operations:

A_1. For *temporary* files, created solely for the current tasks, and for files that will *never* be referenced again, destroy the file by releasing its secondary (and off-line) storage resources and deleting its directory entry.

A_2. For *new* files that are to be retained, i.e., *permanent* new files, insert an appropriate entry in the directory structure.

B. For *permanent* old and new files:
1. Update the file descriptor with any new data resulting from its most recent use; these could include changes to the file such as length, and historical information such as time-last-referenced or time-last-changed.
2. If necessary, insert end-of-file markers after the last record in the file.
3. Store the file identification and location so that it may be copied later for back-up purposes. (These procedures are discussed more fully in Sec. 9.7.)

C. For *all* files:
1. "Rewind" the file and possible unmount the storage device.
2. Remove the file entry from the AFD.
3. Release any buffer space and reserved devices to their respective resource pools.

9.5. MANAGEMENT OF AUXILIARY STORAGE SPACE

We consider allocation strategies and methods for keeping track of space on direct-access secondary memory; the space on a device is assumed to be *shared* among several files rather than entirely dedicated to one file. Not surprisingly, some of the techniques for main storage administration described in Chapter 5 are also applicable, with appropriate modifications, to the auxiliary storage case.

The basic function of the allocator is to satisfy requests for fixed- or variable-length "blocks" of secondary storage. Space is usually allocated in units of *fixed*-size blocks because of the fixed-length physical record organization of many storage media, the large amount of available storage, and the relative simplicity of such a policy. Efficiency of IO is often the main criterion for deciding which of several possible free blocks to select; one wishes to minimize rotational delays and seek times (where applicable) when the acquired blocks are later accessed. Thus, it is desirable to allocate all storage for the same request and same file "close" together. However, the fixed-size blocks need not be allocated contiguously together, but could be linked or indexed in some fashion, as described in Sec. 9.3; the allocation and retrieval of blocks is then analogous to that for *paged* main memory, but without the continual need for dynamic replacements (except perhaps in systems that automatically move files through a hierarchy of secondary storage media). Blocks of secondary storage are freed when a file is moved off-line either as a result of a user request or because of its inactivity, or when a file is purposely destroyed or shrunk in size.

Arguments for and against static versus dynamic allocation are also present here but in somewhat different form than in the main memory case. File size is often not known in advance, so that a static allocation policy must frequently rely on upper bound size estimates. Unless much wasted space can be tolerated, a dynamic method seems necessary for some files, for example, spooled input and output. As we illustrated in Example 2 of Sec. 8.1, such a policy can easily lead to a deadlock situation. For example, in a spooling subsystem, all processes may become blocked waiting for input and output file space. (This type of deadlock could be prevented by using maximum claim information supplied by a user for each job. More commonly, the deadlock is allowed to occur, provided it does not happen too often. The recovery procedure is usually to destroy the input queue of jobs, run one or more of the active jobs to completion, and then manually reload the old input queue. A more complex but satisfying recovery solution is to start printing a job before it is completed.)

There are several ways to keep track of available space. The most obvious method is to link all free blocks together by pointers stored in each free space block. It suffices to maintain in main storage a pointer to the first such block. This has the advantage of simplicity but is severely inefficient. In order to add or remove free space from the lists, extensive IO operations must be executed to find the appropriate number of blocks and to modify the pointers. (Why?) For this reason, it is more common to employ index table techniques, similar to those outlined in Sec. 9.3. A separate table or set of tables containing all free space is maintained on a device basis. The tables can be organized internally as linked lists or as bit arrays. In the former case, one word is allocated for each (fixed-size) block of secondary storage, and all free blocks are linked together. It is relatively easy to release and allocate blocks with this organization, but it consumes a large amount of storage. Much less table space is necessary if each block is represented by a *single* bit in the table—a "1" is interpreted as a free block and a "0" as unavailable. Retrieval of free blocks takes longer than with the linked tables, but the faster release of free blocks and the efficient representation make the bit method generally preferable. With the possible exception of the bit table method, it is usually necessary to store most of the available space records on secondary storage because of their large size; only the currently "active" records are kept in main memory.

Available and used space records provide an opportunity for some useful redundancy. Two separate sets of tables can be maintained—one for free space and the other for used space. This permits some elementary file system consistency checks when hardware and software errors occur; the tables can be matched against each other and the directory entries. These tables are conveniently treated as files; they thus can be accessed through the file system commands, and appear in the file directory.

Example

The HASP II system (Simpson, et al., 1969), widely used for input and output spooling within IBM OS/360, employs an efficient management scheme for direct access devices (disks and drums). Available space is maintained on a "cylinder" basis. A *cylinder* was originally defined for movable head disks as that set of data that may be accessed under one positioning of the heads; the term was extended to include drum and fixed-head disk storage, where it may mean the entire unit or some part of it, depending on addressing conventions. A *Master Cylinder Map* contains a bit table for each device, with each bit representing a single cylinder; a bit value of "1" means that the cylinder is free, and a value of "0" indicates that the cylinder has already been allocated to either a HASP file or some other file. This map is maintained in main storage. The allocation of input and output files associated with each job is kept on a *Job Cylinder Map* with one set of maps per job; a bit value of "1" in a table means that the cylinder is allocated, while "0" means that it is free. These maps are stored on secondary storage until they become active. When a job file dynamically requires more space during either input or output spooling, it receives storage on a cylinder basis for the file but on a track basis for each request. Thus, when a track of space is requested, the allocator will either supply the next track of an allocated (for that job file) cylinder; or, if the cylinder has no more free tracks or this is the first request, it will supply a new cylinder to the job file and give the first track to satisfy the request. To reduce seek times, the system systematically attempts to allocate the cylinder closest to (or equal to) the last cylinder referenced on that device. Space is released for an entire file at once; this is accomplished simply by "ORing" the *Job Map* with the *Master Cylinder Map.*

There is one other component of the auxiliary storage administration subsystem that must be carefully designed. Since the storage is limited in capacity, facilities must be provided for moving inactive files off-line, for example, onto magnetic tape, and for transferring files through a hierarchy of storage devices when one exists. Typically, the bases for moving include the current filing load on the system, the priorities of the file users, the relative activities of the files, and the file sizes. In addition to file movement routines, there is a need for file *copying* to provide back-up capability.

9.6. A HIERARCHICAL MODEL FOR FILE SYSTEMS

The file system organization presented in Sec. 9.2 approximately follows the model described in Madnick (1968) and Madnick and Alsop (1969). Such a model allows, in principle, the systematic design, construction, and comprehension of these complex systems by breaking them into manageable self-contained components. In this section, the details of the model are developed more explicitly. We take the position that the average user need be concerned only with virtual files, structured and accessed according to his application, and that he should be isolated from machine-dependent details, such as the particular device containing his file, storage allocation algorithms, software accessing mechanisms, blocking, and buffering; the latter are the responsibility of the file system.

A file system is decomposed into a number of levels in an hierarchical structure, leading from the actual hardware and IO schedulers at the lowest level to the user interfaces at the most abstract. This is consistent with our descripton of systems in Sec. 1.4.1 and with the design methodology described in Sec. 4.5. Each level represents a successively more abstract machine—in this case, "filing" machine—and is realized by a set of processes; communication is restricted so that any process at level k can send messages only to other processes at the same level, level $k + 1$, and $k - 1$ (Fig. 9-6). The hierarchical structure is useful because it permits one to concentrate on the design of individual processes with well-defined tasks and communication channels to other processes.

The model consists of six functional levels, as illustrated in Fig. 9-7. Below, we specify the tasks within each level, proceeding from the virtual file user interface down to the hardware:

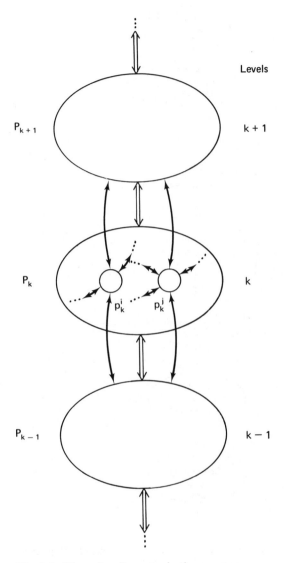

Fig. 9-6 Hierarchy of communicating processes.

L6. *Logical Organization Methods.* The user interface level provides the routines and processes for imposing a logical structure on formatless virtual files (Sec. 9.3). An independent routine or module would normally be associated with each different type of organization.

L5. *Directory Retrieval.* The primary function of the processes at this level is to convert symbolic file names to identifiers, which, in turn, point to

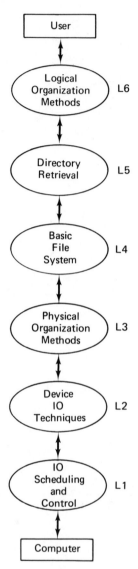

Fig. 9-7 A file system model.

the precise location of either the file, its descriptor, or perhaps a table containing this information. To accomplish this, the directory structure is searched for an entry to the referenced file (Sec. 9.4.1).

L4. *Basic File System.* This part activates and deactivates files by invoking opening and closing routines, and is responsible for verifying the access rights of the caller on each file request, if necessary. The primary task is to retrieve the descriptor for the file (Secs. 9.4.2, 9.4.3, 9.4.4).

L3. *Physical Organization Methods.* The original user request for access to certain logical file addresses is translated into physical secondary storage address requests, reflecting the actual locations and organization of the desired records (Sec. 9.3). Allocation of secondary storage (Sec. 9.5) and main storage buffers is conveniently treated in this level also.

L2. *Device IO Techniques.* The requested operation(s) and physical record(s) are converted into appropriate sequences of IO instructions, channel commands, and controller orders. Local optimizations, for example, to minimize rotational delay within the operations, are performed. (The device processes described in Sec. 7.3 are prototypes of the processes at this level.)

L1. *IO Scheduling and Control.* The actual queuing, scheduling, initiating, and controlling of all IO requests occur at this level which directly "connects" to the IO hardware of the computer system. Basic IO interrupt servicing is also done here.

One reason for this particular choice of levels and functions is the simple communication that exists between levels. The information passed down from the user through successive levels is basically requests for work and the following data:

$$\text{L6} \xrightarrow{\text{(symbolic file name, } A_6)} \text{L5} \xrightarrow{\text{(file identifier, } A_5)} \text{L4} \xrightarrow{\text{(file descriptor, } A_4)}$$

$$\text{L3} \xrightarrow{\text{(physical record list, } A_3)} \text{L2} \xrightarrow{\text{(IO sequences, } A_2)} \text{L1}$$

where the A_i represent other parameters such as type of operation, length, and core address.

The messages passed up the hierarchy would be essentially completion messages. Parts of the hierarchy may often be bypassed within a given system by special classes of users and/or for certain files; for example, some supervisory routines might access the Basic File System or the IO Scheduling and Control modules directly.

Example

Consider again the card file read example given earlier in Sec. 9.2. The correspondence between the various operations performed in response to the user's *ReadaCard* request and the model levels are

$$(2) \longleftrightarrow \text{L6}, \quad (3)_1 \longleftrightarrow \text{L5}, \quad ((3)_2, \quad (3)_3, \quad (3)_4) \longleftrightarrow \text{L4},$$

$$(4)_1 \longleftrightarrow \text{L3}, \quad (4)_2 \longleftrightarrow \text{L2}.$$

The model is a relatively recent offering and clearly requires some further development and specification. Nevertheless, it is presently useful in a pedagogic setting for systematically examining the components and tasks of file systems, and it may prove more beneficial for realizing réal systems. One aspect of file systems design that is *not* included in the model is back-up and recovery from errors. The next section discusses some details of this important problem.

EXERCISE

Select a multiprogrammed OS with which you are familiar and describe its file system in terms of the six levels presented in this section. Where does it agree and where does it deviate from the model?

9.7. RECOVERY FROM SYSTEMS FAILURE

Hardware and software errors can be reduced by building reliable and, often, redundant machine components, and by the systematic logical design, coding, and debugging of programs. Unfortunately, failures or "crashes" are still *guaranteed* to occur in most complex systems. These may be *catastrophic* failures which essentially destroy vital parts of the MS and require extensive reconstruction efforts, or they could be less severe and localized to a small number of tables and/or programs. Modules for analyzing and recovering from such errors should be an integral part of any systems design and not—as is commonly done—be an *ad hoc* patch inserted after the rest of the operating system has been implemented. The basic need is for "graceful" recovery methods that are transparent to the user, execute rapidly, and require little real-time work by systems staff at the time of failure; an extreme example of a nongraceful recovery procedure is simply to reload the most current version of the OS—stored off-line on tape or disk usually—and force users to redefine *all* of their files. (This is a good way for a computer center to lose all of its customers!) It is appropriate to examine the recovery problem in this chapter since, from the point of view of systems reconstruction, the file system contains the most vital information—directories of jobs in progress, locations of all programs and data files, allocation details of on- and off-line storage, accounting records, and other critical data.

First, we briefly review some of the causes and effects of systems failures. Hardware errors may result from failures in any of the computer components as well as the communications lines connecting them. An error can produce a complete breakdown of a component, such as a disk drive, or it may be manifested more subtly as a nonreproducible transient, for example, a storage parity error caused by a fluctuation in power. Hardware failures are normally detected by the hardware itself and, in many instances, can be localized to a small area; an example is the mechanical breakdown of a peripheral unit such as a card reader. Frequently, however, the situation can be much more serious, causing many of the problems discussed below for software bugs; the electronic destruction of information in a memory box or the erasure of parts of a disk due to incorrect functioning of read/write heads or movable arms are in this category.

Systems and user programs are rarely, if ever, bug-free. Typical coding errors are transfer of control to an incorrect, perhaps nonexistent, address, mistakes in operand addressing that result in the retrieval and modification of wrong data items, and "infinite" looping. Careful systems design and a computer with appropriate hardware protection mechanisms should ensure that user errors are totally isolated from the OS and from other users;† attempts to access data in or to transfer control to memory assigned to the system or to other user jobs are normally caught by hardware, while incorrect systems service calls, e.g., through a trap mechanism, are discovered by systems programs. Thus, software failures can be traced mainly to errors in system programs (and design) rather than to those of users. The effects of these bugs may be

1. The complete destruction of critical tables, such as process queues or active directories.

2. Addresses and pointers, for example those in file directories, that do not link to valid list items.

3. Incorrect resource lists, such as the free space tables for auxiliary storage.

4. Even writing or reading the wrong data from the wrong files.

Discovery of the cause and effects of a system failure is generally a very difficult task, since programs have usually progressed far beyond the actual incorrect code at the time the failure becomes apparent. There are few general rules that one can give, at least for isolating the effects. A common technique is to examine all systems data structures for *consistency*. Examples of how consistency may be verified are:

1. *Tracing of Address Entries in Tables.* Normally, the set of addresses to which a pointer may link is fixed and relatively small, and each "node" of a list structure has some identifying header information that can be checked. For example, file directory entries must point to other directories or files, and the pointer structure usually forms a tree with data files as the leaves; the latter can be verified by tracing through the pointers. Another clear example is found in doubly linked lists, where successive forward and backward links

---

†Nevertheless, it is still a challenge and ritual for many computer science students to discover ways to break through the protection schemes into the system.

must point to the same entry. Auxiliary storage addresses in tables are also usually valid only within a small range of possible addresses.

2. *Use of Redundant Information.* It is often convenient for normal processing purposes to maintain several copies of the same information but in different forms. For example, a resource data structure might contain allocation details, such as the name of each process holding some of the resource, while the process descriptors may redundantly contain a list of each resource allocated to the process; the available and used space lists mentioned in Sec. 9.5 also duplicates the same information. This redundancy might also be explicitly designed for consistency checking.

3. *Application of Checksum Methods.* Accountants have long used checksums and hash totals to provide an independent check on the validity of a table of dollar amounts. The idea is to combine *all* of the data in a table or file into a single number, for example, by summing, exclusive "ORing," or some other operation; this is done when the table is first created and whenever it is changed. When the table or file is accessed, the checksum is computed again to ensure that all of the data is still present.

Numerous other examples exist; many of these fall within normal error checking responsibilities of programs, e.g., checking that a count of the number of buffers is nonnegative.

Localized hardware breakdowns that do not subsequently result in software damages and that are not critical to the continued operation of the computer are normally handled by removing records of the hardware resource from the data structures and possibly substituting an equivalent resource; a breakdown of a noncritical peripheral unit falls in this class. For more serious hardware problems and for software failures, graceful recovery requires that up-to-date copies of the operating system, the file system, and even the contents of main storage be available. This *backup* series of files is the center of all recovery procedures. Failures are then handled by the selective loading of backup files in an attempt to recreate the total system as it appeared immediately before failure.† Recovery from catastrophic "crashes" can be accomplished by a systematic but lengthy reloading procedure, while less severe failures are treated on a more *ad hoc* basis in the hope of recovering more quickly and more completely.

Backup procedures that *dump* parts of the system must be both convenient and efficient. To dump the entire on-line set of information at selected time

†Note that a complete reconstruction of the system *immediately* before failure will subsequently result in the *same* crash; thus, the error must be found and then corrected or bypassed, or, in the case of more subtle or transient errors, a slightly less than up-to-date reconstruction is necessary so that the OS can be run while a lengthy systems analysis is made.

intervals is not satisfactory generally because it is both too time-consuming and cannot be done frequently enough to provide up-to-date copies. The standard approach maintains two types of backup dumps: *selective incremental* dumps obtained at relatively frequent time intervals and more complete *checkpoint* dumps occurring over much longer intervals.

The incremental dumps will copy all files that have been either *modified* or *created* since the last such dump; files that have been accessed in a read-only manner are not included. This ensures that the most recent version of any file is available. Dumping can be initiated at a regular fixed time interval, say every few minutes or hours, when the system has nothing else to do, almost continuously at the end of each job or phase within a job, or some combination of these; the second scheme is somewhat dangerous by itself, since no guarantees could be made on the timeliness of the dump. In any case, some record of changed or created files must be maintained. The purpose of checkpoint dumps is to allow a relatively recent version of the system to be loaded quickly so that jobs may be run and further reconstruction can proceed at a more leisurely pace. Typically, this dump copies the *most recently used* parts of the system—both systems and user files. A complete checkpoint dump cycle may be accomplished approximately every few days but could be programmed to copy small portions at a smaller time increment. Records of backup files, containing items such as time, type, and location of the dump, may conveniently be included in file directories; that is, the dumps are treated as files. Of course, we run into a familiar problem here: What happens if the directory is destroyed? One clearly needs an off-line record of the backup file directories; but, since these directories are changing often, they appear in the incremental dumps, and the record is available.

Given the incremental and checkpoint backup files, recovery from catastrophic failures proceeds in the following manner:

1. Reload the system from the most recent checkpoint dump. The reloaded system is now used to control the remainder of the recovery while other user jobs are simultaneously run.

2. Starting from the most recent incremental dump, work backwards in time through the incremental dumps, reconstructing system and user files and directories.

It is not possible at this time to outline a systematic procedure for restoring a system after noncatastrophic failures. However, if errors can be isolated to a small set of files or tables, it is often possible to reconstruct these in a consistent manner so as to affect a small, if not null, set of users and allow almost immediate continued systems operations. For example, if the failure only affects a single job or the current job mix, then one can simply purge the job(s) and rerun it (them); if files are modified during the first failed execution, then either the users will have to be notified about a possible bad file, or, more satisfactorily, the most recent file can be obtained from one of the backup dumps automatically. Similarly, if only a small set of systems files or tables prove erroneous on checking after failure, then it may be possible to correct these and continue. One example might be the files and in-core tables relating to user accounting; if these were partially or fully destroyed as a result of a systems error, they should be easily built from backup files, with the exception of the current job load. Another example is an inconsistency in the available and used space lists in secondary storage; they can be rebuilt by tracing through the directory structures.

Examples

1. The backup procedures of the Cambridge multiple-access system (Wilkes, 1968) employ two sets of tapes—a "primary" cycle set S_1 for frequent incremental dumping and a "secondary" cycle set S_2 for more complete but less frequent dumps; S_1 and S_2 are each used in a cyclic manner. For incremental dumps, the next tape T in S_1 is selected and all new and modified files are copied in T as well as any files on T (from the last cycle) that are not yet in S_2. The secondary cycle selects the next tape U from S_2 and copies all files on U that are not yet in S_2 as well as previous files on U that still have permanent status.

2. The file system in MULTICS (1967) includes incremental and both systems and user checkpoint dumping, with copying done in duplicate for even further protection. Systems checkpoints consist of the current accounting, directory, and OS component files, whereas user checkpoints dump all segments accessed since the last checkpoint. In addition to the reloading process for catastrophic errors, MULTICS has an "on-line salvage" procedure that attempts to correct less severe failures by ensuring that directories and space tables are consistent.

3. The HASP II Spooling System (Simpson, et al., 1969) of IBM OS/360 (see also the example in Sec. 9.5) copies backup information at the completion of each stage of every job and also at a predefined time increment, approximately every minute. The dumped data include the job table, disk cylinder map, and a print checkpoint table that permits the warm start of those jobs being printed.

EXERCISE

Examine the systems tables, data structures, and directories in some MS and develop a catalog of consistency tests for these structures. What additional checking information would you recommend?

Appendix
A MULTIPROGRAMMING PROJECT

A1. INTRODUCTION

The appendix describes a tractable project involving the design and implementation of a multiprogramming operating system (MOS) for a hypothetical computer configuration that can be easily simulated (Shaw and Weiderman, 1971). The purpose is to consolidate and apply, in an almost realistic setting, some of the concepts and techniques discussed in this book. In particular, the MOS designer/implementer must deal directly with problems of input-output, interrupt handling, process synchronization, scheduling, main and auxiliary storage management, process and resource data structures, and systems organization.

We assume that the project will be coded for a large central computer facility (the "host" system) which, on the one hand, does not allow users to tamper with the operating system or the machine resources but, on the other hand, does provide a complete set of services, including filing services, debugging aids, and a good higher-level language. The global strategy is to simulate the hypothetical computer on the host and write the MOS for this simulated machine. The MOS and simulator will consist of approximately 1000 to 1200 cards of program, with most of the code representing the MOS. The project can be completed over a period of about two months by students concurrently taking a normal academic load.

The characteristics and components of the MOS computer are specified in the next section. Section A3 outlines the format of user jobs. The path of a user job through the system, and the functions and main components of the MOS are described in Section A4. The following section (A5) then lists the detailed requirements for the project. In the final Sec. A6, some limitations of the project are described.

277

A2. MACHINE SPECIFICATIONS

The MOS computer is described from two points of view: the "virtual" machine seen by the typical user and the "real" machine used by the MOS designer/implementer.

1. The Virtual Machine

The virtual machine viewed by a normal user is illustrated in Fig. A-1. Storage consists of a maximum of 100 words, addressed from 00 to 99; each

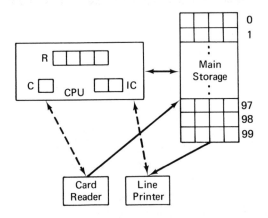

Fig. A-1   Virtual user machine.

word is divided into four one-byte units, where a byte may contain any character acceptable by the host machine. The CPU has three registers of interest: a four-byte general register R, a one-byte "Boolean" toggle C, which may contain either 'T' (true) or 'F' (false), and a two-byte instruction counter IC.

A storage word may be interpreted as an instruction or data word. The operation code of an instruction occupies the two high-order bytes of the word, and the operand address appears in the two low-order bytes. Table A-1 gives the format and interpretation of each instruction. Note that the input instruction (GD) reads only the first 40 columns of a card and that the output instruction (PD) prints a new line of 40 characters. The first instruction of a program must *always* appear in location 00.

With this simple machine, a batch of compute-bound, IO-bound, and balanced programs can be quickly written. The usual kinds of programming errors are also almost guaranteed to be made. (Both these characteristics are desirable, since the MOS should be able to handle a variety of jobs and user errors.)

Table A-1   Instruction Set of Virtual Machine

Instruction		Interpretation
Operator	Operand	
LR	$x_1 x_2$	$R := [\alpha]$;
SR	$x_1 x_2$	$\alpha := R$;
CR	$x_1 x_2$	**if** $R = [\alpha]$ **then** $C := $ 'T' **else** $C := $ 'F' ;
BT	$x_1 x_2$	**if** $C = $ 'T' **then** $IC := \alpha$;
GD	$x_1 x_2$	$Read([\beta + i], i = 0, \ldots, 9)$;
PD	$x_1 x_2$	$Print([\beta + i], i = 0, \ldots, 9)$;
H		$halt$

Notes: 1. $x_1, x_2 \in \{0, 1, \ldots, 9\}$
  2. $\alpha = 10x_1 + x_2$
  3. $[\alpha]$ means "the contents of location α"
  4. $\beta = 10x_1$

2. The Real Machine

(a) *Components*

Figure A-2 contains a schematic of the real machine. The CPU may operate in either a *master* or a *slave* mode. In master mode, instructions from supervisor storage are directly processed by the higher-level language processor (HLP); in slave mode, the HLP interprets a "microprogram" in the read-only memory which simulates (emulates) the CPU of the virtual machine and accesses virtual machine programs in user storage via a paging mechanism. The HLP is any convenient and available higher-level language. (This

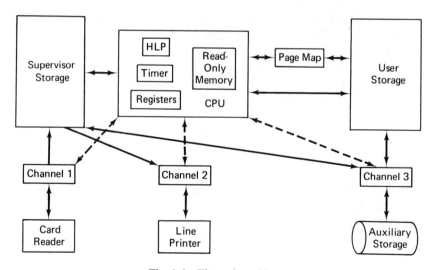

Fig. A-2   The real machine.

organization allows the virtual machine emulator and the MOS to be coded in a higher-level language available on the host system, while maintaining some correspondence with real computers.) The CPU registers of interest are:

C: a one-byte "Boolean" toggle,
R: a four-byte general register,
IC: a two-byte virtual machine location counter,
PI, SI, IOI, TI: four interrupt registers,
PTR: a four-byte page table register,
$CHST[i]$, $i = 1, 2, 3$: three channel status registers, and
$MODE$: mode of CPU, 'master' or 'slave'.

User storage contains 300 four-byte words, addressed from 000 to 299. It is divided into 30 ten-word blocks for paging purposes. Supervisor storage is loosely defined as that amount of storage required for the MOS.

Auxiliary storage is a high-speed drum of 100 tracks, with 10 four-byte words per track. A transfer of 10 words to or from a track takes one time unit. (Rotational delay time is ignored.)

The card reader and line printer both operate at the rate of three time units for the IO of one record. These devices have the same characteristics as the virtual machine devices; i.e., 40 bytes (10 words) of information are transferred from the first 40 card columns or to the first 40 print positions on a read or write operation, respectively.

Channels 1 and 2 are connected from peripheral devices to supervisor storage, while channel 3 is connected between auxiliary storage and both supervisor and user memory.

(b) *Slave Mode Operation*

User storage addressing while in slave mode is accomplished through paging hardware. The *PTR* register contains the length and page table base location for the user process currently running. The four bytes $a_0 a_1 a_2 a_3$ in the *PTR* have this interpretation: a_1 is the page table length minus 1, and $10a_2 + a_3$ is the number of the user storage block in which the page table resides, where a_1, a_2, and a_3 are digits.

A two-digit instruction or operand address, $x_1 x_2$, in virtual space is mapped by the relocation hardware into the real user storage address:

$$10[10(10a_2 + a_3) + x_1] + x_2,$$

where $[\alpha]$ means "the contents of address α" and it is assumed that $x_1 \leq a_1$. *All* pages of a process are required to be loaded into user storage prior to execution.

It is assumed that each virtual machine instruction is emulated in one time unit. All interrupts occurring during slave mode operation are honored at the end of instruction cycles and cause a switch to master mode. The operations

$GD, PD,$ and H result in *supervisor*-type interrupts, that is, "supervisor calls." A *program*-type interrupt is triggered if the emulator receives an invalid operation code or if $x_1 > a_1$ during the relocation map (invalid virtual space address).

(c) *Master Mode Operation*

Master mode programs residing in supervisor storage have access to user storage and the CPU registers. The CPU is *not* interruptable in master mode; however, an appropriate interrupt register is set when an interrupt-causing event (timer or IO) occurs. The interrupt registers may be interrogated and reset by the instruction *Test*(x), which returns a value and has the effect:

> **if** $x = 1$ **then begin** *Test* $:=$ *IOI* ; *IOI* $:= 0$ **end else**
> **if** $x = 2$ **then begin** *Test* $:=$ *PI* ; *PI* $:= 0$ **end else**
> **if** $x = 3$ **then begin** *Test* $:=$ *SI* ; *SI* $:= 0$ **end else**
> **if** $x = 4$ **then begin** *Test* $:=$ *TI* ; *TI* $:= 0$ **end else**
> **if** $(IOI + PI + SI + TI) > 0$ **then** *Test* $:= 1$ **else** *Test* $:= 0$;

All user IO is performed in master mode. An IO operation is initiated by the instruction

$$StartIO(Ch, S, D, n) ;$$

where Ch is the channel number, S is an array of source blocks (10 word units), D is an array of destination blocks, and n is the number of blocks to be transmitted. If a *StartIO* is issued on a busy channel, the CPU idles in a *wait* state until the channel is free, whereupon the *StartIO* is accepted. (Issuing a *StartIO* on a busy channel is generally not advisable.) The status of any channel may be determined by examining the channel status registers *CHST*; $CHST[i] = 1$ if channel i is busy and $CHST[i] = 0$ when channel i is free ($i = 1, 2, 3$).

To switch back to slave mode, the instruction

$$Slave(ptr, c, r, ic) ;$$

is issued. *Slave* sets *PTR* to *ptr*, *C* to *c*, *R* to *r*, *IC* to *ic*, and then switches to slave mode, at the start of the emulator execution cycle.

Master mode instructions are normally executed in *zero* time units. However, it is occasionally necessary to force the CPU to wait for some specified time interval before continuing. This occurs implicitly when a *StartIO* on a busy channel is issued. An explicit wait is effected by the instruction

$$Superwait(t) ;$$

which causes the CPU to idle in a wait state for t units of time.

(d) *Channels*

When a *StartIO* is accepted by the addressed channel i, $CHST[i]$ is set to 1 (busy), and the IO transmission occurs completely in parallel with continued CPU activity. At the completion of the IO, $CHST[i]$ is set to 0 and an *IO Interrupt* signal is raised.

(e) *Timer*

The timer hardware decrements supervisor storage location TM by 1 at the end of every 10 time units of CPU operation. A *timer interrupt* occurs whenever TM is decremented to zero; the time continues decrementing at the same rate so that TM may also have negative values. TM may be set and interrogated in master mode.

(f) *Interrupts*

Four types of interrupts are possible:

(1) program: protection (page table length), invalid operation code

(2) supervisor: GD, PD, H

(3) IO: completion interrupts

(4) timer: decrement to zero

The events causing interrupts of types (1) and (2) can happen only in slave mode; events of type (3) and (4) can occur in both master and slave mode, and several of these events may happen simultaneously. The interrupt-causing event is recorded in the interrupt registers regardless of whether the interrupts are inhibited (master mode) or enabled (slave mode).

The interrupt registers are set by an interrupt event to the following values:

(1) $PI = 1$: protection; $PI = 2$: invalid operation code

(2) $SI = 1 : GD; SI = 2 : PD; SI = 3 : H$

(3) $IOI = 1$: channel 1; $IOI = 2$: channel 2; $IOI = 4$: channel 3; if several IO completion interrupts are raised simultaneously, the values are summed; for example, $IOI = 6$ indicates that both channel 2 and channel 3 completion interrupts are raised.

(4) $TI = 1$: timer.

The following code describes the *hardware* actions on an interrupt in slave mode:

comment Save state of slave process in supervisor storage locations c, r, and ic;

$c := C$; $r := R$; $ic := IC$;

comment Switch to master mode ;

$MODE :=$ 'master' ;

comment Determine cause of interrupt and transfer control;

    if $IOI \neq 0$ **then go to** *IOint* **else**

    if $PI \neq 0$ **then go to** *PROGint* **else**

    if $SI \neq 0$ **then go to** *SUPint* **else**

    go to *TIMint* ;

comment *IOint*, *PROGint*, *SUPint*, and *TIMint* are supervisor storage locations;

Note that the order of interrupt register testing implies a hardware priority scheme; this can be easily changed by master mode software.

A3. JOB, PROGRAM, AND DATA CARD FORMATS

A user job is submitted as a deck of control, program, and data cards in the order:

⟨*JOB card*⟩, ⟨*Program*⟩, ⟨*DATA card*⟩, ⟨*Data*⟩, ⟨*ENDJOB card*⟩.

1. The ⟨*JOB card*⟩ contains four entries:

(1) $AMJ   cc. 1–4, *A M*ultiprogramming *J*ob.

(2) ⟨*job id*⟩   cc. 5–8, a unique 4-character job identifier.

(3) ⟨*time estimate*⟩   cc. 9–12, 4-digit maximum time estimate.

(4) ⟨*line estimate*⟩   cc. 13–16, 4-digit maximum output estimate.

2. Each card of the ⟨*Program*⟩ deck contains information in card columns 1–40. The ith card contains the initial contents of user virtual memory locations

$$10(i - 1), 10(i - 1) + 1, \ldots, 10(i - 1) + 9, i = 1, 2, \ldots, n,$$

where n is the number of cards in the ⟨*Program*⟩ deck. Each word may contain a VM instruction or four bytes of data. The number of cards n in the program deck defines the size of the user space; i.e., n cards define $10 \times n$ words, $n \leq 10$.

3. The ⟨*DATA card*⟩ has the format:

$DTA   cc. 1–4

4. The ⟨*Data*⟩ deck contains information in cc. 1–40 and is the user data retrieved by the VM *GD* instructions.

5. The ⟨*ENDJOB card*⟩ has the format:

$END   cc. 1–4
⟨*job id*⟩   cc. 5–8, same ⟨*job id*⟩ as ⟨*JOB card*⟩

The ⟨*DATA card*⟩ is omitted if there are no ⟨*Data*⟩ cards in a job.

A4. THE OPERATING SYSTEM

The primary purpose of the MOS is to process a batched stream of user jobs efficiently. This is accomplished by multiprogramming systems and user processes.

A job *J* will pass sequentially through the following phases:

1. *Input Spooling. J* enters from the card reader and is transferred to the drum.

2. *Main Processing.* The program part of *J* is loaded from the drum into user storage. *J* is then ready to run and becomes a process *j*. Until *j* terminates, either normally or as a result of an error, its status will generally switch many times among:
(a) *ready*—waiting for the CPU.
(b) *running*—executing on the CPU.
(c) *blocked*—waiting for completion of an input-output request.
Input-output requests are translated by the MOS into drum input-output operations.

3. *Output Spooling. J*'s Output, including charges, systems messages, and his original program, is printed from the drum.

In general, many jobs will simultaneously be in the main processing phase.

The MOS is to be documented and programmed as a set of interacting processes. A typical design might have the following major processes:

Readin_Cards:	Read cards into supervisor storage.
Job_to_Drum:	Create a job descriptor and transfer a job to the drum.
Loader:	Load a job into user storage.
Get_Put_Data:	Process VM input-output instructions.
Lines_from_Drum:	Read output lines from drum into supervisor storage.
Print_Lines:	Write output lines on the printer.

The operating system is normally activated by interrupts occurring during slave mode operation. The interrupt handling routines will typically call the process scheduler (CPU allocator) after they service an interrupt.

A major task of the MOS is the management of hardware and software resources. These include user storage, drum storage, channel 3, software buffers, job descriptors, and the CPU.

The MOS is also responsible for maintaining statistics on hardware utilization and job characteristics. The following statistics are computed from software measurements:

1. *Resource Utilization.* Fraction of total time that each channel is busy, fraction of total time that the CPU is busy (in slave mode), mean user storage utilization, and mean drum utilization.

2. *Job Characteristics.* Mean run time (on VM), mean time in system, mean user storage required, mean input length, and mean output length.

These statistics are to be printed at the end of a run.

A5. PROJECT REQUIREMENTS

Three sets of program modules must be designed and implemented:

1. Major simulators for hardware, including the interrupt system, timer, channels, reader, printer, auxiliary storage, user storage, and the slave mode paging system. (The HLP and supervisor storage is assumed available directly from the host system.)

2. The "microprogram" that emulates the VM.

3. The MOS.

These three parts should be clearly and cleanly separated. It should not be difficult to change the size and time parameters of the hardware, specifically drum and user storage size, IO times, instruction times, and the timer "frequency."

Students should work in small teams of two or three, each team doing the complete project. Several weeks after the project is assigned, a complete design of the MOS as a set of interacting processes is submitted. The design includes a description of the major processes in the system and how they interact, the methods to be used for the allocation and administration of each resource, and the identification and contents of the main data structures.

A batch stream of about 60 jobs (a "run") should be prepared for testing purposes.

A6. SOME LIMITATIONS

The MOS and machine deviate from reality in simplifying some features of real systems and omitting others. Significant features that are lacking include: a more general virtual machine that would permit multistep jobs and the use of language translators, a system to organize and handle a broader variety of data files, an operator communication facility, and master mode operation of the CPU in nonzero time. The project specifications could be expanded in some of the above directions, but there appears to be an unacceptable overhead in doing so. Instead, similar tractable case studies emphasizing other aspects of operating systems, such as file systems or time-sharing, should be designed.

REFERENCES

AHO, A. V., P. J. DENNING, and J. D. ULLMAN (1971). Principles of optimal page replacement. *J. ACM*, **18**, No. 1 (Jan.), 80–93.

ALEXANDER, M. T. (1970). Time sharing supervisor programs. The University of Michigan Computing Center, Ann Arbor, Michigan (May).

BAER, J. L. and G. R. SAGER (1972). Measurement and improvement of program behavior under paging systems. In W. Freiberger (ed.), *Statistical Computer Performance Evaluation*, Academic Press, New York, 241–264.

BATSON, A., S. JU, and D. C. WOOD (1970). Measurements of segment size. *Comm. ACM*, **13**, No. 3 (March), 155–159.

BELADY, L. A. (1966). A study of replacement algorithms for a virtual storage computer. *IBM Syst. J.*, **5**, No. 2, 78–101.

BÉTOURNÉ, C., J. BOULENGER, J. FERRIE, C. KAISER, J. KOTT, S. KRACKOWIAK, and J. MOSSIÈR (1969). Process management and resource sharing in the multiaccess system "ESOPE". *Proc. ACM Second Symposium on Operating Systems Principles*, Princeton University, Princeton, N. J. (Oct.), 67–79.

BOBROW, D. G., J. D. BURCHFIEL, D. L. MURPHY, and R. S. TOMLINSON (1972). TENEX, a paged time sharing system for the PDP-10. *Comm. ACM*, **15**, No. 3 (March), 135–143.

BOETTNER, D. W. (1969). Command (job control) languages for general purpose computing systems. University of Michigan Computing Center, Ann Arbor, Michigan (June).

BRINCH HANSEN, P. (1970). The nucleus of a multiprogramming system. *Comm. ACM*, **13**, No. 4 (April), 238–241, 250.

——— (ed.) (1971). RC 4000 Multiprogramming System, 2nd ed. A/S Regnecentralen, Copenhagen, Denmark.

BURROUGHS (1964). B5500 Information Processing Systems, Reference Manual. Burroughs Corporation, Detroit, Michigan.

——— (1967). B6500 Information Processing Systems, Characteristics Manual. Burroughs Corporation, Detroit, Michigan.

CAMBRIDGE (1967). Cambridge Multi-Access System Manual. University Mathematical Laboratory, Cambridge University, Cambridge, England.

CDC (1969). Control Data 6400/6500/6600 Computer Systems Reference Manual. Control Data Corporation, St. Paul, Minnesota.

——— (1971). Control Data 6000 Computer Systems, SCOPE Reference Manual. Pub. No. 60189400, Control Data Corporation, Sunnyvale, Calif.

CLASP (1971). Users Manual. Office of Computer Services, Cornell Univeristy, Ithaca, N. Y.

COFFMAN, E. G., JR., and L. C. VARIAN (1968). Further experimental data on behavior of programs in a paging environment. *Comm. ACM*, **11**, No. 7 (July), 471–474.

———, M. J. ELPHICK, and A. SHOSHANI (1971). System deadlocks. *Computing Surveys*, **3**, No. 2 (June), 67–78.

——— and L. KLEINROCK (1968). Computer scheduling measures and their countermeasures. *Proc. AFIPS 1968 Spring Joint Comput. Conf.*, 11–21.

COMFORT, W. T. (1965). A computing system design for user service. *Proc. AFIPS 1965 Fall Joint Comput. Conf.*, **27**. Spartan Books, New York, 619–628.

CONTI, C. J., D. H. GIBSON, and S. H. PITKOWSKY (1968). Structural aspects of the System/360 model 85, I General organization. *IBM Syst. J.*, **7**, No. 1, 2–14.

CONWAY, M. (1963). A multiprocessor system design. *Proc. AFIPS 1963 Fall Joint Comput. Conf.*, **24**. Spartan Books, New York, 139–146.

CORBATO, F. J., M. M. DAGGETT, and R. C. DALEY (1962). An experimental time-sharing system. *Proc. AFIPS 1962 Spring Joint Comput. Conf.*, **21**, 335–344.

COURTOIS, P. J., R. HEYMANS, and D. L. PARNAS (1971). Concurrent control with "Readers" and "Writers". *Comm. ACM*, **14**, No. 10 (Oct.), 667–668.

CP-67/CMS (1969). Program 360D-05.2.005, IBM Corp., Program Inf. Dept., Hawthorne, N. Y. (June). See also Meyer and Seawright (1970).

DALEY, R. C. and J. B. DENNIS (1968). Virtual memory, processes, and sharing in MULTICS. *Comm. ACM*, **11**, No. 5 (May), 306–312.

——— and P. G. NEUMANN (1965). A general purpose file system for secondary storage. *Proc. AFIPS 1965 Spring Joint Comput. Conf.*, **27**, Part 1. Spartan Books, New York, 213–230.

DENNING, P. J. (1968). The working set model for program behavior. *Comm. ACM*, **11**, No. 5 (May), 323–333.

——— (1970). Virtual memory. *Computing Surveys*, **2**, No. 3 (Sept.), 153–189.

——— (1972). A note on paging drum efficiency. *Computing Surveys*, **4**, No. 1 (March), 1–3.

DENNIS, J. B. and E. C. VAN HORN (1966). Programming semantics for multiprogrammed computations. *Comm. ACM*, **9**, No. 3 (March), 143–155.

——— (1965). Segmentation and the design of multiprogrammed operating systems. *J. ACM*, **12**, No. 4 (Oct.), 589–602.

DIJKSTRA, E. W. (1965a). Cooperating sequential processes. Mathematics Dept., Technological University, Eindhoven, The Netherlands.

——— (1965b). Solution of a problem in concurrent programming control. *Comm. ACM*, **8**, No. 9 (Sept.), 569.

——— (1968a). The structure of the "THE"-multiprogramming system. *Comm. ACM*, **11**, No. 5 (May), 341–346.

——— (1968b). Co-operating sequential processes. In F. Genuys (ed.), *Programming Languages*, Academic Press, New York, 43–112.

——— (1969). Notes on structured programming. EWD 249, Technological University, Eindhoven, The Netherlands.

EISENBERG, M. A. and M. R. MCGUIRE (1972). Further comments on Dijkstra's concurrent programming control problem. *Comm. ACM*, **15**, No. 11 (Nov.), 999.

ELSPAS, B., K. N. LEVITT, R. J. WALDINGER, and A. WAKSMAN (1972). An assessment of techniques for proving program correctness. *Computing Surveys* **4**, No. 2 (June), 97–147.

FINE, E. G., C. W. JACKSON, and P. V. MCISAAC (1966). Dynamic program behavior under paging. *Proc. ACM 21st Nat. Conf.*, Thompson Book Co., Washington, D. C., 223–228.

FREIBERGS, I. F. (1968). The dynamic behavior of programs. *Proc. AFIPS 1968 Fall Joint Comput. Conf.*, **33**, Part 2, 1163–1167.

GEAR, C. W. (1969). *Computer Organization and Programming*. McGraw-Hill Book Company, New York.

GRAHAM, R. M. (1968). Protection in an information processing utility. *Comm. ACM*, **11**, No. 5 (May), 365–369.

GRIES, D. (1971). *Compiler Construction for Digital Computers*. John Wiley & Sons, New York.

HABERMANN, A. N. (1969). Prevention of system deadlocks. *Comm. ACM*, **12**, No. 7 (July), 373–377, 385.

HAVENDER, J. W. (1968). Avoiding deadlock in multitasking systems. *IBM Syst. J.*, **7**, No. 2, 74–84.

HEBALKAR, P. G. (1970). Deadlock-free sharing of resources in asynchronous systems. MAC-TR-75 (Ph.D. thesis), Massachusetts Institute of Technology, Cambridge, Mass. (Sept.).

HOLT, R. C. (1971a). Comments on prevention of system deadlocks. *Comm. ACM*, **14**, No. 1 (Jan.), 36–38.

——— (1971b). On deadlock in computer systems. Ph.D. thesis, Tech. Rep. 71–91, Computer Science, Cornell University, Ithaca, N. Y. (Jan.).

——— (1972). Some deadlock properties of computer systems. *ACM Computing Surveys*, **4**, No. 3 (Sept.), 179–196.

HORNING, J. J. and B. RANDELL (1973). Process structuring. *Computing Surveys*, **5**, No. 1 (March), 5–30.

IBM (1963). IBM 7090 data processing system multiprogramming package. IBM Special Systems Feature Bulletin L22–6641–3, IBM Corp., White Plains, N. Y.

——— (1965). IBM System/360 Operating System. Concepts and Facilities. Form C28–6535, IBM Corp., Poughkeepsie, N. Y.

——— (1967) IBM System/360 Operating System: Supervisor and Data Management Services. Form C28–6646, IBM Corp., Programming Systems Publications, Poughkeepsie, N. Y.

KILBURN, T., D. B. G. EDWARDS, M. J. LANIGAN, and F. H. SUMNER (1962). One-level storage system. *IRE Trans. EC–11*, 2 (April), 223–235.

KNUTH, D. E. (1968). *The Art of Computer Programming, Vol. 1.* Addison-Wesley, Reading, Mass.

LAMPSON, B. W. (1968). A scheduling philosophy for multiprocessing systems. *Comm. ACM*, **11**, No. 5 (May), 347–360.

LIPTAY, J. S. (1968). Structural aspects of the System/360 model 85, II The cache. *IBM Syst. J.*, **7**, No. 1, 15–21.

MADNICK, S. E. (1968). Design strategies for file systems: a model. Scientific Center Report, 2nd Revision, April 1970, IBM Corp., Cambridge Scientific Center, Cambridge, Mass.

——— and J. W. ALSOP, II (1969). A modular approach to file system design. *Proc. AFIPS 1969 Spring Joint Comput. Conf.*, **34**, AFIPS Press, Montvale, N. J., 1–13.

MATTSON, R. L., J. GECSEI, D. R. SLUTZ, and I. L. TRAIGER (1970). Evaluation techniques for storage hierarchies. *IBM Syst. J.*, **9**, 2, 78–117.

MEYER, R. A. and L. H. SEAWRIGHT (1970). A virtual machine time-sharing system. *IBM Syst. J.*, **9**, No. 3, 199–218.

MILLER, W. F. (1968). Lecture notes, C. S. 246, Computer Science Dept., Stanford University, Stanford, Calif. (unpublished).

MINSKY, M. L. (1967). *Computation: Finite and Infinite Machines.* Prentice-Hall Inc., Englewood Cliffs, N. J.

MORRIS, R. (1968). Scatter storage techniques. *Comm. ACM*, **11**, No. 1 (Jan.), 38–44.

MTS (1967). The MTS Manual, Vols. I and II, University of Michigan Computing Center Publication, Ann Arbor, Michigan (Dec.).

MULTICS (1967). J. L. BASH, E. G. BENJAFIELD, and M. L. GANDY, The Multics operating system—an overview of Multics as it is being developed, Project MAC, MIT, Cambridge, Mass. (May). See also Organick (1972).

NAUR, P. (ed.) (1963). Revised report on the algorithmic language ALGOL 60. *Comm. ACM*, **6**, No. 1 (Jan.), 1–17.

OPPENHEIMER, G. and N. WEIZER (1968). Resource management for a medium scale time-sharing operating system. *Comm. ACM*, **11**, No. 5 (May), 313–322.

ORGANICK, E. I. (1972). *The Multics System: An Examination of its Structure.* The MIT Press, Cambridge, Mass.

RANDELL, B. (1969). A note on storage fragmentation and program segmentation. *Comm. ACM*, **12**, No. 7 (July), 365–369, 372.

—— and C. J. KUEHNER (1968). Dynamic storage allocation systems. *Comm. ACM*, **11**, No. 5 (May), 297–306.

ROSEN, S. (ed.) (1967). *Programming Systems and Languages.* McGraw-Hill, New York.

—— (1969). Electronic computers: a historical survey. *Computing Surveys*, **1**, No. 1 (March), 7–36.

ROSIN, R. F. (1969). Supervisory and monitor systems. *Computing Surveys*, **1**, No. 1 (March), 37–54.

RUSSELL, R. D. (1972). A model for deadlock-free resource allocation. SLAC Report No. 148, Stanford Linear Accelerator Center, Stanford, Calif. (June). Ph.D. thesis, Computer Science, Stanford University.

SALTZER, J. H. (1966). Traffic control in a multiplexed computer system. MAC–TR–30 (thesis), MIT, Cambridge, Mass. (July).

SHAW, A. C. and N. WEIDERMAN (1971). A multiprogramming system for education and research. *Proc. IFIP Congress 71*, North-Holland Publishing Co., Amsterdam, The Netherlands, 1505–1509.

——, N. WEIDERMAN, G. ANDREWS, M. FELCYN, J. RIEBER, and G. WONG (1973). A multiprogramming nucleus with dynamic resource facilities. Tech. Report 72–12–04, Computer Science Group, University of Washington, Seattle, Washington (Revised, April).

SHOSHANI, A. and E. G. COFFMAN (1969). Prevention, detection, and recovery from system deadlocks. Computer Science Lab., Tech. Report No. 80, Dept. of Electrical Engineering, Princeton University.

SIGPLAN (1972). *SIGPLAN Notices 7*, 11 (Nov.). Special issue on control structures in programming languages, B. M. Leavenworth, (ed.).

SIMPSON, T. H., R. P. CRABTREE, R. O. RAY, G. H. PHILLIPS, and R. B. HITT (1969). Houston automatic spooling priority system—II (Version 2). IBM Type III Program No. 360D–05.1.014, IBM Corp., Program Information Department, Hawthorne, N. Y.

TSS (1967). IBM System/360 time sharing system, resident supervisor program logic manual. Form A27–2719–0, IBM Corp., Poughkeepsie, N. Y.

VAREHA, A. L., R. M. RUTLEDGE, and M. M. GOLD (1969). Strategies for structuring two-level memories in a paging environment. *Proc. ACM Second Symposium on Operating Systems Principles*, Princeton University, Princeton, N. J. (Oct.), 54–59.

WATSON, R. W. (1970). *Timesharing System Design Concepts.* McGraw-Hill, New York.

WEGNER, P. (1968). *Programming Languages, Information Structures, and Machine Organization.* McGraw-Hill, New York.

WEIDERMAN, N. (1971). Synchronization and simulation in operating system construction. Ph.D. thesis, Tech. Rep. 71–102, Computer Science, Cornell University, Ithaca, N. Y. (Sept.).

WILKES, M. V. (1965). Slave memories and dynamic storage allocation. *IEEE Trans. EC—14,* (April), 270–271.

——— (1968). *Time-sharing Computer Systems.* American Elsevier, New York.

WIRTH, N. (1966). A note on "Program Structures for Parallel Processing." *Comm. ACM,* **9,** No. 5 (May), 320–321.

——— (1969). On multiprogramming, machine coding and computer organization. *Comm. ACM,* **12,** No. 9 (Sept.), 489–498.

WOLMAN, E. (1965). A fixed optimum cell-size for records of various lengths. *J. ACM,* **12,** No. 1 (Jan.), 53–70.

XDS (1969). XDS 940 Computer Reference Manual. Xerox Data Systems, El Segundo, Calif.

ZURCHER, F. W. and B. RANDELL (1968). Iterative multi-level modeling—a methodology for computer system design. *Proc. IFIP Congress 1968,* North-Holland Publishing Co., Amsterdam, The Netherlands, 867–871.

INDEX AND ABBREVIATIONS